POLITICS

AND OCCULT
THE

THE LEFT, THE RIGHT,
AND THE RADICALLY UNSEEN

POLITICS

AND THE OCCULT

THE LEFT, THE RIGHT, AND THE RADICALLY UNSEEN

Gary Lachman

QUEST

BOOKS

Theosophical Publishing House
Wheaton, Illinois * Chennai, India

First Quest edition 2008

Quest Books
Theosophical Publishing House
P.O. Box 270
Wheaton, IL 60187

www.questbooks.com

Library of Congress Cataloging-in-Publication Data

Lachman, Gary.
Politics and the occult: the left, the right, and the radically unseen / Gary Lachman.—1st Quest ed.
   p.   cm.
Includes bibliographical references and index.
ISBN 978-0-8356-0857-2
1. Occultism. 2. Political science. 3. Civilization—History. I. Title.
BF1439.L325 2008
130.9—dc22   2008021518

6   5   4   3   *   18   19   20   21   22

Printed in the United States of America

For James Webb (1946–1980) and
Robert Anton Wilson (1932–2007),
Illuminati supreme

Nothing could be more dangerous for the human race than to believe that its affairs had fallen into the hands of supermen.

– Colin Wilson, *The Mind Parasites*

Contents

ACKNOWLEDGMENTS

Many people helped in making this book possible. I'd like to thank Richard Smoley for approaching me with the idea of doing another book with Quest and for his sympathetic reading of the first draft. Joscelyn Godwin went above and beyond the call of duty in suggesting fruitful areas of inquiry and in passing me on to Marco Passi, who generously shared his forthcoming work on Aleister Crowley with me. Students of occult politics should be thankful that two such incisive thinkers are at work in their fields. Thanks go to Christina Oakley-Harrington for inspiring the book's subtitle, taken from a talk I gave at her wondrous bookshop, Treadwells, here in London. Warm appreciation goes to my old friend John Browner, his wife Lisa Yarger, their daughter Greta, and their pets for making me feel at home in Munich and Ascona, where I researched the Schwabing–Monte Verità set. Thanks also to Emilio Alvarez for his thoughtful comments on the Thulegesellschaft and for introducing me to some brown shirt haunts. Many friends, too numerous to mention adequately, deserve thanks for enduring my obsessive pursuit of these dark matters; I trust their tolerance continues. Special appreciation goes to Andy Zax for enabling me to continue work on the book in style while in Los Angeles; thanks go to my great friend Lisa Persky, too, for the use of her laptop while there: may they both enjoy the rich happiness they deserve. Maja d'Joust of the Philosophical Research Society in Los

Angeles kindly opened its doors when I visited on a day it was closed. Thanks also go to my old alma mater, the Bodhi Tree Bookstore, who opened its doors for a talk I gave on related themes. Adam Simon's insights into the religious Right were profitable, if chilling. Christopher McIntosh's remarks on the Rosicrucians, made at a talk at the Theosophical Society in London, were, it goes without saying, helpful, and I was glad to renew our acquaintance, first made ages ago at the Rosicrucian Conference in Czesky Krumlov in the Czech Republic. My sons, Joshua and Maximilian, remain inexhaustible wells of inspiration, and I'd like to thank their mother, Ruth Jones, for our many constructive and rewarding Caffé Nero conferences. We'll always have Domodossala.

Introduction

Hidden Superiors and the Retreat from the Modern World

I first became interested in the relationship between politics and the occult through reading a remarkable book published in the 1970s by the occult historian James Webb. In *The Occult Establishment*, Webb, who is generally skeptical of most occult claims, argues that at the turn of the nineteenth century, and especially after World War I, a variety of social pressures produced in Europe and America what he called a "flight from reason," leading to an embrace of the irrational and a rejection of the modern world. For Webb, the occult revival of the late nineteenth century, which produced such significant movements as the Theosophical Society, the Hermetic Order of the Golden Dawn, and Rudolf Steiner's anthroposophy, was in fact a reaction to the shifts in society brought about by the rise of modernity. This in turn led to what he calls "illuminated politics," "a politics that has a religious complexion and obeys a transcendental scale of values"—"illuminated" taken, perhaps, from the infamous Bavarian Illuminati.[1]

To many at that time, the secular, materialist world rooted in science, rationalism, and economics seemed bent on destroying age-old traditions that had hitherto given life and society a secure meaning. Religion was on the way out, and the rise of industrialism and an increasingly rapid technological progress, which continue today, were bringing about sudden social changes. The move to cities, the loss of contact with nature, the disintegration of the family, the loosening of the organic ties that had previously bonded individuals into a community: these were the elements of a strange, new world. The confusion and dismay accompanying these transformations is perhaps best expressed in Karl Marx's remark that in the modern world, "all that is solid melts into air." Marx's analogy gives the impression of a dizzying social free fall, but the sociologist Max Weber voiced an equally distressing concern in a radically different metaphor, calling the modern world an "iron cage" of rules and regulations that casts its lonely inhabitants into a "polar night of icy darkness."

We may regard these and other gripes against the modern world, from William Blake's "satanic mills" to the "liquid modernity" of the contemporary social philosopher Zygmunt Bauman, as the whining of misfits unable to get with the program. But it is difficult to ignore the philosopher Leszek Kolakowski's remark that today "it seems as though we live with the feeling of an all-encompassing crisis without being able, however, to identify its causes clearly."[2] Kolakowski is right, I think, and this is the modern condition.

As someone who believes that interest in the occult, the esoteric, the metaphysical, and the spiritual is not necessarily prompted by anxiety, a crisis of identity, or weakness of mind, I took Webb's thesis with a few grains of salt, which nevertheless didn't prevent me from appreciating the remarkable amount of research he had put into his book, or the slightly wry humor with which he presented his evidence. I had enjoyed very much Webb's *The Harmonious Circle*, a near-exhaustive study of Gurdjieff, Ouspensky, and their followers, although having been involved for a time with the Gurdjieff "work," I once again had my doubts about his conclusions.[3] Webb seems to have had his own doubts about his skeptical rationalism, and although we may never know for certain, those cracks in his rational armor may have had something to do with the mental unbalance that led to his suicide in 1980 at the age of thirty-four.[4] In many ways this present book is written in return for the profit and enjoyment I received from reading Webb's work.

OCCULT FASCISM

One reason that Webb's book came out when it did was that by the late '70s, a subgenre of books about the Nazis and the occult had acquired a wide readership. Webb, like more recent researchers in this field, was skeptical of many of these claims, and in his book he undermines many of the myths surrounding "occult Nazism." Yet the association persists, and for most people who consider the idea at all, "occult politics" invariably means some form of fascism. While some, perhaps even most, occultists who dabbled in politics, or politicians who dipped into the occult, had right-wing, reactionary, and even fascist leanings, it is by no means true that all did. One of the things I hope to show in this book is that there was a progressive, left-wing occult politics as well, although, to be sure, it has gone comparatively unnoticed.

Although for writers like Umberto Eco, who makes great use of the link in his esoteric novel *Foucault's Pendulum*, occult politics *is* fascist politics, the truth, as far as I can tell, is more complicated. Occult politics, like politics in the real world, is hardly ever straightforward and simple, and the categories of "right" and "left" are increasingly inadequate aids in understanding its complexities. Webb himself, who seems to have held liberal, left-of-center views, recognized this and rejected any unqualified equation of occult or illuminated politics with fascism or its frequent fellow traveler, anti-Semitism. "Fascist movements could and did contain illuminates"—Webb's term for those geared toward occult politics—"but . . . the illuminates were by no means necessarily fascist." And again, "Illuminated politicians are by no means necessarily anti-Semitic," but "neither necessarily or predominantly Fascist or anti-Semitic, the illuminated politicians deserve a classification of their own."[5] This notion of a *new* kind of politics, however vague, appeals to me, and in showing that some occult politics was of a progressive stamp, I hope it will be clear that I'm not arguing for one side and against another. Clarity is needed here, not scoring points for one set of outmoded terms at the expense of another.

The Old New Age

One of the things that struck me in Webb's book was his account of the fascinating brew of alternative ideas about reality, society, and politics that was bubbling in the underground of German-speaking countries before National Socialism's devastating rise to power. Many of the themes associated with the counter-culture of the 1960s—back to nature, health, vegetarianism, youth culture, feminism, interest in "primitive" cultures, spirituality, meditation, communal living, free love, the occult, the irrational, Theosophy, and the "wisdom of the East"—had a much earlier airing in the bohemian underground of cities like Munich in the years leading up to and following World War I. Had he lived to see it, Webb no doubt would have added material about the New Age—an outgrowth of the 1960s—to a later edition of his book. In *Turn Off Your Mind: The Mystic Sixties and the Dark Side of the Age of Aquarius*, a book I wrote with the work of Webb and other occult historians, specifically Joscelyn Godwin and Nicholas Goodrick-Clarke, in mind, I explored parallels between the '60s liberation ethos and some of the ideas circulating around the cafés of pre-Nazi Germany.[6] That the book was criticized by people strongly associated with the sixties counter-culture, specifically about these dark resonances, suggests to me that the similarities struck home.[7]

This isn't to say that interest in the counter-culture, organic foods, and the beneficial properties of sun worship, for example, unavoidably leads to fascism—an unfortunate and hasty association made by many who view these matters superficially and against which I argue above. What it does point to is the fact that in the world of occult politics, nailing down an unqualified good is rarely easy and that for every yang there is usually an inextricable yin, making things, for the honest investigator, difficult but also interesting.

GOOD GUYS SAYING BAD THINGS

That hardly anything in the world of occult politics is clear-cut or unalloyed will become apparent when we look at some of the figures in this book. I give one example here of someone I won't be looking at in any detail further on: the mythologist Joseph Campbell, who rose to posthumous celebrity in the early 1990s with the famous series of television interviews *The Power of Myth*, which brought spiritual, mystical, and transcendental concerns to millions of viewers who might otherwise have been unaware of them and who encouraged us all to "follow our bliss." In the early 1930s, Campbell was more than ambivalent about Hitler, and criticized his hero, the German novelist Thomas Mann, when he spoke out against the Nazis. In the 1950s, Campbell didn't condemn Joseph McCarthy's communist witch hunt, and while the Vietnam War was going on, he spoke critically of the anti-war demonstrators and had nothing but disdain for flower power.[8] He's also been criticized for his supposedly anti-Semitic remarks. My point isn't that Campbell is "bad" because of these actions—their meaning continues to be debated—but rather that they suggest a sensibility not usually associated with clichéd ideas about spirituality. We'd assume that someone associated with New Age or spiritual ideas wouldn't have such right-wing views, which are more or less considered "bad" in our current politically correct climate, while left views—pacifism, anti-Americanism (at least in the sense of America as an imperialist bully)—are tacitly assumed to be "good." Yet, as I expressed it to a friend one evening at a London pub, what I've discovered in doing the research for this book is that, on more than one occasion, the "good guys" were saying "bad" things.

The Right Stuff

One reason why occult or esoteric politics has been generally lumped in with the right can be found in Webb's definition of *illuminated politics*: "a politics that has a religious complexion and obeys a transcendental scale of values." For the last few centuries, religion, and more specifically the Church, has, rightly or wrongly, been seen as an agent of oppression and authoritarianism, an obstacle in the way of progress and personal freedom. Karl Marx famously called religion the "opium of the people," and Voltaire, the leading mind of the Enlightenment, in his hatred of the Church said to *écrasez l'Infâme*, "crush the Infamy." The "transcendental scale of values" that Webb associates with occult politics is, in the modern world, seen as a means of control used by the Church to stay in power.

In his pornographic work *Philosophy in the Bedroom*, the Marquis de Sade, a man for whom personal freedom was an end-all and be-all, included a political pamphlet entitled, "Frenchmen, One More Effort If You Wish to Become Republicans." In it he argued that if the French really want to abolish superstition, they shouldn't stop at the execution of Louis XVI but should finish the job by killing off God as well. Evidence that this antipathy to religion hasn't lessened, even after more than a century of scientific and secular dominance, can be seen in the success of books like Richard Dawkins' *The God Delusion*, as well as in the fear that any criticism of a scientific dogma like the Darwinian version of the theory of evolution must necessarily lead to equally unsatisfactory (from the esoteric point of view) fundamentalist positions like Creationism.

To be clear, a transcendental scale of values is one based not on animal needs or material goods—a higher standard of living, more consumer choice, the liberty of free enterprise—nor on scientific facts about human nature or the structure of society, nor on the increase of personal freedoms (although it's not necessarily opposed to this), but on non-material, spiritual, "higher" ideals. We can look at the transcendental scale of values as an *idealistic* one, as opposed to the *practical* values of a secular scale.

The left, then, has generally been associated with progress, freedom, egalitarianism, and anti-authoritarianism, and these "goods" have been linked to a non-religious, non-transcendental, scientific materialist world view. The left has its own brand of authoritarianism—Stalinism, for example, or the Reign of Terror—but the opposition to this is generally a more economically and individually "freer" form of materialism, for instance, capitalist democracies.

The right, on the other hand, is seen as an agent of tradition, which is non-progressive, authoritarian, and hierarchical. In his essay "Ur-Fascism," Umberto Eco identifies the first ingredient of what he calls "Eternal Fascism," a kind of fundamental form of fascistic thinking, not linked to any particular historical expression of it, as "the cult of tradition," and he goes on to link this with the syncretism of the Hellenistic period when "people of different religions (most of them indulgently accepted by the Roman Pantheon) started dreaming of a revelation received at the dawn of human history."[9]

TRADITION

The revelation received at the dawn of human history that Eco refers to is in fact the basic idea of tradition in occult philosophy, the notion that an ancient wisdom, once available to mankind but subsequently lost, can still be accessed. The occultist's or esotericist's job is to discover its traces in the historical record and follow them to the source. The truth was given once, in an original revelation, and our job is to get back to this primal disclosure. This scheme is also the basis of the church, but although it is an agent of tradition, many of the figures we will encounter in this book found it as oppressive and authoritarian as the secularists did and fought against it as well, although for different ends—another example of the complexities involved in our study.

AGAINST MODERNITY

An irony I discovered while researching this book is that, although sworn ideological enemies, the radical extremes of the left and the right frequently meet in a shared detestation of modernity. The Traditionalists, for example, associated with the work of the esotericist René Guénon, make no bones about their disgust with the modern age. They find popular culture particularly offensive. In this, and in some other ways, they are reminiscent of more recent exponents of "tradition," such as Christian and Islamic fundamentalists.

In his book *Ride the Tiger: A Survival Manual for the Aristocrats of the Soul*, Julius Evola, one of the most articulate of the Traditionalists, talks specifically about jazz. "It is with good reason," he writes, "that the present epoch, besides being called the 'age of the emergence of the masses' . . . has also been called the 'Jazz Age.'" He goes on to speak of jazz as "something mechanical, disjointed, altogether primitively ecstatic and even paroxysmal," writing darkly of the "hundreds of couples" in dance halls, "shaking themselves to the syncopation and driving energy of this music," linking its "convulsive-mechanical" rhythms to those of machines.[10] The neo-Marxist philosopher Theodor

Adorno, who made no secret of his antipathy to anything occult—"Occultism is the metaphysics of dunces," he once proclaimed[11]—would have gagged at the title of Evola's book. But to read Adorno's attacks on the "culture industry," which keeps the masses docile by pandering to and even creating their tastes, and especially his scathing critiques of popular culture and music—jazz in particular—and then to turn back to Evola, is an enlightening experience. Adorno's famous critique of the modern age, *Dialectic of Enlightenment*, written with the sociologist Max Horkheimer, finds common cause with the Traditional critique of the "scientification" of human experience; both, in their own ways, see this as dominated by what Guénon called the "reign of quantity." And although the neo-Marxist left and the esoteric right offer radically different alternatives to the problem, they share a surprisingly similar notion of some philosophical or cultural elite, a vanguard of individuals who can steer the unenlightened masses toward the new dawn.

THE OCCULT AND THE MODERN WORLD

Paradoxically, while traditionally seen as rooted in the ancient past, the occult is in many ways a product of the modern world. As I argue in *A Dark Muse*, it wasn't until the rise of science and the modern world view that the occult became what it is for us today.[12] If, as James Webb argues, "the occult consists of an amalgam of theories which have failed to find acceptance with the establishments of their day,"[13] becoming what he calls *rejected knowledge*, then modernity can be seen as the process of rejecting occult knowledge, previously regarded with respect. One example may suffice. The occult notion of tradition, at least in its modern form, has its roots in the fifteenth century. It was born when Cosimo de' Medici, patron of the great Renaissance magician and scholar Marsilio Ficino, commanded his scribe to break off translating Plato into Latin and to concentrate on a newly found batch of manuscripts purported to be the work of Hermes Trismegistus, a mythical figure associated with Thoth, the Egyptian god of magic, but who in Ficino's day was believed to be a flesh-and-blood contemporary of Moses (whose own historical reality is itself a matter of debate). That Plato, to whom, as the philosopher Alfred North Whitehead once remarked, all subsequent Western philosophy is but a series of footnotes, took second place to Hermes indicates the importance given to occult and hermetic knowledge at the dawn of the modern period. Ficino's translations are a kind of ur-text for all subsequent occultism and may be the single most important link between the esoteric knowledge of the past and modern times. As Christopher McIntosh writes in his important study of the Rosicrucians, Ficino "started the habit of talking in terms of a special wisdom handed down from sage to sage,"[14] an occult trope that would emerge in different forms in centuries to come.

We can also recall that Isaac Newton, father of the modern scientific worldview and no doubt familiar with Ficino's work, occupied himself more with writing about alchemy and with Biblical exegeses than with the theory of gravity. And if we recall that *occult* means "hidden" or "unseen," then Newton's great discovery pointed to an occult force we encounter every day, for who has seen gravity?

I'm not arguing that the occult didn't exist until four or five centuries ago. I'm saying that the disciplines, practices, and theories that we call "occult" hadn't yet become part of the great reservoir of "rejected knowledge" that anyone interested in the occult draws on today. When they did, the occult, which in many ways had been the establishment, became *subversive*. This subversive character of occultism constitutes a great part of its modern appeal, and in *Turn Off Your Mind*, I explored its links to the revolutionary sensibility of the 1960s. In a wider sense, it's remained a weapon in the ongoing battle between scientism—the dogma that scientific materialism can explain *everything* in the universe—and the lingering sense of mankind's spiritual nature, a battle that, in *A Dark Muse*, I look at in terms of the literature of the last two centuries. This subversive character of the occult is the subject of this present book, albeit here I look at it in a more specifically political sense.

THE COSMIC STATE

Occult politics, however, is as old as politics itself. A look at Nicholas Campion's exhaustive and illuminating *The Great Year: Astrology,*

Millenarianism and History in the Western Tradition, which examines the role of astrology in Western political history, shows how central something that we consider occult was to notions of the state in previous times. As Campion argues, in the "cosmic state"—which he locates first emerging in ancient Sumer[15]—the gods and goddesses decided the future and communicated their decisions to humanity through cosmic and earthly events: the pattern of stars, an earthquake, the shape of a cloud. Diviners read these portents and advised their monarchs accordingly. The monarchs then enacted laws that were in harmony with the edicts of the gods. The human/political, natural/cosmic, and divine/spiritual worlds were one, and politics, religion, and the occult—the art of interpreting the divine will, in this case, astrology—formed a seamless whole.

Something along these lines continued for the greater part of human history, until the rift between the human and the spiritual opened up considerably in the modern period. Shakespeare's Cassius in *Julius Caesar*, a play written in 1599, says that "the fault lies not in our stars but in ourselves," showing that by Shakespeare's time, human consciousness was moving further away from the idea that its future was written in the heavens. A little further on, and the idea that God or the divine will played a part in human politics became very shaky. To give one example, the divine right of kings was put in question when the philosopher John Locke argued that we are all born as *tabula rasas*, "blank slates," empty consciousnesses waiting for experience to "write" on us. When in *An Essay Concerning Human Understanding* (1690) Locke maintained that there was "nothing in the mind that was not first in the senses," he not only jettisoned the Platonic and, more to Locke's point, Cartesian, notion of "innate ideas"—a belief in inherent psychic contents that would re-emerge in the modern world in the form of C. G. Jung's archetypes—he also paved the way for our modern, democratic notion of egalitarianism, enshrined in the American Declaration of Independence. All men and women are created equal—equally blank—in the sense that no one has anything special implanted in them at birth that sets them apart as natural rulers. From here it wasn't a particularly long step to the French Revolution and Louis XVI's grisly end. And if there's some doubt as to when, exactly, modernity began, most accounts agree that post Louis XVI's execution, it had certainly arrived. It was at this point too, I would say, that occult politics in its modern, subversive sense, began to appear.

FROM PROGRESSIVE TO REACTIONARY

In the chapters that follow I look at examples of illuminated politics in the modern period, roughly the last four centuries, beginning with the mysterious appearance—or actually non-appearance—of the Rosicrucian Brotherhood in the early 1600s and leading up to relatively contemporary times. This is by no means an exhaustive survey, nor a strict history of occult politics. Considerations of space and time—those two perennial tyrants—demand a limited selection. So as not to disappoint a reader who is expecting a different sort of book, I should point out what this book *isn't* about, a practice most publishers frown on, but which I feel may be appropriate here. It isn't, for example, an exposé of secret societies whose occult machinations are behind the political movements of today. Nor is it a rummaging through the occult closets of famous politicians in order to uncover some hermetic skeletons. (That Ronald Reagan, for example, employed an astrologer may be an interesting bit of gossip, but it tells us little about the nature of occult politics. Likewise, the fact that Aleister Crowley, probably the most famous magician of modern times, wrote pro-German propaganda during World War I tells us more about Crowley than it does about politics.) It's also not about any conspiracy to infiltrate earthly governments involving UFOs, although it is true that in 1960, aliens took an interest in U.S. politics and backed a candidate for the presidency.[16] I've also not focused on occult politics in the sense of the politics of special interest groups, for instance, how neo-pagans fit into contemporary society or the relationship between Wicca and some forms of contemporary feminism. These and no doubt other equally deserving elements are missing from my study, and I look forward to being enlightened about them by interested readers.

The narrative of occult politics in the modern age follows a broad arc. The general stream seems to begin with a progressive character. This carries on until that devastating watershed in Western history, World War I. Then a strong reactionary turn appears, which isn't surprising, given that a similar *volte face* gripped other manifestations of Western consciousness at that time. The enthusiasm for the new, for the future, that characterized what elsewhere I call the "positive *fin de siècle*,"[17] vanished in the face of the barbarism the modern world had unleashed upon itself. A great revulsion sickened the West and in many ways prompted what I call in the title of this introduction a "retreat from the modern world." Readers familiar with the Traditionalist literature may notice in this an allusion to two classics of that school.[18] The echo is intentional, a nod to the kind of occult politics that Webb put at the center of *The Occult Establishment*.

Another significant theme endures in different ways in our own time. Whether it's the Secret Chiefs, the Inner Circle of Humanity, the Hidden Masters, the Ascended Masters, the Great White Brotherhood, the Unknown Nine, or any other variant, the idea is the same. Behind the everyday world, secluded in the remote fastness of the Himalayas, in a sunken city beneath the Gobi Desert, or on some occult plane inaccessible to ordinary consciousness, there exists an elite, a coterie of occult adepts, who guide human affairs, steering an unwieldy humanity in its spiritual evolution. In paranoid versions, some dark ulterior motive drives their activities, but for the most part, the "unknown superiors" spoken of in different ways in this book have our best intentions at heart. But the kind of revolution they and their followers have in mind isn't one that merely shifts the burden of tyranny from one shoulder to another, as Bernard Shaw pithily puts it. The revolution they speak of is a spiritual revolution, one in which mankind and the earth itself is transformed and transfigured and in which a true New Age begins, or, conversely, a past Golden Age returns. That the idea of a Golden Age hasn't been absent from more conventional politics is clear from the various utopias—Marxist, socialist, and others—that have been behind several conventional revolutions. But these have been shadows, echoes of the genuine item. The paradise aimed at by conventional revolutions is only a metaphor. The one occult politics works toward is for real.

1

ROSICRUCIAN DAWN

In 1614, a pamphlet appeared in Cassel, Germany, announcing the existence of a strange secret society, the Fraternity of the Rosy Cross, and inviting its readers to seek it out and to join it in its work. Soon other documents relating to this mysterious organization appeared, and within a few years a "Rosicrucian furor" had broken out across practically half of Europe. Exactly who or what the Rosicrucians were remains a mystery, and to this day historians of the occult and of secret societies debate whether in fact they ever existed. In his classic work, *The Secret Teachings of All Ages*, the occult scholar Manly P. Hall asks "Who were the Rosicrucians?" and offers several possibilities. "Were they," Hall asks, "an organization of profound thinkers rebelling against the inquisitional religious and philosophical limitations of their time?" Or "isolated transcendentalists united only by the similarity of their viewpoints and deductions?" Were they a "religious and philosophical brotherhood, as they claimed to be?" Or was this a front for their true aim, "which possibly was the political control of Europe?"[1] Other similar questions fill Hall's chapter, and I leave to interested readers the pleasure of discovering them.

Like all good occult historians, Hall leaves the matter open. But the *Fama Fraternitas*, the document announcing their arrival, has no doubts about the Fraternity's existence or mission. It tells the story of one Christian Rosencreutz and his adventures in the East, where he studied secret esoteric lore. It also speaks of his return to Europe and his desire to bring about a "reformation" of all Western arts, sciences, politics, and religion. This "brother C.R." was also the protagonist of a later, even more mysterious document, *The Chemical Wedding of Christian Rosencreutz*, published in 1616, a kind of esoteric novel that in alchemical and often surreal language presents a series of dream-like evocative tableaux.

Exactly what transpires in the *Chemical Wedding*, like the significance of the Rosicrucians themselves, is still a matter of debate, although the general sense is that it relates in symbolic form the Great Work of spiritual transformation that is at the heart of all esoteric teaching. But the Rosicrucian message, which combines elements of alchemy, hermeticism, astrology, and other occult disciplines, wasn't limited to the transformation of the individual alone. It also aimed to transform European society as a whole. It was, as the historian Frances Yates argues, "an apocalyptic message of universal reformation leading to a millennium."[2] The *Fama Fraternitas* was, in short, a powerful and influential polemic of occult politics that in many ways set the tone for similar works to come.

ROSICRUCIAN ENLIGHTENMENT

The story of Christian Rosencreutz's travels and search for secret knowledge has become an archetype of the Western spiritual path, informing most, if not all, of the esoteric currents that followed, as well as the plethora of conspiracy theories and spiritual revolutions that came in their wake; the theme of "hidden superiors" that runs throughout occult politics has Rosicrucian roots. His "esotourism," to coin an awkward term, appears, for example, in the eighteenth-century figure of the "noble traveler" and finds echoes in Madame Blavatsky's journeys to the Himalayas, G. I. Gurdjieff's through Central Asia, and those of thousands of lesser-known seekers who hit the hippie and later New Age trails in search of the mystic East. Yet aside from the Rosicrucian documents, there's no record of his ever existing. He's thought to have been born in 1378 and to have lived until 1484, making him 106, a remarkable age, but also a number said to have cabalistic significance. Though descended of noble parents, he was born in poverty, and at the age of five he was placed in a cloister where he learned Latin and Greek. He was apprenticed to a monk who was determined to visit the Holy Land. Making his pilgrimage, his mentor died in Cyprus, but Christian continued the journey to Jerusalem. He fell ill in the mysterious city of Damcar, where he remained for some time, learning much from the Turks, meeting the wise men of Arabia, and continuing his studies in spiritual and esoteric knowledge.

The wise men suggested he visit Damascus, and, changing his plans, Christian headed there. He arrived and was welcomed "not as a stranger" but as one "long expected."[3] He learned Arabic and translated a strange book, "M," into Latin; henceforth he would carry this with him wherever he went. He also perfected his knowledge of physics and mathematics.

After visiting Egypt, where he studied plants and animal life, Christian sailed to Fez. Unlike the envious and petty minds of Europe who kept their knowledge to themselves, the sages Christian encountered in the East seemed to be in agreement with each other and were happy to share what they knew. Here the author(s)[4] of the *Fama* may be suggesting that the knowledge the Eastern sages shared was part of the *prisca theologia*, the lost ancient wisdom that began to be recovered when Cosimo de' Medici asked Marsilio Ficino to translate the newly discovered *Corpus Hermeticum*. That this wisdom comes from the East, specifically Muslim countries—Arabia and Morocco—suggests it was part of the "treasure" thought to have been brought back to Christian countries by the Order of the Knights Templar, a powerful religious and political society that emerged from the Crusades in the early twelfth century. In esoteric history, the Rosicrucians come more or less in between the Knights Templar and modern Freemasonry, which, in the eighteenth century, carried on the Rosicrucian tradition of occult politics.

HOUSES OF THE HOLY

After two years in Fez, Christian returned to Europe. In Spain he "conferred with the learned," showing them their errors and how to correct them. They only laughed, more concerned about their reputations than about the truth, a problem Christian found elsewhere. Finding no recipients for his reforming zeal, Christian returned to Germany, where he built a house and meditated on his journeys. Five years later he set out again, this time with a few followers, the original Brothers of the Rosy Cross. In the end they separated, each brother going to a different country to spread the word, taking upon themselves certain vows: to heal the sick without payment; to wear the dress of their adopted country; to meet each year on an appointed day at the house, *Sancti Spiritus*, or "House of the Holy Spirit" that Christian had built; to seek another to replace oneself when the time came; to use the initials "C.R." as a secret mark; and to keep the existence and work of the Fraternity a secret for one hundred years.

THE SECRET TOMB OF CHRISTIAN ROSENCREUTZ

Years passed and Christian died. Knowledge of the society was handed down to younger seekers until all that remained of the founders was legend. When the hundred years of silence had ended, a senior member informed the newer recruits—the author(s) of the *Fama*—that "the Fraternity shouldn't remain hidden, but should come forth and be helpful to the whole German nation."[5] He then decided to do some home improvement on the House of the Holy Spirit, and move a brass memorial containing the names of previous brethren to a more suitable location. Behind the memorial they discovered a hidden door leading to a secret room, and within this was the tomb of Christian Rosencreutz. The author(s) of the *Fama* remark: "As our door was after so many years wonderfully discovered, also there shall be opened a door to Europe (when the wall is removed) which already doth begin to appear, and with great desire is expected of many."[6]

Within a seven-sided vault illuminated by a kind of miniature sun, Christian's body lay. Although it had rested there for more than a century, miraculously it showed no signs of decay.[7] Geometrical figures covered the walls, and within were many treasures, including works by the sixteenth-century Swiss healer and alchemist Paracelsus, bells, lamps, mirrors, and something they call "artificial songs"—reference, perhaps, to a form of mechanical marvel popular at that time. The vault resembled a kind of time capsule, the idea being that "if it should happen after many hundred years the Order or Fraternity should come to nothing, they might by this only vault be restored again."[8]

In Christian's hand they discovered a parchment book, "I," which, next to the Bible, they counted as their greatest treasure. At the end of the book they found this inscription: "We are born of God, we die in Jesus, we live again through the Holy Spirit," suggesting that Christian may have been a follower of Joachim of Fiore. Born in Calabria in 1135, Joachim was a monk, mystic, and theologian who prophesied a new age of spiritual freedom, due to arrive in 1260. He died in 1202, too early to know if he was right or not. Joachim saw history unfolding in three stages: the Age of the Father, characterized by the Old Testament and obedience to the laws of God; the Age of the Son, beginning with the advent of Christ and continuing to 1260, during which man becomes the Son of God; and the Age of the Holy Spirit, when mankind would achieve *direct* contact with God and experience the spiritual freedom that is the true message of Christianity. Joachim believed that at this stage the hierarchy of the Church would be unnecessary and the true, rather than merely literal, meaning of the Gospels would prevail. Thomas Aquinas argued against his ideas, but Dante placed Joachim in Paradise, and his beliefs inspired Christian breakaway sects like the Brethren of the Free Spirit.[9] The Church, understandably, wasn't that happy with his prophecies—it rarely appreciates any challenge to its authority. But they were precisely the sort of thing the Rosicrucians looked forward to.

Rejoicing in their discovery, the author(s) of the *Fama* suggest that their readers might also find the lost tombs of other deceased brethren and that other doors in Europe might be opened. Convinced that the "general reformation" will take place, the author(s) are confident that others will join them and increase their numbers. Accepting the "Roman Empire" as their "Christian head," they are nevertheless aware of "what alterations be at hand" and promise to "help with secret aid this so good a cause." They claim that their philosophy, which Adam received after his fall and which Moses and Solomon put to good use, is in agreement with Plato, Pythagoras, Enoch, Abraham, and, importantly, the Bible. Their remark that the wisdom of these sages "makes a sphere or Globe, whose total parts are equidistant from the Center,"[10] again suggests the *prisca theologia*, the ancient wisdom at the core, handed down from initiate to initiate.

The brethren shouldn't be confused, however, with those who concern themselves with common gold-making, a fraudulent practice sadly prevalent at the time, a dig at the "puffers" and mountebanks who ingratiated themselves into the courts of influential figures like the Holy Roman Emperor Rudolf II and gave alchemy a bad reputation. The true alchemist, they know, works to transform *himself*, not lead, into gold: the spiritually regenerated man. In closing, the *Fama*'s author(s) entreat those who hear their call to seek them out, assuring that if seekers "behold the present time with diligence," their desire to reach the brethren will be known.

THE FUROR CONTINUES

If the appearance of the *Fama* caused a furor, this only increased the next year when a follow-up document appeared, the *Confessio Fraternitas*. Although the *Fama* was published in German, the *Confessio* appeared in Latin and was aimed at a more learned audience. Doubtless the declaration that its author(s) "do now altogether freely and securely, and without hurt, call the Pope of Rome Antichrist"[11] made the most powerful impression on its readers. This reference to the "end time" announced in the Book of Revelations was reinforced by the remark that Jehovah, "seeing that the Lord's Sabbath is almost at hand," "doth turn about the course of Nature."

Along with the Pope, "Mahomet" (Muhammad), too, is charged with blasphemy against Jesus. Yet the Fraternity itself, the author(s) insist, is innocent of the least heresy or conspiracy against the worldly government. Readers of the *Fama* shouldn't reject its message out of hand, nor believe in it too hastily, they advise, but consider it seriously and deeply. And the remarkable accomplishments of Christian Rosencreutz are now placed in a context of what seems a project of social regeneration. Such knowledge as the Fraternity possesses, we are told, could free mankind from a host of perennial worries. "Were it not good," the author(s) ask rhetorically, "that we needed not to care, not to fear hunger, poverty, sickness and age?"[12] The brethren could "release" the world "from innumerable miseries."[13] One sign that such a transformation of earthly life is at hand are the "new stars" in the constellations Serpentarius and Cygnus, which were first sighted in 1604, the year Christian Rosencreutz's tomb was supposedly discovered. These, the author(s) tell us, clearly indicate that "the World shall awake out of her heavy and drowsy sleep," to meet "the new arising Sun."

THE INVISIBLES

This somewhat detailed account of the Rosicrucian documents may, I hope, convey the strange atmosphere their appearance created. Yet perhaps the strangest thing is that after sounding a clarion call to join them in their work of reformation, the Brothers of the Rosy Cross were nowhere to be found. That such famous figures as the philosophers Robert Fludd, René Descartes, and Gottfried Wilhelm Leibniz are associated with the Rosicrucians makes their obscurity all the more intriguing. All attempts to contact them seem to have failed, and their absence led to the name "the Invisibles." At the time this made them even more mysterious and attractive, but in later years it encouraged doubts about their existence. Most historians of the period conclude that the whole thing was a hoax. And that as a teenager, Johann Valentin Andreae, author of the *Chemical Wedding* and possibly responsible for the earlier manifestos, had written a version of the *Chemical Wedding* that he later admitted was a *ludibrium*, or joke, albeit a serious one, suggests that, in one of his contemporaries' phrases, it was all "much ado about nothing."

Yet Frances Yates in *The Rosicrucian Enlightenment* makes clear that, whatever the truth behind the occult claims of the Rosicrucians, the political and religious climate in which the *Fama*, *Confessio*, and *Chemical Wedding* appeared was very serious indeed. The Rosicrucian furor emerged during the years of struggle between Catholics and Protestants that led to the devastating Thirty Years War (1618–48). Many at the time hoped the schism fracturing the Church might be healed. In 1555, the Peace of Augsburg brought about a temporary calm in hostilities and gave official status to Lutheranism within the Holy Roman Empire. According to its edict, *cuius regio, eius religio*: literally, "whose region, his religion," the religion of a particular ruler would be the religion of his land. While this satisfied some Protestant groups, others, like the Calvinists and Anabaptists, had to wait until 1648 and the Peace of Westphalia to be recognized. Many others simply felt that Rome had lost its way and indeed become the seat of the Antichrist.

In 1517, a century before the *Fama*'s appearance, Martin Luther had nailed his *Ninety-Five Theses* to the door of the Wittenberg church (although whether he actually did this or not is a matter of debate), declaring his contempt for Rome's practice of "indulgences." These were basically bribes accepted by priests in return for assuring ones' salvation or that of a deceased loved one, a procedure that smacks of magic: for a price, a priest will use his "powers" to make things right between you and the gods. This nauseated Luther; he knew the indulgences did nothing for one's salvation and that the money was really used by Pope Leo X to rebuild the basilica of St. Peter in Rome, further evidence that the Church had moved away from Christ's true teachings to become a symbol of worldly power. Like Joachim of Fiore, Luther believed that the hierarchy of Rome had become an obstacle to the true Christian message, a belief the Rosicrucians—whoever they were—shared. It's been suggested that the rose of the Rosicrucians is taken from Luther's own emblem, in which a heart and a cross rise up from a flower. Alternative theories suggest that *Rosicrucian* is derived from the alchemical *Ros* (dew) and *Crux* (cross), or that it is linked to the chivalric Order of the Garter, a ceremony that Johann Valentin Andreae is said to have witnessed in his student days, at the time when he wrote the first *Chemical Wedding*. Yet symbols are elusive and their origins difficult to nail; the rose has a history of mystical associations that precedes its links to Luther. It was an important symbol for the Islamic mystics, the Sufis, and through them passed to the troubadours, and later reached Dante. Further associations link it and the cross to the *yoni* and *lingam* of the Tantric mysteries, emblems of natural generation and of spiritual re-generation, processes that clearly interested the Rosicrucians.

Yet Andreae was a Lutheran pastor, and his Protestant sympathies were obvious. He came of age in a time when "religious and social upheavals had gone hand in hand"[14] and Germany especially "was the great focal point in Europe of messianic and millennialist ideas."[15] It was also a time when, according to Christopher McIntosh, there was "a strong tendency to form secret or semi-secret societies," which were "very often closely linked with a burgeoning German nationalism."[16] Indeed, McIntosh suggests that the French seer and astrologer Nostradamus may even have predicted the coming of the Rosicrucians. In 1555—the year of the Peace of Augsburg—Nostradamus wrote that

> A new sect of Philosophers shall rise
> Despising death, gold, honours and riches,
> They shall be near the mountains of Germany,
> They shall have abundance of others to
> Support and follow them.[17]

Whether or not Nostradamus was speaking of the Rosicrucians, the period leading up to the manifestos seems to fit his prediction. Paracelsus, whose works were found in Christian Rosencreutz's tomb, tried to launch a reformation in the scientific and religious sensibilities of his time, which for him were hopelessly mired in outmoded beliefs and dominated by a decadent, authoritarian church. In his fascinating biography of the Swiss alchemist and healer, Philip Ball points out that after Paracelsus' death in 1562, brotherhoods of a Paracelsian character sprang up in Germany. Although Ball rejects the idea that Paracelsus was the "spiritual founder" of the Rosicrucians, opting for the link with Martin Luther's rose instead (even so, he admits that the "Paracelsus connection remains puzzling"),[18] he certainly sees the alchemist as the inspiration for groups like the German *Orden der Unzertrennlichen* (Order of the Inseparables), out of whom he suggests the Rosicrucians themselves may have emerged, a possibility that McIntosh offers, too. The Inseparables were also linked to the oddly named—for English speakers—*Fruchtbringende Gesellschaft* (Fruit-Bringing Society), of which Andreae was a member.[19]

Earlier echoes of the Rosicrucian theme can be seen in Wolfram von Eschenbach's Arthurian poem *Parzival*, written in the 1190s. Here, a brotherhood of knights live in a mysterious, hidden castle called Munsalvaesche, reminiscent of Christian Rosencreutz's Sancti Spiritus. Like the Rosicrucians, the knights are celibate, trained to work for the good of mankind and to pass among the population unrecognized, dressed in the clothes of their adopted country. Both the *Chemical Wedding* and *Parzival* include many astrological references, and both refer to a strange stone. In *Parzival*, the Grail itself is spoken of as a stone, linking it to the alchemical "philosopher's stone," and on the Seventh (and last) day of the *Chemical Wedding*, the beautiful virgin Virgo Lucifera tells the wedding guests—including Christian Rosencreutz—that they are all now "Knights of the Golden Stone." Gold, along with the stone, is a central alchemical symbol.[20]

ALCHEMICAL EMPEROR

As well as being a pastor and a writer, Johann Valentin Andreae was a devotee of alchemy, a passion for which he acquired from his father and tutors. After his father's death, his mother became court apothecary to Frederick I, Duke of Württemberg, and early exposures at the court to charlatans and puffers who ingratiated themselves with royalty may have prompted Andreae's staunch defense of true alchemy in the *Fama*. Andreae grew up in a time when alchemy and other occult disciplines were respected and their practitioners sought after, perhaps nowhere more fervently than in the court of Rudolph II, Holy Roman Emperor, whose Bohemian capital, Prague, was an occultist's dream. (Rudolph II is the "Christian head" of the "Roman Empire" mentioned in the *Fama*.) Although a weak, indecisive ruler, Rudolph was a keen devotee of the arts and sciences, and also of astrology, alchemy, and magic. His court attracted many of the greatest minds of his time: the astronomer Tycho Brahe, the mathematician Johannes

Kepler, the hermetic philosopher Giordano Bruno, the painter Giuseppe Arcimboldo, and the astrologer and magus John Dee. Rudolph also advocated religious tolerance, and although he vacillated in this as he did in practically everything else, under his rule Protestants and Jews received fairer treatment than anywhere else in Europe.

Because of his Renaissance passion for knowledge, Rudolph encouraged freedom of thought and expression, and although he was responsible for maintaining the temporal power of the Catholic Church, his liberal, humanist view brought him into conflict with it. Combined with his pathological indecisiveness, this eventually led to his downfall at the hands of his brother, Matthias, who became emperor after Rudolf's death. Matthias himself proved a mediocre ruler, and on his death only a few years after Rudolph's, the title of Holy Roman Emperor passed into the hands of the fanatically intolerant Catholic Hapsburg Ferdinand II. Ferdinand II was educated by the Jesuits, and not surprisingly he immediately annulled all of Rudolph's policies of religious tolerance. Nevertheless, during Rudolph's reign hopes had grown that the hegemony of the Catholic church, embodied in the political and military power of the Hapsburgs, might be loosened.

HERETICS

The Church had already seen considerable opposition to its rule and had dealt with it ruthlessly. Even at its start, it had to eliminate a rival interpretation of Christ's teaching advocated by the various early Christian groups known as the Gnostics. The Christians whose views eventually became those of the official church read the Gospels as *literal* truth, but the Gnostics read them *symbolically*. For them, Christ's crucifixion and resurrection weren't historical but spiritual events; all true Christians would experience them in their own lives as a spiritual death and rebirth. The Gnostics were known to shake their heads at the fanatical Christians who believed they would enter heaven by letting themselves be mauled by Roman lions. Where the literalists saw faith and obedience as the essence of salvation, the Gnostics looked to knowledge and spiritual experience; their name is derived from the Greek *gnosis*, "knowledge," and has become a synonym for occult practice today. Where the Church moved toward a hierarchical structure, the Gnostics remained loosely knit and individualistic and, unlike the Church, regarded women as equals with men. Probably most offensive to the Church was the Gnostic belief that the world is the creation of an idiot demi-urge, or half-god, associated with the Jehovah of the Bible. Salvation for the Gnostics meant escape from the demi-urge's trap through awakening the spark of the divine substance that slumbered within, a trope central to all subsequent occult and esoteric disciplines.

Similar beliefs were shared by later "heretical" sects that were also eliminated. The Bogomils, for example, in tenth-century Bulgaria, whose name means "beloved of God," and the Albigensians and Cathars (the "purified"), who were prominent in the eleventh, twelfth, and thirteenth centuries in the Languedoc region of France, fell afoul of the Church's belief that it alone could offer a sinful mankind a sure path to God's love, even if securing its salvation meant meting out the kind of violence responsible for the Cathar massacre at Montségur in 1244.[21] Some occult historians suggest there's a direct link running through the Gnostics, Cathars, and Rosicrucians. Whether or not there is, they do seem to share a sympathy of ideas and beliefs.

Less mystical opponents also proved considerable thorns in the Church's side. Jan Huss (1373–1415) preached egalitarianism, rejected violence, and practiced a kind of fundamentalism based on the life of the early Christians, uniting small groups together in closely knit communities. The Church frowned on his activities, and he was burned at the stake by the Inquisition in 1415, thus inaugurating the Hussite Wars. It was in this climate that Luther's theses found their way to the door of the Wittenberg church.

PANSOPHIA

By the time the Rosicrucian manifestos appeared, the tensions surrounding the Reformation had reached a crisis point, and the Counter-Reformation had begun. Some sudden shift in the state of things seemed to be at hand, and the "pursuit of the millennium," in the historian Norman Cohn's phrase, was rife. *Pansophia*, or "universal wisdom," was much discussed. Pansophia was a movement of learning that, according to the esoteric scholar Joscelyn Godwin, combined "the natural and the supernatural sciences for the betterment of mankind,"[22] an enterprise with clear echoes of the Rosicrucian experiment. Paracelsus was an early pansophist, as was John Dee. Dee's work was a major influence on the Rosicrucian manifestos, especially the *Confessio*; his forays into occult politics led him to the court of Rudolf II and to coining the phrase "the British Empire," much to the delight of Queen Elizabeth I. Pansophists shared a desire to bring together the growing discipline of empirical science and the insights of the esoteric tradition, a unity many felt was blocked by the hegemony of the Church.

CONFEDERATIO MILITIAE EVANGELICAE

Another pansophist was the obscure scholar and mystic Simon Studion, born in Urach, Württemberg, in 1543. He's remembered today for his strange work *Naometria*, or "The Measurement of the Temple," which didn't appear in print but was widely circulated in manuscript. In *Naometria*, Studion adapts Joachim of Fiore's system of three ages to make predictions about his own time. One is that the third age, which Studion, like Joachim, believes will begin in 1620, will be symbolized by a cross. Studion presented his work as a gift to the Duke of Württemberg in 1604, which, we know, was an important year for crosses and roses. Perhaps more interesting is that Studion speaks of a mysterious order, the Confederatio Militiae Evangelicae, founded in Lüneburg in 1586. Whether any such organization ever existed is unclear, but Studion describes it as a Protestant alliance between the King of Navarre, the King of Denmark, and the Queen of England, formed to block the Catholic League's attempts to prevent Henry of Navarre's accession to the French throne. In his dedication to the Duke of Württemberg, Studion remarks that the Duke himself had a position of some importance in this confederation.

In his *Brotherhood of the Rosy Cross*, the occult scholar A. E. Waite argues that the *Naometria* and the Confederatio Militiae Evangelicae are key sources for the Rosicrucian manifestos. Waite studied the *Naometria* manuscript and claims that a rose and cross design found in it was the model for the Rosicrucian symbol. Later researchers are less sure, but Frances Yates agrees that the Rosicrucian movement was linked to an alliance of Protestant sympathizers eager to obstruct the Hapsburg Catholic League. In his *Turris Babel*, published in 1619, Andreae draws on the *Naometria* for its prophecies of future events, specifically that the year 1620 will see the downfall of the Pope and the end of the reign of the Antichrist, and that the new millennium will begin in 1623. Like Studion, Andreae links his speculation to Joachim of Fiore and to other visionaries, like Paracelsus. Echoes of the *Naometria* appear in the *Confessio* as well.[23]

Andreae may have been introduced to Studion's work in his student days as a member of what McIntosh dubs the "Tübingen circle," a group of devout Lutheran intellectuals with socialist leanings. Christoph Besold, a member of the circle, was a cabalist and something of a mentor to Andreae. He may have shared with him his vision of a Europe free of religious strife and renewed through a union of the new sciences with the true Christian faith. Other members were disciples of the Italian former Dominican friar Tommaso Campanella, author of the pansophic work *The City of the Sun*. Although not published until 1623, after the Rosicrucian manifestos appeared, the work was written in around 1602. Campanella depicts a utopia run along Gnostic and Rosicrucian lines, an egalitarian society with men and women as equals. The city has seven walls, recalling the seven-sided vault that housed Christian Rosencreutz's tomb; that it is a "city of the sun" recalls the miniature sun found in the tomb. At its heart is an Hermetic priesthood who use Ficinian star magic for the benefit of its inhabitants. In 1600, Campanella had put his visionary politics into practice and in southern Italy led a revolution against the Spanish occupiers. The revolution failed, and Campanella was arrested, tortured, and then imprisoned for twenty-seven years; it was while in prison that he wrote *The City of the Sun*. Two of Campanella's disciples who visited him in prison were Tübingen friends of Andreae, and they carried manuscripts of Campanella's work, including *The City of the Sun*, back to Germany with them.[24]

FREDERICK AND ELIZABETH

Andreae wasn't the only Protestant who took Studion's predictions seriously. At the time of the Rosicrucian furor, hopes for a serious challenge to Hapsburg and Catholic dominance rested on Frederick V, the Elector Palatine of the Rhine. (The Palatinate, a state in western Germany, was part of the Holy Roman Empire; as elector, Frederick had a vote in who would become Holy Roman Emperor.) Frederick enjoyed the Rosicrucian blend of Protestantism and hermetic science and was himself something of a visionary. His castle at Heidelberg, renovated by the architect and hydraulics expert Simon de Caus, was decorated in an occult fashion and included several mechanical marvels, such as water organs and singing fountains—reminiscent of the "artificial songs" found in Christian Rosencreutz's tomb—set in fantastic gardens and grottos. Arranged in allegorical and mythological designs, the gardens were based on the ideas of the classical architect Vitruvius, rediscovery of whose work formed part of the Renaissance. Combining music, mathematics, and science, they were spoken of as an "eighth wonder of the world."

In 1613, Frederick married Princess Elizabeth, daughter of King James I of England, and for their wedding in the royal chapel at Whitehall, "all the treasures of the English Renaissance were outpoured." Their return to Heidelberg was triumphant. Pageants and celebrations went on for several days. Frederick, dressed as Jason, "sailed" in a chariot made up as the Argos in search of the Golden Fleece, a symbol from Greek mythology with alchemical correspondences. The Fleece was known to cure ills and to revive the dead, and the union of the Protestant Frederick with the English Princess Elizabeth suggested that a Europe debilitated by religious dissension and Hapsburg rule might soon be rejuvenated. Elizabeth's father, James I, was known to be anti-Hapsburg, and it was believed that in a crisis, he would come to his daughter and son-in-law's aid.

THE BOHEMIAN TRAGEDY

The idea that Frederick would lead a campaign against the Hapsburgs seems to have been masterminded by Christian of Anhalt, chief adviser to Heidelberg and, like so many other Protestant noblemen at the time, a student of the hermetic arts. Anhalt was a patron of the cabalist Oswald Croll and a close friend of Count Rotmberk, whose Bohemian estates near Trebon had been home for a time to John Dee during his mission to Rudolph II. Rotmberk was a Rudolphine liberal and a student of alchemy and the occult. It's likely that Dee's ideas of "mystical imperialism" reached Anhalt through Trebon. Anhalt had already been involved in plans laid by Henry IV to end the Hapsburg dominance, and when Henry died, Anhalt turned to Frederick. Although young, Fredrick had much to suggest him for the job. Coming from a tradition of Protestant activism, he was a natural choice for head of the Union of Protestant Princes. He had strong connections with powerful French, German, and Dutch Protestants. And he was married to the daughter of James I. Thought of the English monarch no doubt prompted echoes of Anhalt's earlier British connection with Dee, and the Elizabethan magician's own visions of pansophia were more than likely linked to what seemed to be the destiny of the Elector Palatine.

When Ferdinand II became king of Bohemia in 1617, the era of religious tolerance was over. One of his first acts was to suppress the Bohemian Church, which had carried on the work of Jan Huss, and the Bohemian Brethren, a mystical sect associated with it. The long tension kept in equilibrium by the Peace of Augsburg had snapped, and the anti-Hapsburg forces knew that they had to act quickly. A diplomatic attempt by Catholic liberals to stop the suppression proved futile; Ferdinand's Jesuit advisers fiercely opposed any leniency. An equally determined reaction stiffened the Protestants. At a thunderous meeting in Prague, two Catholic advocates were thrown out a window, an incident known as "the Defenestration of Prague." The Bohemian rebels maintained that the crown of Bohemia was an elective seat and not hereditary, as Ferdinand and the Jesuits insisted.[25] On August 26, 1619, they asked Frederick if he would accept the crown. A month later he agreed.

His spiritual convictions decided him. The poet John Donne and the Archbishop of Canterbury both advised Frederick to accept the responsibility. Writing to his uncle, the Duke of Bouillon, a Huguenot leader and one of the French Protestants whose support he counted on, Frederick said, "It is a divine calling which I must not disobey." "My only end," he said, "is to serve God and His Church."

This open defiance of the Hapsburgs soon proved disastrous. Not long into Frederick's reign as king of Bohemia, the Hapsburgs brought their forces against him. The support he and Anhalt had counted on from James I didn't arrive; the English king was in fact courting favor with Frederick's enemies. The few who stood by Frederick weren't enough, and on November 8, 1620, at the Battle of the White Mountain, his army was decimated. The Thirty Years War had begun, and among its many casualties were the fantastic gardens of Heidelberg. These were destroyed, and with them, one could say, the hopes of a Rosicrucian dawn.[26]

A ROSICRUCIAN TRAGEDY?

There's much to suggest a link between the Rosicrucian experiment and the Bohemian Tragedy. The Rosicrucian manifestos called for a great "reformation," and although they recognized the "Roman Empire" as their "Christian head," they were also aware of "what alterations are at hand." The tolerant Rudolph II was still Holy Roman Emperor when the *Fama* was written (although published in 1614, the *Fama* seems to have been written in 1610 and to have circulated in manuscript for some time); hence the gesture of respect. Yet its author(s) were aware of the hopes gathering around Frederick V, and as we have seen, Andreae was a keen reader of Studion's *Naometria*, with its predictions of a coming new age. Talk of "doors" opening in Europe, of the "secret aid" the Rosicrucians would offer, and of the "wall" that would soon be "removed" point to some expectation of a specific change. Cassel, where the manifestos were published, is near the Palatinate, and as Frances Yates points out, it shared the same occult and Protestant sympathies. Württemberg, where Andreae lived, was another neighboring Protestant principality.

Textual evidence also suggests a connection. References in the *Confessio* to "eagle's feathers" "hindering" the Rosicrucian effort is an allusion to the Hapsburgs, whose emblem was a double eagle. The Pope as Antichrist was a common Protestant epithet. The magical gardens mentioned in the *Chemical Wedding* may be an allusion to the hermetic gardens of Heidelberg. Although first written in his student days, the *Chemical Wedding* was rewritten in parts before appearing in 1616, and as an "eighth wonder of the world," reports of the Heidelberg gardens would have reached Andreae. The emblem of a lion, a symbol of the Palatinate, plays a major role in the *Chemical Wedding*. And like the *Chemical Wedding*, Frederick's and Elizabeth's own wedding was a dream-like, fairy tale affair.[27] That no further Rosicrucian communications appeared after the fateful year of 1620 suggests that their campaign ended when Frederick's did.

Most convincing is the flood of vilification that followed Frederick's ignominious defeat, linking his hopeless cause with the Rosicrucians, a smear tactic that would be used against future devotees of occult politics. Satirical cartoons and pamphlets showed the Hapsburg eagle victorious over the Palatinate lion and his hermetic accomplices. Humiliated, Frederick and Elizabeth fled their devastated Palatinate. For the rest of their lives they lived as exiles in The Hague.

Yet if the defeat at White Mountain spelled an end to the Rosicrucian attempt at a "hermetic reformation" of Europe—to bring the esoteric into the full light of the exoteric stage—in other, less obvious ways the Rosicrucian experiment continued. And as befits an invisible order, the politics involved were not quite so out in the open.

2

INVISIBLE COLLEGES

A feeling for the despair following the defeat of Frederick V can be found in one of the most moving works to emerge from the Rosicrucian aftermath. While hopes were high, even while in prison, the pansophist Tommaso Campanella could write about the "city of the sun." Now darkness had fallen. One response to the confusion was the Bohemian philosopher, educator, and scientist John Comenius' work *The Labyrinth of the World*. Like many who responded to the Rosicrucian call, Comenius, known as the "teacher of nations" and "father of general education," had believed that a new dawn of enlightenment and universal regeneration was at hand. But instead of walking the broad avenues of science and true Christian faith, Comenius found himself circling in a labyrinth of illusion and deceit—literally, as he was forced to flee Bohemia and spend the rest of his life in exile. *The Labyrinth of the World*, which depicts a society in which "everything is wrong," and in which "all the sciences of man lead to nothing,"[1] may be the first example of a "dystopia" in modern literature. It is certainly a heartbreaking response to the end of the Rosicrucian dream.

But was the Rosicrucian dream really over? The vilification the Rosicrucians received after the defeat of Frederick V made many think twice about admitting any association or "fellow-traveling" with them. And by this time, even some who had been essential to the Rosicrucian experiment seemed to have changed their minds.

TRUE LIES AND SERIOUS JOKES

Some writers have argued that Johann Valentin Andreae was really hostile to the Rosicrucian hoax from the start. They take his admission that the *Chemical Wedding* was a kind of joke as evidence that he was actually satirizing the gullible who took the *Fama* at face value. Others have suggested that he was in some way trying to Christianize the Rosicrucian myth.[2] Yet the truth may be more subtle. In *Turris Babel* Andreae seems to confess that the whole Rosicrucian furor was a mistake. "In vain do you wait for the coming of the Brotherhood," he writes, "the comedy is over." Frances Yates points out that Andreae was passionate about the theater, plays, and performances. This seems to clinch that, rather than being a utopian alchemist who tried to ignite a mystical regeneration of Europe, Andreae was really enjoying himself with a literary practical joke that unfortunately got out of hand. Even before the defeat at White Mountain, the Rosicrucians were getting a bad reputation. Their invisibility made them a hoax, and the associations claimed between them and witchcraft and other evils didn't help. Andreae would certainly have wanted to avoid being tarred with this brush. Yet even this perfectly sensible explanation for his apparent *volte face* isn't quite satisfying.

The key here is Andreae's use of the term *ludibrium*. The word can mean a "plaything," a "trivial game," or an "object of fun" or of "scorn and derision." At the time of the Rosicrucian experiment, the notion that, to quote again from Andreae's illustrious contemporary, "All the world's a stage, and all the men and women merely players" wasn't unusual; it was in fact a common theme of the hermetic philosophy the Rosicrucians pursued. In *The Theatre of the World*, *The Art of Memory*, and *Giordano Bruno and the Hermetic Tradition*, Frances Yates examines the enormous importance that "the art of memory" had for the ancients, which was rediscovered in the Renaissance. One frequently used trope to master this difficult art was a theater. A practitioner would "erect" an imaginary theater in his mind (employing a power of visualization sadly rare in our time) and then ascribe to different "parts" of it the contents of whatever work he wished to remember. "Looking" at his mental theater, he would, in a sense, have the work "in front of him" and could "read" it as if were a book. Again, one of the influences on the Rosicrucian philosophy was an extraordinary work of spiritual alchemy by the hermetic philosopher Heinrich Khunrath, *The Amphitheatre of Eternal Wisdom*, which reached them through the link with John Dee.[3] The earliest theater in the West emerged from the Dionysian mysteries, and the Greek tragedies at the foundation of Western literature have roots in spiritual and occult initiations.

In our time, the theater, although a place of illusions, has been used to great effect for very concrete political purposes, in the work of the Marxist playwright Bertolt Brecht and on a larger and perhaps more "revolutionary" scale, by the Situationists, the anarchist group who turned the streets of Paris into a theater of revolt in May 1968. In fact, the recognition that what one sees in a theater *is* a fiction can be used to bring home very serious truths, as Brecht did with his famous "distancing" technique. The philosopher Friedrich Nietzsche remarked that "the great man is the play actor of his own ideal," meaning that in order to become, as Nietzsche put it, "what one is," one must first *pretend* to be it. The theater, then, can be a medium to communicate, as the title of an Arnold Schwarzenegger film has it, "true lies," which to me doesn't seem too far away from "serious jokes."

THE REAL ROSICRUCIANS

Andreae was a literary man, aware of the dangers of being literal. In denying the *factual* reality of the Rosicrucians, he was warning against the dangers of a too-literal reading of his work, much as the Gnostics avoided a literal interpretation of Christ's crucifixion and resurrection. What was true about the Rosicrucian experiment were its ideals as well as its recognition of the need for a regeneration of Lutheran Protestantism, which had become just as inflexible as the Roman church it rejected. This was true whether or not there was any "actual" Brotherhood. What was important were the Rosicrucian sensibility, the Rosicrucian outlook, and, quite possibly, the Rosicrucian "state of mind," an altered state of consciousness, achieved through the hermetic disciplines the "Rosicrucians" pursued. This suggests that to ask who the Rosicrucians "really" were may be misguided, and that more recent inquiries into the "truth" behind similar secret societies may be as well.

Seeing that his serious joke had spawned a clamor for wonder workers and magicians, as well as a dangerous backlash, Andreae distanced himself from this too-literal reading of the Rosicrucian idea. But also he wanted to ensure that the serious part of the joke wasn't lost. This wasn't new; if Andreae had had a hand in the *Fama*, he had already warned against linking the Brotherhood with those puffers and their patrons who wanted to turn real lead into gold. Even if some alchemists, like Michael Maier, believed that the Brotherhood possessed the secret of making actual gold, his real concern was with the spiritual transformations this involved.

Yet the question of the literal existence of a secret Brotherhood or "initiatic chain" continues today. Some occult philosophers have been of two minds about it. In *Tertium Organum*, the Russian philosopher P. D. Ouspensky wrote that humanity was evolving into a new form of consciousness and that people in whom this new consciousness was emerging were "beginning to recognize one another." "Watchwords, signs and countersigns are already being established,"[4] Ouspensky said, and the "selection goes on in all races and nations of the earth." This suggests that the "new consciousness" Ouspensky recognized was widespread, not located in a specific group. Yet, after writing *Tertium Organum*, Ouspensky spent the rest of his life searching for what he called the "Inner Circle," an *actual* society of "awakened" human beings, a kind of Rosicrucian Brotherhood, an idea he absorbed in his early days in the Theosophical Society.[5] That secret or occult societies have existed, and continue to exist, isn't denied; writing this book would be difficult if they didn't. Yet, I wonder if the sensibility or state of mind associated with some of these groups require *actual* contact and "initiation" into them. Can one have a Rosicrucian sensibility without ever having met an "actual" Rosicrucian? The Tarot and Cabala scholar Paul Foster Case thought so. "One *becomes* a Rosicrucian," he wrote, "one does not *join* the Rosicrucians."[6]

Some proponents of "illuminated politics" would argue with this. It raises an important question in what we might call the "politics of occultism": whether one adopts a "liberal" approach to esoteric ideas or a more "conservative" one. For all the trappings of an elite, secret order, the Rosicrucian impulse was, I think, a democratic, progressive one, and the Rosicrucian call, even with its subtle *ludibrium*, was addressed to anyone who shared its sensibility.

CITIES OF THE SUN

Andreae's subsequent career saw the creation of what he called Christian Societies—exoteric, visible expressions of the Rosicrucian ethos, minus the hermetic paraphernalia of the manifestos. Most of these were soon lost in the chaos of the Thirty Years War, but one did lead to a later society that would, in an edited form, fulfill part of the Brotherhood's mission. That Andreae hadn't abandoned the Rosicrucian cause and was actually working to promote it, albeit in a very different way, is seen in a work many consider his most important—his own "city of the sun," the utopian *Christianopolis*.

It's difficult to think of a work with a vision further from Comenius' *The Labyrinth of the World*; when we reflect that Comenius knew Andreae and was influenced by him, the disenchantment of his *Labyrinth* becomes even more poignant. *Christianopolis* presents the utopia the Rosicrucians hoped to bring about. In the preface, Andreae rejects the manifestos, yet, for those subtle enough to see it, he also affirms this new work's links with them. He remarks on the confusion brought about by the Rosicrucian furor; yet he deplores the dominance of Antichrist over the Church and applauds the effort to reform it, calling for a new reformation that will go beyond Luther's, clearly one of the Brotherhood's aims.

Christianopolis is a city based on the sacred geometry of the circle and the square. Its inhabitants are pious Christians, devoted to science and its practical application. Mechanical arts and music feature prominently, which reminds us of the "artificial songs" discovered in Christian Rosencreutz's tomb. Medicine, too, is important, and we recall that healing the ill was one of the Rosy Brethren's vows. Mathematics is central, as is the theater as an educational tool: much of the teaching involves the pictures decorating the city's walls. Architecture is crucial, reminiscent of the hermetic gardens of Heidelberg. Angels also play an important role, as they did in John Dee's philosophy and in the Christian cabala that emerged from the Renaissance. Indeed, the combination of angels, with whom the inhabitants of Christianopolis have intimate and frequent contact, and the inhabitants' own zeal in carrying out socially conscious activities, resembles the heavenly society portrayed by the Swedish scientist, philosopher, and theologian, Emanuel Swedenborg. Swedenborg claimed to have visited heaven while in profound, meditative trance states, and we will hear more of his own links to occult politics further on.

A reader of *Christianopolis*, whether a fellow seeker of utopia or a Hapsburg censor, would have noted Andreae's disdain for a "certain fraternity," which was in his opinion "a joke." Less obvious is that the way to his pious, technological paradise is by a boat marked with the zodiacal sign of Cancer. This astrological vessel, as Yates points out, is the same one Christian Rosencreutz voyages in at the close of *Chemical Wedding*.

ESOTERIC WRITING

In *Persecution and the Art of Writing,* the philosopher Leo Strauss, in recent years tagged as an intellectual forefather of neoconservatism, argues that philosophers before the modern period developed a form of writing he calls "esoteric"—not in the hermetic sense, but as a way of avoiding persecution while at the same time reaching their audience. A text could have a surface meaning that raised no alarm with the censors, but below or within this, the attentive reader could detect the real kernel of communication. Strauss believed such works force readers to think actively, to tease out the meaning and not simply absorb information passively. This safeguards against accepting dangerous ideas too quickly. Recalling that Andreae—if indeed he was one of its authors—cautioned readers of the *Confessio* not to reject the *Fama*'s message out of hand or to accept it too hastily, and that his *ludibrium* of the Brotherhood may be what Strauss called a "noble lie"—a myth proposed to achieve a desirable end—it seems possible that this perpetrator of serious jokes was practicing Straussian tactics centuries in advance of any neoconservative agenda.

BACON'S *NEW ATLANTIS*

Andreae's wasn't the only city of the sun associated with the Brotherhood. Francis Bacon, the father of experimental science, isn't usually considered particularly "occult." Yet his *Advancement of Learning* seems to share some of the Brethren's educational ideals. In it, Bacon argues that just as there are "brotherhoods" in families and those associated with certain skills (crafts guilds), there should also be a "fraternity in learning and illumination."

The Bacon-Rosicrucian connection inevitably spills over into the Bacon-Shakespeare controversy, the contention that Bacon is the true author of Shakespeare's works. Proponents of this theory have combed Shakespeare's plays for Baconian-Rosicrucian evidence. The results are inconclusive at best; at worst, they border on the absurd—see for example F. W. C. Wigston's *Bacon, Shakespeare and the Rosicrucians* (Wigston calls Shakespeare "the phantom Captain Shakespeare, the Rosicrucian mask"). Manly P. Hall contends that "it is quite evident that William Shakespeare could not, unaided, have produced the immortal writings bearing his name"[7] and marshals evidence for this claim. For Hall, Bacon "was a Rosicrucian, some have intimated *the* Rosicrucian." Hall backs away from the idea that Bacon was "the Illustrious Father C.R.C.," yet he concludes that he was "certainly a high initiate of the Rosicrucian Order."

The Bacon-Shakespeare argument, fascinating as it is, can't detain us, yet many scholars have indeed detected esoteric elements in the plays. Hall even argues that they contain Rosicrucian "secret teachings," as well as the "true rituals" of the Freemasons, who we will be meeting shortly. John Dee is often considered the model for Prospero in *The Tempest*, and *Love's Labors Lost* includes a group of celibate scholars dedicated to a life of learning. Given that the play was first performed in 1595, it couldn't have been directly influenced by the Rosicrucian manifestos. Nevertheless, it suggests that the ideas that would surface two decades later were percolating in the zeitgeist.

The evidence that Bacon was at least a Rosicrucian fellow traveler comes from his *New Atlantis* (1626), which depicts a utopian society discovered by sailors in an uncharted land. Like *Chemical Wedding*, *New Atlantis* is a fiction, a *ludibrium*. Its inhabitants are, like the Rosicrucians, pious Christians dedicated to the furthering of learning, which they use for the benefit of mankind. When Bacon's mariners reach the unknown land, they're handed a scroll of instructions stamped with a curious image: an angel's wings hanging down near a cross. The *Fama* ends with the motto, "Under the shadow of Jehovah's wings," and as Yates points out, wings are a kind of Rosicrucian trademark. The inhabitants treat sick mariners and refuse payment for their service. Travelers from New Atlantis visit other lands to gather news about the outside world; dressed in the native style, they journey undetected. An official who meets with the mariners wears a white turban surmounted by a small red cross. The red—rosy—cross is obvious, but is it redundant to point out that the turban suggests a native of "the East," where Christian Rosencreutz sought out esoteric knowledge?

These and other "clues" suggest that although he wasn't Christian Rosencreutz and didn't "belong" to the Rosy Brethren in any factual sense, Bacon knew of the manifestos and adopted some of their imagery and themes for his own purposes.

Yet one Rosicrucian enthusiast, who even celebrated his membership in the Brotherhood, was convinced of Bacon's affiliation. John Heydon was an astrologer, alchemist, and utopian; for his picture at the National Portrait Gallery in London he's even listed as a "Rosicrucian." In his *Holy Guide* (1662), Heydon interprets Bacon's *New Atlantis* as an undoubted work of Rosicrucian philosophy, making direct references to the order. He identifies the man in the white turban with the red cross as "a Christian priest, and of the Order of the Rosie Cross." The inhabitants of New Atlantis claimed to possess some of the lost works of Solomon; Heydon remarks that they are really referring to the book "M" found in the hidden tomb of Christian Rosencreutz and that this book had been written in New Atlantis (in the *Fama*, of course, this is the book C.R. translates in Damascus).[8] Heydon, who did much to promote the image of the Rosicrucians as magicians and wonder-workers, claims to have translated this work into English, or so he says in his strange book *The Wise-Man's Crown, Set with Angels, Planets, Metals, etc., or The Glory of the Rosie Cross.*[9]

That Bacon probably knew of the *Fama* and that his *New Atlantis* exhibits Rosicrucian ideals doesn't mean he was a Rosicrucian, John Heydon's arguments notwithstanding. But these possibilities do suggest that the idea of a general reformation and a new, utopian Christian society dedicated to a progressive political ethos was "in the air."

Maier and Fludd

Another Rosicrucian enthusiast was the alchemist and healer Michael Maier (1568–1622), at one time Rudolph II's personal physician. Born at Rendsburg, in Holstein, after finishing his medical studies Maier went to Prague—a natural choice, given that, like Paracelsus before him, Maier combined alchemy with medicine: following the great Swiss savant, Maier was the most important figure in "alternative health" of the time. After Rudolph died in 1612, Maier traveled to England, where it's thought he met the philosopher Robert Fludd, one of the Rosicrucians' most outspoken defenders. We know he met William Paddy, James I's physician, and that he sent the king a curious Christmas greeting. On a three-by-two-foot piece of parchment, with bits of verse and some conventional greetings, Maier drew an eight-petaled rose prominently in the center. The Latin message reads: "Greetings to James, for a long time King of Great Britain. By your true protection may the rose be joyful."

It's unclear if Maier ever had an audience with the king; as Rudolph II's former physician, it wouldn't have been unusual. What's interesting is that James received his proto–Christmas card two years before the *Fama* appeared in print—although the manuscript had been circulating during this time—and well before his daughter's wedding. Did Maier see James as a supporter, even a protector, of the Rosicrucian cause, or did he want him to be? James I was notoriously hostile to witchcraft; he even wrote a book against it, his *Demonologie*, which is understandable, given that a "coven" of witches had confessed to trying to sink the ship in which he and his queen, Anne of Denmark, returned to England after their wedding. Yet he may have been open to more spiritual practices. Shakespeare and Bacon (or, depending on your view, possibly just Bacon) flourished during his reign, as did the arts in general, and until the catastrophe at White Mountain, James was seen as a protector of Protestantism. Yet James's attitude to John Dee was less than encouraging. When Dee petitioned for an audience, the king wouldn't receive him and in effect sentenced Dee to a kind of internal banishment. Dee, once the "Queen's conjuror" and one of the most brilliant and accomplished men of his age, died in poverty and neglect. Yet until the Bohemian Tragedy, more than one Hermetic philosopher courted James for support or wished to create the impression he already had it.

Maier is best known for his exquisite alchemical work *Atalanta Fugiens* (Atalanta Fleeing), a kind of multi-media text inspired by Ovid's telling of how Hippomenes pursued Atalanta until he ravished her in a temple dedicated to Zeus, who promptly turned them both into lions. With poetry, images, and music, Maier focuses his readers' faculties on the alchemical narrative, portraying the *coniunctio oppositorum*, the union of the opposites, and the alchemist's need to reject temptation while persevering with the Great Work.

Maier believed the Rosicrucians were the inheritors of an ancient esoteric tradition; in his *Themis Aurea* he depicts them as dedicated scientists and physicians using their knowledge to create a better world. Yet in specifics he's less than concrete. He tells us that he "cannot set down the places where they meet, nor the time," yet recalls "Olympick Houses not far from a river" and a city that might be called "S. Spiritus" or perhaps "Helicon or Parnassus," which is where Diana bathed herself, with Venus, Saturn, and the flying horse Pegasus in attendance—a dreamy, non-committal rhetoric.[10] When he explains that an intelligent reader will know what he means but the ignorant will be confounded, we're reminded of Andreae's Straussian technique of "esoteric" writing.

Peter Marshall reports that Maier once performed psychic healing on a favorite of Rudolph II.[11] Maier's time in England, his meeting with Fludd, and the fact that his first book, *Arcana Arcanissima* (Secret of Secrets), was published there in 1614 are signs that the Rosicrucian impulse, which, as Yates argues, had its start with John Dee's "mission to Prague," was returning to its source. Sadly, Maier, like the fantastic gardens at Heidelberg, was a victim of the Thirty Years War. By all accounts he died during the siege of Magdeburg in 1622.

It's debated if Maier actually met Robert Fludd (1547–1637) during his time in England, but it's likely he did. Maier's *Arcana Arcanissima* was dedicated to the English physician William Paddy, a friend of Fludd's, and we know Maier met Paddy. Though significant, the esoteric community in Europe was small, and at that time networking meant something more than checking your email. Travel was for education and to meet similar minds, and it's unlikely that Maier would have missed the opportunity to meet a mind like Fludd's. Maier and Fludd shared a common publisher, Johann Theodore De Bry, at Oppenheim, a city in the Palatinate.[12] That the ample works of both men appeared in rapid succession suggests that the bulk of them were written well before publication. That their publisher was located in the Palatinate also suggests sympathy with the rising hopes surrounding Frederick V. And while not propaganda, the works of both writers would have helped spread the Rosicrucian sensibility favorable to the expected "general reformation."

Like Maier, Fludd stressed that he wasn't a member of the Brotherhood; with the exception of John Heydon, this is a tactic adopted by most Rosicrucian sympathizers. His sympathies were made obvious, if in a long-winded way, in the title of his first published work, *Apologia Compendiaria Fraternitatem de Rosea Cruce suspicionis et infamiae maculis aspersam, veritatis quasi Fluctibus abluens et abstergens* (A Compendius Apology for the Fraternity of the Rosy Cross, pelted with the mire of suspicion and infamy, but now cleansed with the waters of truth"). As "flood" or "waters" in Latin is *fluctibus*, Fludd was making a joke of his own name; but the book itself was very much in earnest. Here, and in the rest of his Rosicrucian output, Fludd links the Brotherhood to the *prisca theologia*, brought to light by Ficino, and argues that the "magic" it employs is strictly "scientific" and "holy."

This first effort and the one that followed, the *Tractatus Apologeticus* (Apologetic Treatise of the Integrity of the Society of the Rosy Cross), were out-and-out defenses of the Brotherhood, as well as attempts to contact it. Yet if Fludd, like Maier, believed the Brotherhood actually existed, he also, like Andreae, argued against a too-literal understanding of it. In his *Summum Bonum*, replying to attacks by the French monk Marin Mersenne, Fludd restates the case against confusing the Rosicrucians with the "impostors" who debased true spiritual magic with false claims to gold-making and other spurious wonders. Just as the true Church is made up of devout believers, so the Spiritus Sancti isn't made of mortar and bricks but of belief in the Rosicrucians and their ideals. The Fraternity offers spiritual, not blood, kinship.

Fludd's Rosicrucian kinship is evident in his colossal *Utriusque Cosmi Historia*, published by De Bry in 1617, a history of the "two worlds," the macrocosm and the microcosm. Just as Maier expressed the alchemical aspect of Rosicrucian thought, Fludd, harnessing the work of Dee, Paracelsus, Ficino, and the other Renaissance Hermeticists, synthesized the ideas of man as a "little universe." The work was dedicated to James I and salutes him as "Ter Maximus," a title given to Hermes Trismegistus himself, equating the king with the founder of the very science the work celebrates. As Maier did with his Rosicrucian Christmas card, Fludd seems to have tried to bring James on board, or to give the impression that he was already sympathetic to the works' ideals and its associations with the Palatinate and his son-in-law.[13]

Fludd possibly links the Rosicrucian experiment with another, much more visible fraternity that was to have its own entanglement with occult politics. Whether or not Fludd was a Freemason is still debated. Following A. E. Waite, Christopher McIntosh suggests he was, although the evidence for this is circumstantial.[14] Yet the works of other Rosicrucian followers suggest possibly strong connections between the two.

The Paradise of the Heart

If Maier and Fludd carried the hermetic-alchemical Rosicrucian torch, other sympathizers continued the utopian, educative impulse. One such was John Comenius, with whose despairing *Labyrinth of the World* this chapter began. Comenius' name may not be familiar to most English-speaking readers, but in central Europe he's a national hero. His birthday is a national holiday. In Hungary, a teachers' college and an adult education program are named after him. Rembrandt painted his portrait. Although a symbol of Czech nationalism, Comenius is an international figure as well, as is appropriate for a Rosicrucian thinker. He was asked to be the first president of Harvard University, and UNESCO offers a Comenius Medal for outstanding achievements in education. With this in mind, his epithet of "teacher of nations" is apt.

Comenius belonged to the Bohemian Brethren, the mystical strain of Protestantism that began with Jan Huss; when the Counter-Reformation attacked, he was one of its targets. With the fall of Frederick V, Spanish troops captured his hometown; they burned his house, his library, and all his manuscripts. He led the brethren into exile, traveling through Sweden, Lithuania, Transylvania, the Netherlands, Hungary, Poland, and England—again, the labyrinth in the title of his book was no mere metaphor. En route to the city of Brandeis, where he would find protection for a time on the estate of Count Zerotin, a Bohemian patriot who nevertheless hadn't supported Frederick V, Comenius's wife and one of his children died. It was here that he wrote *The Labyrinth of the World*.

Comenius, like Campanella, was a pansophist and, like Andreae, the theater was an important theme for him. His first pansophic work was *A Theatre of All Things in the World*. It's possible he and Andreae met in Heidelberg, where he studied at the university. He graduated in June 1613, only days after the arrival of Elizabeth, Frederick's bride, and he's likely to have witnessed the magnificent procession and festival that greeted her. Many of Comenius's professors had strong links to the Heidelberg court, and they may have told their young students of the great changes the marriage of Frederick and Elizabeth presaged.

At Heidelberg, Comenius also met George Hartlib, whose brother, Samuel Hartlib, would be of great help to Comenius in England.

Many of the Rosicrucian ideals would have been familiar to Comenius from his association with the Bohemian Brethren, who were noted for their benevolence, good works, and piety. And although his retreat from the failure of the Rosicrucian dream was more extreme, like Andreae, Comenius found refuge in his Christian faith. The labyrinth that his Pilgrim—the protagonist of his book—faces is vast and confusing, but he's saved from its darkness by a voice, which bids him to leave the maze and enter "the Paradise of the Heart." Just as Andreae abandoned the Rosicrucian *ludibrium* for more straightforward efforts like the creation of his Christian Societies, Comenius turned away from the collapse of his dreams to find new hope in Christ. At the book's close, Comenius (who we must assume is the Pilgrim) has a vision of angels. They are, he sees, the guardians of them who are good, but they are also their teachers. "They often give them secret knowledge of diverse things," Comenius writes, "and teach them the deep secret mysteries of God." Because of these angelic instructors, "nothing that a godly man can wish to know can be secret to them, and with God's permission they reveal that which they know."[15]

Comenius' angels form a kind of "invisible college," one that the inhabitants of Andreae's *Christianopolis* also attend. Like Andreae, Comenius jettisoned the form of his early utopian ideals but not the ideals themselves. With Dee, Andreae, and Fludd, he believes the search for knowledge includes both the earthly and the spiritual realms. This knowledge should be shared by those who devote their energies to acquiring it and disseminated in the service of an enlightened, philanthropic cause. The Rosicrucian furor was a letdown, and Frederick V a lost cause, but the progressive vision of an enlightened, liberated humanity is still at the heart of Comenius's paradise.

THE ENGLISH CONNECTION

Samuel Hartlib belonged to one of the Christian Societies promoted by Andreae, a mystical, philanthropic sect that would feel the Hapsburg's wrath. When he had to flee his home in Poland to avoid the Counter-Reformation, Hartlib went to England. Like many who had held on to the Rosicrucian dream, Hartlib was among those who, like Comenius, frequented the court of Elizabeth, the exiled former queen of Bohemia, in The Hague. After Frederick's death in 1623, the lingering hopes for a return of the Palatinate lion hung on her.

Hartlib shared Comenius' belief in education and seems a living, breathing Rosicrucian brother, uniting a passionate Christian piety with a fierce scientific sensibility and a commitment to help his fellow man. He set up a school in Chichester; when this proved unsuccessful, he returned to London. By this time Comenius had started a community of exiled Bohemian Brethren in Poland and had begun to write and publish educational works promoting his pansophic ideal. Another in Hartlib's circle was the Scots preacher John Dury, who had met Hartlib in Elbing and become infected with his enthusiasm for social and scientific reform. He too kept in close touch with Elizabeth in The Hague.

The England Hartlib discovered in many ways mirrored the Bohemia preceding the Rosicrucian debacle. On the brink of a catastrophic civil war, England's intellectual and political climate was strangely liberal and expansive. Hartlib took advantage of this situation to launch a monumental kind of networking; he was known as an "intelligencer" who kept up to date in a dizzying number of fields and distributed his knowledge among his wide circle of correspondents. One of his pet ideas was what he called an "Office of Addresses," a "citizen's information bureau," which made available material on a number of different subjects—a kind of seventeenth-century version of Google.

In 1640, Hartlib addressed Parliament, telling them about his own city in the sun, his *Description of the Famous Kingdom of Macaria*—"Macaria" being the name of the imaginary country in Thomas More's *Utopia*, from which the term *utopian* derives. As it is with other Rosicrucian utopias, Hartlib's yokes religious piety to scientific and spiritual learning. Like Andreae's, it's a *ludibrium* expressing the Rosicrucian dream; yet it also includes more practical proposals, ones a legislative body like Parliament could act on. Hartlib must have felt that his speech was successful; encouraged, he urged Comenius and

Dury to come to England. It seemed that here, finally, years after the *Fama* first set the Rosicrucian ball rolling, the general reformation and regeneration of the world could begin.

Fate was against it. When Dury and Comenius joined Hartlib in London in 1641, they were warmly received by his prestigious associates. Excitement was in the air. But by the following year, all plans for the "general reformation" were shelved. Civil war erupted. The chaos wasn't as devastating as that on the continent, but it was horrific enough, especially for men like Hartlib and Comenius, who had lived through it already. The brief Rosicrucian enlightenment faded again into darkness. Comenius left for Sweden; Dury for The Hague. Comenius must have felt a double sorrow. In *The Way of Light*, written while Comenius was in England, he had again called for the spread of universal wisdom, for a "college" of scholars and thinkers to work together for the common good. But death and destruction had once more trumped this cause.

ROYAL SOCIETIES

The call for a "college" was answered, but not in the way that Comenius and his comrades expected. Around 1645, in the middle of the civil wars, some scientific enthusiasts gathered in London. One was Theodore Haak, Comenius's London agent. An exile from the Palatinate and one of Hartlib's contacts, Haak is thought to have first proposed the meetings. Although not mentioned in the "official" account of its origins, these gatherings were possibly the start of what would eventually become the Royal Society, the oldest and most prestigious scientific society in the world. If the Haak-Hartlib-Comenius connection isn't enough to place the Royal Society in a line of descent from the *Fama*, letters concerning the meetings written in 1646 and 1647 by the eminent scientist Robert Boyle—considered the father of modern chemistry—offer stronger evidence. Writing to his former tutor, Boyle asks for certain books that will make him "extremely welcome to our Invisible College." Boyle describes the members of this "Invisible" or "Philosophical College" as men of "capacious and searching spirits" who "endeavour to put narrow-mindedness out of countenance" and "who take the whole body of mankind to their care." In another letter, written to Hartlib, Boyle, who himself professed strong Christian beliefs, speaks of the philanthropic and civic-minded plans of the "college."[16]

The Royal Society was founded in 1660, and although it fulfilled some Rosicrucian expectations, it wasn't run along Rosicrucian lines. By this time, the angelic science promoted by Dee, Fludd, and others had been discredited, both as science and for being somehow demonic. In 1659, Dee's *Spiritual Diary*, with its accounts of his communications with angels, was published, and a preface by Meric Causabon had accused Dee of consorting with devils. (Earlier, Meric's father, Isaac, had dampened Hermetic enthusiasm by dating the Hermetic texts translated by Ficino to the second or third century AD, thus showing they couldn't have been written by Hermes himself.) A general antipathy to Rosicrucian-Hermetic science spread, and religious and political paranoia flared. Members of the Royal Society had to watch their step; prudently they distanced themselves from ideas about "universal wisdom" and a "general reformation" and got down to doing science in the "real" world. Bacon himself, although included in the Rosicrucian clan, argued against Dee's "mathematical magic," and the hard-nosed empirical approach associated with science today became dominant.

Yet occult dreams of secret wisdom weren't far away. One of the original members of the Society was the antiquarian Elias Ashmole, best known today for the Ashmolean Museum in Oxford that houses his collection. An astrologer, alchemist, and Hermetic philosopher, Ashmole was a firm believer in the Rosicrucian ethos. He copied out English translations of the *Fama* and the *Confessio* by hand, and in Latin he wrote a strange letter to the Rosicrucian Brotherhood, asking to join the Fraternity. Not surprisingly, he never sent it—what was the address? But among his curious claims to our attention, one in particular stands out. In October of 1646, Elias Ashmole became a Freemason.

3

MASONIC MANEUVERS

The origins of Freemasonry have inspired more theories than perhaps those of any other group in the Western esoteric tradition. The Freemasons themselves have added to this uncertainty and at different times in their history have embraced or rejected an association with the occult. The taint of conspiracy that attached itself to the Masons in the eighteenth century still remains, yet modern Masons reject the claim that they are "a society of men who take the most solemn oaths, enforceable by horrible penalties, to further their own interests against those of the 'cowans' (non-masons)."[1] The infamous *Protocols of the Elders of Zion*, published in Russia in 1905, accused the Masons of having plans for world domination. Supposedly a secret document outlining a scheme for financial world conquest, written by a governing body of international Jews, the *Protocols* linked Freemasonry with two other targets of virulent paranoia: the Jews themselves and a relative newcomer, communism. All three were later targets of Adolf Hitler, a great reader of the *Protocols*, who gave speeches on them in Munich in the early days of National Socialism and refers to them approvingly in *Mein Kampf*. After Hitler came to power and Freemasonry was banned, the *Protocols* became a required text in German schools, and they remain required reading among many right-wing conspiracy theorists today. The fact that in 1921 a series of articles in *The Times* showed the *Protocols* to be a work of plagiarism and forgery hasn't altered their status as a classic work of both anti-Semitism and Masonic paranoia.

In 1924, the charge of world domination against Freemasonry returned in *Secret Societies and Subversive Movements*, by the conspiracy theorist Nesta Webster. Another seminal text for modern-day conspiracy hunters, its first readers included a future British prime minister, the Freemason Winston Churchill.[2] Fifty years later, Webster found a new, if more discerning, readership through the work of the late esoteric humorist Robert Anton Wilson, coauthor of the classic modern *ludibrium*, the *Illuminatus!* trilogy, which features the nefarious Bavarian Illuminati, a Masonic offshoot, in a series of hilarious esoteric escapades. Yet Webster was grimly serious about the Jewish-Masonic threat, which she linked with Theosophy and socialism and her role in battling it; according to one account, she would only answer her door with a loaded pistol in her hand.[3]

For most Masons today, such concerns border on the insane, yet the Masons have never dispelled the notion that they are involved in something underhanded. In the 1970s and 1980s, books like Stephen Knight's *The Brotherhood*, which "exposes" the secret aims of Freemasonry, and *Jack The Ripper: The Final Solution*, which argues that the blood-curdling murders of several prostitutes in the 1880s in the East End of London were the work of the Masons, renewed suspicion. In the 1990s in Great Britain, scandals surrounding Masonic "corruption" in the police, politics, and banking filled tabloid pages and led to calls for legislation compelling Masons to make "transparent" their affiliations—not unlike the edict in Nazi Germany forcing Jews to wear a yellow star, or the demand, in Joe McCarthy's America, that "communists" confess their "red" sentiments. In more recent times, the Masonic threat has evidently reemerged in high places, with Hillary Clinton being "exposed," along with her ex-president husband, as a member of the Illuminati and other secret societies.[4]

MASONIC POLITICS

Whether or not it wants to take over the world, of all the esoteric movements looked at in this book, Freemasonry has had perhaps the most sensational association with occult politics, being linked to the American, French, and other European revolutions. Participants in the Boston Tea Party and many signatories of the Declaration of Independence were, or soon after became, Masons. Some writers, like David Ovason and Robert Hieronimus, argue that the United States is—or at least was originally planned to be—the kind of utopia aimed at by the Rosicrucians, and that Washington, D.C., is laid out according to the precepts of sacred geometry, a discipline associated with Freemasonry.[5]

For Manly P. Hall, "the signature of the Mysteries may still be seen on the Great Seal of the United States," which includes "a mass of occult and Masonic symbols."[6] If Hall, as an occultist, may be biased, consider this remark by Charles Eliot Norton, the respected scholar, man of letters, translator of Dante, and professor of art history at Harvard University. Speaking of the Great Seal, Norton says, "The device adopted by Congress . . . can hardly (however artistically treated by the designer) look otherwise than as a dull emblem of a Masonic fraternity."[7] Hall links Bacon's *New Atlantis* to the New World and states that "it cannot be doubted that the secret societies of Europe conspired to establish upon the American continent 'a new nation, conceived in liberty, and dedicated to the proposition that all men are created equal.'"[8] For Hall, again, the founding of the United States was the work of "that *silent body* which has so long guided the destinies of peoples and religions." He comments darkly that those nations that succeed in embodying this secret society's high ideals prosper, but those that vary from this course "vanish like Atlantis of old." He even offers some interesting if unverifiable evidence for his belief. According to Hall, when designs for the American flag were being discussed, George Washington, Benjamin Franklin, and others on the committee visited a house where a mysterious stranger, referred to as "the Professor," was staying. Through some secret signs, Washington and Franklin recognized him and asked him to join them. He did, and all of his suggestions about the flag were adopted. The Professor then vanished, never to be seen again. Washington and Franklin were of course Masons, and Hall suggests that Franklin was a Rosicrucian as well. Who the Professor might have been is unclear.

MASONIC ORIGINS

As mentioned, accounts of Freemasonry's beginnings vary. The "Old Charges," a Masonic text dated to 1400 and found in what is known as the Cooke and Regius manuscripts, claims that Masonry goes back to antediluvian times; its secrets were recovered after the Flood and were the source of Hermes Trismegistus' and Pythagoras' knowledge. Another account tells the story of Hiram Abiff, the master builder of Solomon's Temple who was murdered by three lower-grade masons when he refused to disclose the secret "Mason's word." In recent years, a spate of popular books have linked the origins of Freemasonry to a number of things: the Shroud of Turin, the ancient Egyptian pharaoh Seqenenre, the Ark of the Covenant, John the Baptist, the Essenes, the apocryphal Book of Enoch, the Priory of Sion, and an ancient sea-faring civilization that circumnavigated the globe and produced maps of the planet at a time when, by the official account, we were still living in caves.[9] The linchpin holding these and other speculations together is the Order of the Knights Templar. The Order was suppressed in 1307 and finally dissolved in 1312. But some theorists, like John Robinson in *Born in Blood*, argue that many Templars escaped capture and fled to Scotland, where they were welcomed, and that it's from this forced immigration that Freemasonry as we know it today emerged.

A BRIEF HISTORY OF THE KNIGHTS TEMPLAR

The Order of the Knights Templar was established in 1118 to ensure the safe passage of Christians in the Holy Land during the Crusades. Hugh de Payens, a French nobleman from the Champagne region, gathered eight of his knights and approached King Baldwin II of Jerusalem with the idea. Baldwin must have liked it. He allowed the knights to set up their headquarters in the Al Aqsa Mosque, on the Temple Mount, a location sacred to Christians, Jews, and Muslims. The ruins of the Temple of Solomon are said to be there, as is Mount Moriah, where Jehovah asked Abraham to sacrifice his son, Isaac. The Dome of the Rock, the Muslim shrine that houses the stone from which Muhammad ascended to heaven, is also there. Orthodox Jews regard this same stone as the one on which Jacob dreamed of angels and his own ladder to heaven, though there is some debate about this. The knights renamed the mosque "Templum Domini," the Temple of the Lord, hence the name *Knights Templar*.

The Knights asked for donations to fund their enterprise. The charitable would help defend the Holy Land against the heathens, but they would also assure themselves a good seat in heaven, an early version of the indulgences that would upset Martin Luther a few centuries later. Although the Knights took a vow of poverty, and later, when their numbers increased, lived communally, they received considerable contributions of money, land, matériel, and volunteers. All nobles who joined had to donate their lands and wealth to the order. Eventually, the Templars became fabulously rich, with immense properties; at one point they "owned" Cyprus. Officially sanctioned by the Church at the Council of Troyes in 1129, they also received the important patronage of Bernard of Clairvaux, the most respected churchman of the time. Bernard, in effect, gave them, like James Bond, a "license to kill." Much of the criticism of "killing for Christ" dissipated after he wrote a treatise defending the "warrior monks."

In 1139, Pope Innocent II issued a papal bull, *Omne Datum Optimum,* granting the Knights free passage across any border, exempting them from taxes, and making them answerable to no one but himself. The Knights' military prowess was legendary; and along with being something like a medieval version of the Green Berets they were also powerful bankers, and much of modern banking has it roots in the Order. Although usury—something the Jews got a bad reputation for—was banned by the Church (as was killing), the Knights were sophisticated and powerful enough to get around this edict.

Yet the Knights' very success began to make them suspect in some eyes, especially after the Crusades finally failed—the Templars' efforts notwithstanding—and the Christian Kingdom of Jerusalem collapsed. When Acre, the last Christian outpost, fell to the Egyptian Mamluks in 1291, their *raison d'etre* vanished and the Templars returned to Europe. A wealthy, well-trained, independent army with no immediate mission and answerable only to the Pope would have caused considerable nervousness on the Continent, and when the Templars spoke of acquiring their own lands in the Languedoc (home, as mentioned, of the Albigensians and the Cathars), there was some consternation. Most concerned was the French king Philip IV, called Philip the Fair. He was already in debt to the Templars, and when he asked them for more money to carry on his war with England, they refused.

Accounts of what happened next vary, but most likely Philip, envious of the Templars' riches, persuaded Pope Clement V, his childhood friend, to "investigate" them. Trumped up charges of heresy were duly made. They were accused of denying Christ's divine nature, spitting and urinating on the cross, homosexuality, consorting with demons, worshipping a deity called Baphomet, and also worshipping a severed head. On October 13, 1307—a Friday, giving birth, by some accounts, to the belief that it is an "unlucky" day—Templars were arrested all over France. Arrests were made in other countries as well, but not with the alacrity displayed by the French. Confessions of indulging in the heretical practices were obtained through torture, inflicted by a corps of professional interrogators called Inquisitors. No Templar who wasn't tortured confessed, and the charges were very similar to those Philip had wished to make against Pope Boniface VIII in a failed kidnap bid when Boniface had earlier refused to make a move against the Templars. It seems likely that the Templars were innocent of these heresies and that Philip simply used them as a means of getting at the Templar wealth. Although the Church dragged its heels in moving against the Knights, when reports of their "heresies" reached the people, a public outcry arose, and there were calls for their punishment.

In 1314, Jacques de Molay, the last Grand Master of the Knights, and Geoffrey de Charnay, his immediate subordinate, were burned at the stake in Paris, on the Îlot des Juifs, the tiny island in the Seine near Notre Dame. To insure that no relics would remain, their ashes were dumped into the river. As he burned, de Molay is believed to have placed a curse on Philip and Clement, saying that both would stand before God in judgment within a year. He was correct; both men died less than a year after de Molay. The Church's position, at the time and to this day, is that the accusations against the Templars were false and that Clement was forced to act because of pressure from Philip and "popular demand." In 2007 the Vatican announced that the Chinon Parchment, a record of the Templar heresy hearings, had been found after being misplaced for centuries. The document exonerates the Templars from all charges and argues in favor of the theory that the "heresies" were part of their training to prepare for "the humiliation the knights would suffer if they fell into the hands of the Muslim leader Saladin."[10]

TEMPLAR TREASURE

Various accounts suggest that along with their considerable wealth, the Templars also had another kind of treasure. They're known to have used a series of tunnels beneath their Temple Mount stronghold, and some sources argue that they engaged in significant excavations themselves—and that the excavations in the Al Aqsa Mosque were the reason they went there in the first place. As in the legend surrounding the Cathars, some of whom are thought to have escaped the massacre at Montségur carrying away a mysterious treasure, the exact nature of the Templar treasure is unclear. For some, it was a collection of scrolls, originating from the same source as the famous Dead Sea Scrolls, discovered in 1947 in Qumran, on the West Bank, and believed to have been written by a Jewish mystical sect, the Essenes. These Templar scrolls are thought to provide damning evidence against the established Church, showing that the Church as we know it is not the true church of Christ, and that the original teachings of Jesus were considerably different from what we've been taught.

For others, the scrolls contained material inspiring the central symbols of Freemasonry. Still others believe the treasure discovered by Hugh de Payens and his knights were maps constructed by, as mentioned, an ancient sea-faring civilization showing the location of, among other places, America, and that some Templars used these to reach the New World well in advance of Columbus. Others say that the treasure was, or had to do with, the Ark of the Covenant.[11]

Another suggestion is that the treasure, which the Templars came to possess in the Holy Land, wasn't a particular object or thing but a teaching: the Hermetic philosophy, kept alive in Arab lands when it was lost to the West. This would have included sacred geometry and mathematics, necessary in the architecture of something as significant as the Temple of Solomon, the building of which is a principle element in Masonic legend.

THE SCOTTISH CONNECTION

Whatever the mysterious Templar treasure may have been, a considerable number of Templars were thought to have fled Philip the Fair's crackdown. Some may have found a haven in Switzerland. When Leopold I of Austria tried to get control of the St. Gotthard Pass not long after the dissolution of the Order, his army of five thousand men was ambushed and defeated by some fifteen hundred peasants. Folk tales speak of the "white knights" who came to aid the peasants; not known as fighters, the Swiss henceforth gained a reputation as fierce warriors. But the land where legend most suggestively places the exiled Templars is Scotland.

In 1312, Scotland had been placed under excommunication, and Robert the Bruce, a Scottish lord, had himself been excommunicated in 1306 for murdering a rival in a church. This left Rome powerless in Scotland, or at least in those areas controlled by Bruce. Scotland was barely fending off an English invasion, and when the fugitive Templars looked for a destination, where better than there? Not only was it beyond reach of the Pope, they could even find work. In *The Temple and the Lodge*, Michael Baigent and Richard Leigh suggest that the Scots repelled the English at the decisive battle of Bannockburn in 1314 because of a surprise contingent of Templar reinforcements.

Like many esoteric orders throughout history, the Templars were forced to go "underground," but their presence, Baigent and Leigh argue, can be detected in the strange architecture of Rosslyn Chapel, located not far from Edinburgh. One account describes its interior as "a fevered hallucination in stone . . . a petrified compendium of 'esoterica.'"[12] One carving seems to depict a Masonic initiation ritual, and William St. Clair, who started construction of the chapel in 1446, is thought to have been a Templar. The Sinclair family, as they were later known, became, "perhaps more than any other in Britain . . . associated with later Freemasonry."[13] Some see evidence for the Templar-Mason "Scottish connection" in the supposed "Apprentice Pillar," whose dragons and curling vines suggest a link to the vegetal symbolism of the Green Man.[14] According to legend, when a model of the pillar had arrived from Rome, the master mason felt unable to make a copy of it without viewing the original and went off to see it. In his absence, his apprentice went ahead and did it. When the master returned and saw his apprentice's handiwork, he grew jealous and murdered the boy. A carving of the murdered apprentice, with a gash in his right temple, is over the west door of the chapel. Nearby is the head of the master mason, and also that of a woman, the widowed mother. The inference is that the murdered boy is a "son of the widow," a phrase in Masonic ritual, and that the murder echoes that of Hiram Abiff.

There is additional evidence for a Templar-Mason link. The eighteenth-century German Baron Karl Gottlieb von Hund, who we will meet again further on, promoted a peculiar brand of Freemasonry known as Strict Observance. This, he claimed, was a "restoration of the Temple." Curiously, in his early Masonic days, the Traditionalist René Guénon was involved in a brief resurrection of the Templars. In 1908, after receiving a command supposedly from Jacques de Molay himself during a séance, Guénon established the Renewed Order of the Templars in Paris. The group consisted of Guénon and some Martinists—followers of the ideas of Martines de Pasqually—and was very short lived.[15] (Incidentally, Guénon had some odd ideas about the Rosicrucians as well; he believed they abandoned Europe after the Thirty Years War and went to Asia.)[16] Not surprisingly, the Templars remained an important influence in French esoteric and occult circles and were considered a key source for the curious political ideas of the French occultist Alexandre Saint-Yves d'Alveydre.

Rosicrucian Revival?

The Templar-Masonic Scottish connection seems strong, and, as we will see, Freemasonry had close links with Scottish politics. But as

Richard Smoley points out in *Forbidden Faith*, there are a few holes in the argument. For one thing, the Templars were soldiers before all else. This doesn't preclude the notion that some of them may have had esoteric knowledge, but this probably had little to do with sacred architecture or geometry. The historian Jasper Ridley points out that "the ideas of the speculative masons in the 18th century . . . had nothing in common with those of the Templars." "The 14th century Templars were not deists," as Freemasons later became. "They were not even Protestant heretics," as the Rosicrucians were. So while Ridley believes that the story of the Templars winning the Battle of Bannockburn is "certainly nonsense," he agrees that "it is not impossible that some Templars escaped to Scotland" and that "their descendants . . . joined Freemasons' lodges." He denies, however, that they had any part in "the development of speculative Freemasonry in Scotland and England."[17] And as Freemasonry's own legacy has it, there's a clear connection between ancient builders and those of the time of the "Old Charges."

There's also the Rosicrucian link. In a long poem written in 1638 by the Scot Henry Adamson, "The Muses Threnodie," we find these lines:

> For what we presage is not in grosse,
> For we be brethren of the *Rosie Crosse*;
> We have the *Mason Word* and second sight,
> Things for to come we can foretell aright.[18]

This is one of the earliest references to Freemasonry as it is known today—indeed, it's the first printed reference to the "Mason's word."[19] It's also one of the first to link Freemasonry to the Rosicrucians and to suggest that the Masons, along with the Rosicrucians, possess occult powers, in this case, "second sight," a form of precognition. And in 1676, a Masonic pamphlet featured this comic reference to a dinner party with some unusual guests: "To give notice, that the Modern Green-ribbon'd Cabal, together with the Ancient Brotherhood of the Rosy Cross; the Hermetick Adepti and the company of Accepted Masons intend all to dine together on the 31 of November next. . . ." The notice cracked the old Rosicrucian joke, suggesting that those attending should bring their spectacles, otherwise some of the guests may appear invisible.[20]

One Masonic researcher was convinced that Freemasonry's origins lay with the Rosy Brethren. In his long essay on the Rosicrucians, Thomas De Quincey, the "English opium eater," concluded that "the original Freemasons were a society that arose out of the Rosicrucian mania, certainly within the thirteen years from 1633 to 1646, and probably between 1633 and 1640." De Quincey agrees that there was no "actual" Rosicrucian order, calling it a "hoax played off by a young man of extraordinary talents," but for "a more elevated purpose than most hoaxes involve;" nevertheless, he believed that the Rosicrucian impulse led to Freemasonry. "Freemasonry," for De Quincey, "is neither more nor less than Rosicrucianism as modified by those who transplanted it to England."[21] We've seen who some of those "transplanters" may have been: Fludd, Comenius, Hartlib, and Haak.

The Rosicrucian impulse clearly shows a "family resemblance" to Freemasonry, but it can't be the complete answer. The "Old Charges" of 1400 argue against this, as does evidence from William Schaw, who in 1583 was appointed master of works by James VI of Scotland, soon to become James I of England. Responsible for the organization of the nation's lodges, Schaw called for a curious addition to the mason's practice, requiring each new lodge applicant to be tested "in the art of memorie and the science thereof."[22] Was this the same art of memory practiced by the Renaissance adepts? Perhaps Schaw was referring to the everyday memory any workman would need, necessary to memorize rituals and passwords. Yet would something so commonplace need to be tested? And would Schaw refer to it as an "art"? If indeed this was the Hermetic art of memory, then at least some Freemasons knew of it before the Rosicrucian diaspora.

FROM OPERATIVE TO SPECULATIVE MASONRY

If nothing else, Schaw's memory testing suggests that the standard account of the origins of Freemasonry—that it grew out of the medieval stonemasons' guilds—is still perhaps the best. In the Middle Ages there was, according to one writer, a "general feeling " that the masons were "different from other people."[23] While most people hardly ever left their village, the masons had to travel to work on the few buildings that were made of stone: castles, cathedrals, abbeys, churches. They were employed in sacred work by the Church, the king, and the nobles, and the elite masons who did the ornamental carvings on the great cathedrals formed something like guild of their own. In France they were one of the *Compagnonnages*, which also included the *Carbonari*, or "charcoal burners"; in Germany they were known as the *Steinmetzen*, whose work may have included esoteric symbols.[24] These specialists worked in what was called "freestone," which allowed for finer carving, while the "rough masons," who laid a building's foundations, worked in hard stone. Hence the name "freestone masons," or "freemasons."[25] They needed to recognize fellow masons when they traveled, hence the secret passwords, handshakes, and signs; these also helped to ensure their jobs, since only masters of the craft learned them. That they worked on sacred sites linked their efforts to the great religious monuments of the past, like Solomon's Temple.

Between 1550 and 1700 Freemasonry mysteriously changed, becoming what's known as "speculative Freemasonry." Unlike the "operative" masons, who actually worked with stone, the "speculatives" speculated on the *meaning* of architecture. The transformation was similar, but oddly opposite, to the shift from alchemy to chemistry happening at the same time. While spiritual alchemy focused on inner transformation, the chemistry that emerged from it concentrated on the "hands-on" experience of understanding changes in matter. Freemasonry began with the "hands-on" experience of working with actual stone and graduated to the spiritual speculations of Freemasonry today.

Numerous theories have tried to account for this transformation, but it seems to share in the same awakening of religious and spiritual liberalism that accompanied the Rosicrucian experiment. The earliest Charges, or regulations a mason must follow, included not sleeping with the master's wife or daughter and observing complete fealty, first to the Church and then to the king. Whether the regulations about sleeping with the master's wife or daughter changed or not isn't known. But toward the beginning of the eighteenth century, the masons went from being a "trade union" that "accepted all the doctrines of the Catholic Church" and pledged absolute obedience to the king to an "organization of intellectual gentlemen who favoured religious tolerance and friendship between men of different religions, and thought that a simple belief in God should replace controversial theological doctrines."[26]

Suddenly, noblemen and aristocracy took an immense interest in what the lowly masons were doing, as if today's Fortune Five Hundred became fascinated with construction workers overnight. It wasn't unusual for trade guilds to accept as members men who had nothing to do with the trade, which, according to one account, is how the St. Clair family at Rosslyn established a "hereditary right to exercise authority over the masons of Scotland."[27] But this was different. The popularity of the new vernacular Bible in the wake of the Reformation lessened the Church's control, and its account of the building of Solomon's Temple also led to an interest in the masons' work. Somehow, "the possibility of friendship between men of different religions,"[28] a Rosicrucian goal, attached itself to the masons, as did ideas about sacred architecture.

The secret origins of masonry collected in James Anderson's *Book of Constitutions* weren't published until 1723, six years after the formation of the English Grand Lodge, but they had more than likely been in circulation well beforehand. Among other things, these depicted God as a kind of mason, the Divine Architect, an idea found in Plato's *Timaeus* and rooted in Pythagoras' belief that numbers lie at the heart of creation. Abraham was said to have taught geometry to Euclid. Other Biblical stories account for other aspects of Freemasonry. The need for secret signs and codes, for example, arose out of the linguistic chaos following the collapse of the Tower of Babel, lending the "Mason's word," originally a way Scottish masons distinguished between master and apprentice, an aura of mystery. It was used in thrilling initiation rituals and secret ceremonies, but was it also in that mysterious tongue that predated the fall of that monument to man's hubris? Later the search for this *Ursprache*, which many associated with the "correspondences" of Swedenborg, would be linked to renewed ideas of a general social reformation.

JACOBITE FREEMASONRY

Mention of Swedenborg brings us to Jacobite Freemasonry, forms of Masonry linked to the political movement dedicated to restoring the Stuart line to the English and Scottish thrones. In 1710, during his first visit to London, Swedenborg is thought to have been initiated into a Jacobite lodge. And in the 1740s, prior to his transformation from an Enlightenment scientist to a mystical seer, Swedenborg is believed to have renewed contacts with this and other secret societies in London.

Jacobite derives from "Jacobus," the Latin equivalent of *James*, and the Jacobite cause began in 1688 when James II (also known as James VII of Scotland) was deposed by his daughter Anne and her husband, William of Orange (of Holland). Briefly put, James II had become a fervent Catholic, and when he finally and unexpectedly produced a male heir by his second wife, the English nobility was horrified at the idea of a possible Catholic dynasty. The nobles invited William to force James II to abdicate in favor of Anne, William's own wife and James II's Protestant daughter. William agreed, and when he landed in England with his troops, James II escaped to the Continent, where he remained in exile.

For the next sixty years, until the final defeat of Charles Edward Stuart (also known as "Bonnie Prince Charlie," James II's descendant and the "Young Pretender" to the throne), at the battle of Culloden in 1745, the Stuart cause found support from France, Spain, and other countries that had a stake in restoring the Stuarts to power. The cause received romantic expression in the works of Sir Walter Scott and Robert Burns and gave rise to a variety of secret, subversive societies, some of which had strong connections to Freemasonry.

By the early eighteenth century, Freemasonry, at least in England, began to settle into the mainstream. Soon after the Grand Lodge of England—established in 1717—coordinated the activities of separate lodges, Freemasonry was increasingly seen to inculcate values associated with a well-ordered society: sobriety, responsibility, and propriety, but also a certain egalitarian spirit, a sense of personal liberty, and civic consciousness. In what seems a historical irony, sober England was a model of an enlightened society for Voltaire, whose writings helped spark the anything but sober French Revolution. As Baigent and Leigh write, "By the third decade of the 18th century, English Freemasonry, under the auspices of Grand Lodge, had become a bastion of the social and cultural establishment."[29]

To arrive at this "upstanding" position, English Freemasonry had to jettison certain elements, much as the Rosicrucian impulse had to purge itself to become the Royal Society. This meant getting rid of the Jacobites, which in the public's eye had given Freemasonry a sinister character. Prominent Freemasons like the Duke of Wharton and the Earl of Lichfield were not only key supporters of the Stuart cause, they were also cofounders of the notorious Hell Fire Club (later popularly associated with Sir Francis Dashwood, who formed a version of it in 1746), a pagan society known, as its name suggests, for its orgiastic carousing. Alerted to the club's lascivious activities and the sedition breeding in the Jacobite lodges, in 1721 the government issued a edict against "certain scandalous clubs and lodges";[30] the Grand Lodge responded by expelling its radical elements. It wanted to assure the government that it was no threat and, in fact, was wholly supportive of the current Hanoverian regime. This eighteenth-century Patriot Act led to James Anderson's *Constitutions*, an attempt to once and for all allay fears of Masonic subversive activity.

Following this political winnowing, English Freemasonry limited itself to the three "Craft" degrees: Entered Apprentice, Fellow Craft, and Master Mason. The so-called "optional" or "higher" degrees remained the property of the renegade lodges linked to the Jacobite cause, and a seeker of higher initiation had to go to them. The connection between these more esoteric degrees and subversive politics led to a long-running distinction between English and Continental Freemasonry. English Freemasonry still carries a taint of suspicion, but it did find a place within the system. On the Continent, and especially in France, this never happened. Freemasonry was, and still is, seen as rabidly anti-clerical and anti-establishment, a continual threat to a law-abiding, God-fearing society. Hence, what we might call "Continental esotericism" has always carried a certain aura of political and social danger.

UNKNOWN SUPERIORS

One Mason who may have been particularly indisposed by the end of the Stuart cause was Baron Karl Gottlieb von Hund, founder, we recall, of the Strict Observance form of Freemasonry. Strict Observance got its name because the rite required a vow of absolute obedience to those whom Hund called "unknown superiors," high-ranking secret Grand Masters of an extreme esoteric Freemasonry that had its roots in the Knights Templar. Hund was a typical eighteenth-century "noble traveler," journeying to different European capitals and visiting various Masonic lodges. He claimed he had been initiated into this new Templar Masonic rite while in Paris in 1743 by a "superior" known to him only as "the Knight of the Red Feather." Hund also claimed that he had been introduced to Charles Edward Stuart, who, he was given to believe, was perhaps the most superior "unknown" of them all, the hidden Grand Master of all the Masons.

Yet in the early 1750s, while promoting his Strict Observance, Hund was asked for more information about this mysterious rite. He confessed that he had none; the unknown superiors, he explained, had vanished. They had assured him they would return and provide further instructions, but he never heard from them again and had no idea how to contact them. Like the Rosicrucian brothers (or the Scarlet Pimpernel), they were nowhere to be found. Understandably, Hund's claims were doubted.

Baigent and Leigh suggest that Hund's story is probably true and that his unknown superiors were more than likely important Jacobites. When he was initiated, the Jacobite cause was still alive and the Stuarts were still prestigious figures on the Continental scene. But by the 1750s, Stuart hopes had faded and Hund's "unknown superiors" were either dead, in prison, or in hiding.[31]

Yet the notion of "unknown superiors," so crucial to occult politics, cannot be done away with that easily.

4

EROTIC ESOTERIC REVOLUTIONS

In 1723, a group of Bohemian Brethren, followers of the ideals of Jan Huss and Comenius, who had been living in Moravia after fleeing Bohemia, arrived at the Berthelsdorf estate of Count Nikolaus Ludwig Zinzendorf, in eastern Germany, and asked if they could establish a community on his land. The Bohemian Brethren were dedicated to the simple life and to the kind of piety associated with the Rosicrucians; other aspects of their religious practice that differentiated them from more orthodox Christians included having both bread and wine as part of the communion sacrament and having their liturgy written in the national language, rather than in Latin. Zinzendorf, a young, idealistic pietist committed to helping the poor and needy, agreed, and the Moravians, as the Brethren came to be called, started a village that they called Herrnhut, "the Lord's Watch."

Although dedicated to communal living and sharing a strong religious passion, the Brethren faced difficult times, and a period of squabbling almost wrecked their experiment. Then a seeming miracle happened. During one particularly intense meeting, the Moravians suddenly underwent a group transformation in which all dissension vanished and a profound calm and mystical unanimity spread among them. They later believed that the experience was like the visit of the Holy Spirit described in the Bible as the Pentecost. Believing that this transformation and renewal of faith should be brought to all churches, the outcast Moravian community became the center for a worldwide Protestant missionary movement.

Curiously, although the Moravians eventually established their own church, the *Unitas Fratum*, or "Unity of the Brethren," this wasn't their initial aim. The Brethren's first plan was to join other, established churches and bring their Pentecostal experience to them. This tactic of "infiltrating" established churches is oddly reminiscent of the Bavarian Illuminati, whose members joined various Masonic lodges in order to convert suitable Freemasons to their own peculiar political ideals. Indeed, the Moravians faced precisely these criticisms about their missionary activities, which many saw as an attempt to erect a kind of "secret church" within the Church.

The Moravians may have felt that something more than chance had led them to Zinzendorf's door. Not only did the young count let them make a new home on his land, he soon joined the Brethren himself and became one of their most important leaders. Working diligently to spread the word, Zinzendorf sent Moravian missionaries to North and South America, Africa, and the Far East. Zinzendorf himself visited the New World and, among his successes, converted Chief Tomochichi of the Creek Indians. Other early Moravian missionaries established churches among the slaves in the West Indies. During one visit to America, Zinzendorf helped unify the German Protestants living in Pennsylvania. This led to the founding of the town of Bethlehem, where Zinzendorf's daughters would later start the Moravian College. But the Moravian mission important to our story was the one established in Fetter Lane in London in 1738.[1]

COUNT ZINZENDORF
AND THE ORDER OF THE GRAIN OF MUSTARD SEED

In hindsight, Count Zinzendorf and the Moravians almost seem to have been made for each other. Zinzendorf was born into a noble family in 1700 in Dresden, Saxony; his father died when he was an infant, and the boy was brought up by his pietist grandmother. A deep religious faith manifested early in his life and later led to a clash between his spiritual, mystical nature and his duties as a count. Although outwardly accepting the demands of his station, inwardly the young count nursed a strong desire to join the ministry and spread the Gospel. This tension was relieved somewhat in his late teens, while a student at Halle Academy. There Zinzendorf and some fellow students formed a secret society, the Order of the Grain of Mustard Seed, taking their name from the Gospel parable that likens the kingdom of God to a mustard seed, which, although very small, produces a great tree with many branches.

The idea behind the order was that its members, all of whom were nobles destined for important positions in society, would secretly use their influence to spread Christ's message. All shared a profound sense of brotherhood with their fellow men and took as their motto, "No one lives for himself," which they had inscribed on the rings they wore as a sign of their commitment. In later years when Zinzendorf reactivated his youthful order, he brought into the fold the archbishops of Canterbury and Paris, as well as Christian VI, king of Denmark. This later version of the order was linked to both Freemasonry and the Rosicrucians and operated on a kind of need-to-know basis: a candidate didn't know the identity of the brother who interviewed him, and members often didn't know the identity of other members.[2]

Zinzendorf had a kind of mystical experience during his Grand Tour, then a *de rigueur* "gap year" for all young aristocrats. In a museum in Dusseldorf, Zinzendorf saw a painting by the Baroque artist Domenico Feti, showing Christ with the crown of thorns on the way to the crucifixion. Entitled *Ecce Homo* (Behold the Man), its inscription read: "This I have done for you—now what will you do for me?" Zinzendorf couldn't answer this, but, even more deeply, the painting brought home the reality of Christ's suffering and humiliation in a way he had never felt before. This was a fully humanized Christ, and Zinzendorf could almost feel his fleshly nature. It was the exact opposite of the belief, often attributed to the Gnostics and known as *Docetism*, that Christ's mortal body and crucifixion were a kind of illusion, that he was wholly spiritual and not mortal at all. On the contrary, for Zinzendorf, only through a deep grasp of and participation in Christ's humanity could we join, literally, in his mystical body.

For Zinzendorf this mystical-human body of Christ included not only the wounds he suffered during his passion but also his sexuality. It may seem odd to us, and it certainly seemed scandalous to some of Zinzendorf's contemporaries, but during what became known among the Moravians as the "Sifting Time"—referring to a period of egalitarianism, communal living, esoteric practices, and sexual antinomianism—Zinzendorf preached that deep meditation on Christ's sexual organs, as well as his wounds, would lead to a mystical experience. Yet "meditation" may be too sedate a term for the kind of worship the Moravians in London, and elsewhere in Europe, practiced, seeing that it involved activities we would usually associate with Tantra and other forms of sacred sexuality. As one commentator remarked, in Zinzendorf's peculiar form of worship "all the senses must be mobilized, the whole body must participate,"[3] an admonition Zinzendorf's congregation certainly followed.

SEXUAL METAPHYSICS

By the time Zinzendorf established the Fetter Lane mission, he was convinced that the mysticism of the Jewish cabala—the esoteric reading of the Jewish holy books—could bring Jews and Christians as well as Catholics and Protestants together. His belief that followers of different faiths could unite in a common piety chimed in many ways with Masonic notions of universal brotherhood and a common belief in a Supreme Being, and it certainly resonated with the Rosicrucian ethos. His epiphany in Dusseldorf concerning Christ's carnal nature seemed to prime him for cabalistic notions of what we can call "sexual metaphysics." According to the cabalists, the unmanifest source of creation, the *Ein Sof*, performed an act of love when "He" manifested his essence in the male and female emanations that make up the ten *sephiroth*, or "vessels," of the Tree of Life. The sexual polarities expressed in the different *sephiroth* lead from the Godhead to the material world, and in meditating on their combinations—usually through visualizing the letters of the Hebrew alphabet as male and female figures in various sexual positions—the cabalist can unite the emanations and trigger a vision of the androgynous source of things. But this unifying vision wasn't reached via inward meditation alone; as in forms of Tantric spirituality, sex itself was a means of both unifying the opposites and of mirroring the original act of creation.

As in spiritual alchemy, for the cabala, in sexual union, the male and female overcome the rifts in the fallen world and achieve an ecstasy that echoes the original unity of being. Likewise, the climax of intercourse, when the male explodes into the female, echoes the Godhead's original emanation of the *sephiroth*, which gave birth to the cosmos—a rather different take on the big bang. God himself has sex, the cabalists believe, in the cosmic lovemaking he enjoys with his *Shekhinah*, his female emanation. Zinzendorf Christianized this cabalistic holy marriage and declared that the Holy Spirit was feminine, the Mother of Christ. Sex wasn't sinful and degrading, as the Church preached; for the cabalists it was perhaps the most important part of religious life—provided, of course, that one's spiritual intention, one's *kawwanah*, remained pure and didn't sink into mere carnal satisfaction, an accusation that, understandably, Zinzendorf and his followers had to face on more than one occasion.

HOLY SINNING

Another influence on Zinzendorf were the ideas of the then late followers of the "false Messiah" Sabbatai Zevi.[4] When Sabbatai was arrested in Constantinople in 1666 for attempting to overthrow Sultan Mehmet IV, many of his followers were crushed by his prudent decision to convert to Islam and renounce his messianic claim rather than be tortured to death. Others saw his defeat in another light, rationalizing Sabbatai's renunciation as a version of Christ's crucifixion. Both had to undergo debasement and humiliation, and both had to perform a tremendous sacrifice: Christ by allowing himself to be crucified, Sabbatai by ignominiously adopting a false religion. Yet both were able to rise up and proclaim the true faith. This embrace of pain, suffering, and in some sense "evil" led to a theology of radical reversal among some of Sabbatai's followers, who believed that only by abandoning the tepid path of self-righteousness would the new mystical dispensation arrive. Thus sin paved the way for the millennium.

Earlier "heretical" sects, such as the Gnostics, Cathars, and, of course, the Knights Templar, all participated in, or were thought to participate in, similar antinomian beliefs, and it isn't difficult to see Christ himself, who preferred the company of prostitutes and other riff-raff to that of the self-satisfied "righteous," as the original antinomian savior. Later mystical religious groups, from the Russian Khlysty, with whom the notorious Rasputin, the "Holy Devil," is associated, to the gruesome followers of Charles Manson, who in 1969 committed several murders later claimed to be done "out of love," expressed some form of "holy sinning." The idea is that in order to achieve the unified consciousness transcending duality one must, in Nietzsche's much-abused formula, go "beyond good and evil." One antinomian work was both a criticism of some of Swedenborg's ideas and also a handbook for "holy sinning": Blake's early prose poem *The Marriage of Heaven and Hell*. The title alone suggests a reversal of mainstream morality, and its "Proverbs of Hell" offer "dangerous" maxims like, "The road of excess leads to the palace of wisdom" and "If the fool would persist in his folly he would become wise," as well as "Sooner murder an infant in its cradle than nurse unacted desires."[5] The problem with this is that it's not always easy to know whether you're going "beyond good and evil" as a saint or as a sinner, an argument that the orthodox make against the pitfalls of "enthusiasm" and the followers of mystical spirituality. If "anything goes," then the most questionable practices can be excused as expressions of a more profound spirituality that adherents to the safe path of righteousness simply fear.[6]

Zinzendorf's followers certainly took this message to heart, literally, and his new *Herzenreligion* (religion of the heart) emphasized the importance of a "heartfelt" regeneration over obedience to rigid moral standards. Followers were urged to confess their sins in full, joyously, in fact—some even added a few more just to be safe—and then open themselves to the salvific grace transferred through loving meditation on Christ's wounds. In what may appear to us, and did appear to many of Zinzendorf's detractors, as a revolting form of spiritual sadomasochism (or the equivalent, as the term had yet to arise), Zinzendorf taught his followers to visualize Christ's wound, from the infamous spear of Longinus, as a kind of vagina and the spear itself as a kind of phallus whose union made possible spiritual regeneration. Coupled with his own fully male sexuality, the "side hole," as Christ's wound came to called, in effect transformed him into an androgynous being, an earthly manifestation of the cabalistic cosmic man, Adam Kadmon, who enjoyed the primal unity of the sexes that the cabalists, and in a different way the spiritual alchemists, desired.

Among other practices, which included mentally kissing and licking the "side hole" in order to receive the revivifying blood, Zinzendorf urged his followers to visualize Christ's wound as a womb and themselves as children, safe within it, but their peculiar form of eroto-spirituality also took less bizarre, if not less scandalous, forms. At the Fetter Lane Chapel, the Moravians spoke openly about their sex lives and were advised by Zinzendorf and his agents on how to improve it, how the women could achieve ecstasy more easily and satisfactorily, and how the men could perform their spiritual labors with greater perseverance. The meetings, often known as "love feasts," seem to have included couples making love in view of the other parishioners, and the singing, dancing, and general joyous exultation of the senses—necessary in order to fully appreciate the human nature of Christ—may have ended in a communal unification of the opposites. As the male followers enjoyed an identification with Christ through their own genitals, and as Christ's "side hole" allowed the women to identify with him as well, their mutual satisfaction was a vibrant, powerful, and ecstatic means of sharing the regenerating love of the Savior.[7]

SWEDENBORG AND THE MORAVIANS

One who appreciated Zinzendorf's ideas about erotic spirituality and the possibility of uniting Christians and Jews through the cabala—and thus bringing about the millennium—was the Swedish scientist and visionary Emanuel Swedenborg. If Swedenborg is remembered today, it's for his strange accounts of his journeys to the spiritual worlds, which he communicated at length in books like *Heaven and Hell*, and for his ideas that gave rise, after his death, to the New Church, which Swedenborg himself had nothing to do with. But in his lifetime, Swedenborg was one of the most respected scientists in Europe, and on his many travels he met some of the leading minds of the age, including members of the Royal Society.[8] A man of many hats, besides being a scientist and visionary theologian Swedenborg was also a politician, an active member of the Swedish parliament, where he frequently supported progressive causes that met with opposition. He is, in fact, a good example of an occultist who was also a politician, or vice versa.

In 1744, Swedenborg arrived in London on one of his many visits, ostensibly either to oversee publication of one of his many works or to meet with other scientists. As mentioned, he had, some thirty years earlier, joined a Jacobite Masonic lodge during his first visit to London, and during his later travels to Paris he's thought to have participated in other Jacobite-Masonic activities. Throughout his travels, Swedenborg sought out scientists of a Rosicrucian and Masonic bent, motivated by his desire to effect the kind of religious, scientific, and social reform associated with the Rosicrucians. There's reason to believe that this latest visit coincided with an intelligence mission, something he had done before. Sweden had an interest in the Jacobite cause, and in 1744, England was preparing for an ultimately disastrous French-Jacobite invasion aimed at putting Charles Edward Stuart on the throne. On arrival, Swedenborg's companion, a Moravian, was arrested and questioned, and Swedenborg worried that he too was under suspicion.[9] He wouldn't have been the only occult figure under surveillance then. In 1745, the celebrated Comte de Saint-Germain was arrested in London during the Jacobite scare, suspected of spying. Among his occult credentials, Saint-Germain claimed to have given Cagliostro, whom we will meet shortly, the material for his influential Egyptian Rite Freemasonry; he's also thought to have perfected the alchemical *elixir vitae*, an all-purpose curative and bestower of immortality, and to have transformed base metals into gold. Like several eighteenth-century occult adventurers, Saint-Germain seems to have combined esoteric pursuits with fine living; more than likely he supplemented his income with some occasional espionage.

But neither politics nor science was really uppermost in Swedenborg's mind. Although for the "official" sources Swedenborg exhibited the utmost propriety, even sanctity, like Zinzendorf, he had a deep insight into and interest in spiritualized sex. Although he remained a bachelor, Swedenborg kept mistresses, and in one of his last books, *Conjugial Love*, written in his eighties, he argued in favor of concubinage and extramarital sex, relating that in heaven, angels enjoy continuous and mutually satisfactory lovemaking.[10] One source for Swedenborg's robust views on angelic sex were the Moravians.

During his 1744 visit, Swedenborg lodged with Johann Brockmer, an important member of the Fetter Lane congregation, who lived in Salisbury Court, near the chapel, and Swedenborg regularly attended the services.[11] Swedenborg had met with Moravians in other countries and visited their congregations as well. His researches into scientifically demonstrating the reality of the soul—a project that obsessed him for years—had included the works of both contemporary anatomists and neo-Platonic and Hermetic philosophers, one of whom was Comenius, who had made his own attempt to understand the soul using a kind of hieroglyphics.[12] In Prague, Swedenborg met with cabalists and Sabbatians who had relations with the local Moravian community, and in Hamburg he met Arvid Gradin, a Swedish Moravian who told him about their attempts to draw Jews into their congregation. Like many during the "occult Enlightenment," Swedenborg embraced the idea of uniting Jews and Christians in a shared faith, and the Moravians were perhaps the most active promoters of this religious reform.

He appreciated the Moravians' piety and their desire to intensify faith so that it became a "total worship, embracing the whole man."[13] The hypocrisy of the "inner and outer man," who could "say" one thing but "think" another, troubled Swedenborg all his life. In his accounts of the "spirit world," an intermediate realm between earth and heaven, this hypocrisy is impossible; there one's "true affections" are absolutely clear, and what you see is what you get.[14] It's not surprising that for him the Moravians' "total worship" was a refreshing expression of spiritual honesty. Yet although "total worship" attracted him, the Moravians' communal life was too sectarian for Swedenborg, and their justification through faith and meditation on Christ's wounds repellent. Swedenborg was too scientific to be satisfied with Zinzendorf's emotional, ecstatic worship, but he would pursue an erotic spirituality throughout his life.

SWEDENBORG LITE

Most "official" Swedenborg sources downplay his sexual and occult interests. This characterization is due mostly to the highly edited version of Swedenborg's life and ideas that was produced by Robert Hindmarsh, who in 1788 started a Swedenborgian chapel in Eastcheap in London and against whose watered-down version of Swedenborg William Blake would rail. Hindmarsh, a Wesleyan who had lost his position in the ministry, was, according to one account, "at pains to separate his Swedenborgian church from the occultists, and to make it a dissenting church of an unthreatening type, with prayers, hymns and a paid hierarchy,"[15] none of which Swedenborg himself had any interest in. Like the Gnostics, Swedenborg rejected the literal interpretation of the Bible. Moreover, he had nothing but scorn for the Catholic Church and its doctrine of the atonement, which he saw as besmirching the dignity of man. As Christ was for Zinzendorf, Swedenborg's Christ was fully human, and Swedenborg went Zinzendorf one better when he spoke of God and the universe as the Great Man. Swedenborg's "church" was "a new Jerusalem, given by God, as an open community where regenerated men and women would find rules for life through divine grace and love,"[16] an ideal Blake would affirm more concretely when, arguing against Hindmarsh, he declared that "the whole of the New Church is in the Active Life & not in ceremonies at all."[17] Blake was a great reader and critic of Swedenborg, and as the historian Marsha Keith Schuchard points out, his parents were members of the Fetter Lane congregation. Blake himself would practice forms of erotic esotericism and would mingle with other practitioners in a milieu that Schuchard describes as a "motley crew of Moravians, Swedenborgians, Kabbalists, alchemists and millenarians who populated the clandestine world of illuminist Freemasonry in London."[18] It was out of this milieu that Blake's own esoteric politics, embodied in his poems *America, A Prophecy* and *The French Revolution*, emerged.

Attempts to "de-occultize" Swedenborg aside, as Joscelyn Godwin remarks, "If two of the primary objects of ceremonial magic are to converse with angels and to know the hidden causes of things, then . . . Swedenborg was every inch a magician."[19] Swedenborg talked with angels via methods of breath control and meditation that enabled him to maintain an erection and to sustain an orgasmic trance for prolonged periods. As it was for Zinzendorf, crucial to his understanding of these matters was the cabala.

THE MYSTERIOUS RABBI FALK

Swedenborg's travels led him not only to the Moravians but to Jewish communities, too; he's known to have visited the Jewish districts of Amsterdam, Hamburg, Prague, and Rome. But his most significant Jewish encounter was with the rabbi and cabalist Samuel Jacob Chayyim Falk, an enigmatic character who seems to have been at the hub of esoteric life in London in 1744, and during Swedenborg's later London visits as well as his last days there. (Swedenborg died in London on March 29, 1772, the very day he predicted he would.)

Falk was at the center of an occult community comprising Freemasons, cabalists, Rosicrucians, and alchemists, as well as members of Zinzendorf's Fetter Lane Chapel. In his reminiscences of the Hermetic Order of the Golden Dawn, the most famous occult society of the late nineteenth century, the poet William Butler Yeats spoke of "unknown superiors" from whom the order's legitimacy derived, a phrase we encountered earlier when looking at the unfortunate Baron Hund's abandonment by these curious figures. It's been suggested that one of the unknown superiors Yeats speaks of was Falk; the idea can't be entirely ruled out, but it's doubtful.[20] Yet given that Falk was a prodigious traveler, he could have been in Paris in 1743, when Baron Hund was initiated into "Templar Freemasonry," and might possibly have been Hund's own "unknown superior." As Schuchard argues in *Restoring the Temple of Vision: Cabalistic Freemasonry and Stuart*

Culture,[21] cabalistic and hermetic philosophy dominated the Stuart court life, and the milieu that Swedenborg, Hund, and others moved in would have offered an eclectic menu of esoteric beliefs. That a Jewish cabalist could initiate a German Freemason into a Scots-Templar order in Paris wouldn't have been out of the question. The Fetter Lane Chapel itself was suspected of Jacobite sympathies and during the heyday of its erotic worship had been the target for anti-Papist mobs on more than one occasion, its sexual radicalism exacerbated by accusations of political conspiracies.

We know that Falk was born into a Sabbatian community in Galicia (Poland) and that he was known there as a Ba'al Shem, "Master of the Divine Name," a title given to practicing cabalists. Falk must have gotten into some trouble, as he was almost burned for heresy. He was banished from Westphalia, from where he traveled to Holland; he arrived in London in 1742. Falk set up an alchemical laboratory on the old London Bridge—then lined with storefronts—and from his house in the East End started a kind of esoteric school, teaching classes in cabala, alchemy, astrology, and other esoteric disciplines.

Swedenborg's relationship with Falk was close. It was through one of his Moravian contacts that he first met the Ba'al Shem, and the two "good Israelites" that Swedenborg tells us were with him in his rooms in Salisbury Court when he entered a trance state may have been Falk and his associate Hirsch Kalisch. At this house in July 1744, Swedenborg evidently suffered a mental breakdown, part of which involved the belief that he, like Sabbatai Zevi, was the Messiah, and that it was his destiny to be crucified for the Jews. The day after this peculiar revelation, Swedenborg apparently went to a drainage ditch, undressed, rolled in the mud, and then tossed money to the crowd. By this point Swedenborg had practiced a variety of spiritual and erotic cabalistic meditations taught by Falk, and the strain of maintaining control over his physical and psychic reactions could easily have thrown him over the edge. A few months earlier he had experienced a visitation by Christ, an event that marked the start of what we can call his "ministry."

A year later, in 1745, Swedenborg began to have the visions that led to the mission that occupied him for the rest of his life: to reveal the true meaning of the scriptures, communicated by the angels and

God himself, an aim shared also by cabalists and John Dee. By that time, Swedenborg had rooms in Wellclose Square, in London's East End, near Falk's mansion. Many modern Swedenborgians resist the idea, but it seems quite possible that the journeys to heaven, hell, and the spirit world that inform Swedenborg's reading of scripture and provide the basis for the New Church that grew out of his work might not have taken place without the "unknown superior" Rabbi Falk.

Another of Falk's students was the Sicilian adventurer, cabalist, and purveyor of Egyptian Freemasonry, Cagliostro, who may have met Swedenborg in the "Scandinavian da Vinci's" last days. Cagliostro first visited London in 1772, Swedenborg's last year, and Swedenborg remained lucid until the end, a result, perhaps, of his pursuit of "perpetual virile potency" through Falk's and Zinzendorf's techniques. Cagliostro was one of the *illuminati* who inhabited the dizzying warren of occult societies that gave a peculiarly esoteric flavor to the days leading up to the Revolution. Yet before the *ancien régime* fell to the thudding guillotine, a different revolution would take place across the ocean that many would see as the beginning of a very real "new world order."

SWEDENBORG'S LEGACY

As we've seen, after Swedenborg died, one aspect of his work was taken up by Robert Hindmarsh, and the New Church emerging from his interpretation of Swedenborg's doctrines became more or less the "official" view of Swedenborg's teachings. Yet other, more "illuminated" Swedenborgians rejected Hindmarsh's tame rendition. In the years preceding the French Revolution, Swedenborg's accounts of spiritual powers blended with the beliefs of other mystical visionaries to form radical social and political doctrines. The Austrian healer Franz Anton Mesmer's "science" of "animal magnetism," for example, argued that health depends on the unimpeded flow within our bodies of a vital magnetic energy that permeates the cosmos, a notion similar to the "orgone energy" of the renegade Freudian Wilhelm Reich and the Taoist concept of *ch'i*. From his work, which had groups of people submitting to "magnetic passes" performed by Mesmer and his disciples, comes the word *mesmerize*. Mesmer's student, the Marquis de Puysegur, discovered that "animal magnetism's" effectiveness issued not from any vital magnetic fluid but from the trance states the passes induced. A half century after his discovery, the Englishman James Braid coined the term *hypnotism*.

One of Swedenborg's most influential ideas is his doctrine of "correspondences," the belief that our physical world is a reflection of the heavenly one and that things and events here are symbols for spiritual realities, a doctrine Swedenborg learned from the angels.[22] It may seem a long leap from animal magnetism and speaking with angels to radical politics, but as one student of the period remarks, "In the eighteenth century, political outsiders often turned to the doctrines of Swedenborg and Mesmer in order to imagine new, more inclusive social orders."[23] As the historian Robert Darnton explains, for some, Mesmerism and Swedenborgianism "offered a serious explanation of nature, of her wonderful invisible forces, and even, in some cases, of the forces governing society and politics."[24]

One group promoting a more radical approach to Swedenborg's ideas was the London Theosophical Society, started by the Reverend Jacob Duche in 1783—no relation, aside from the name, to the later Theosophical Society founded by Helena Blavatsky and Henry Olcott in New York in 1875; *theosophy* here refers to the writings of Jacob Boehme and his followers. An American of Huguenot background, Duche was the rector of Christ Church in Philadelphia, and his fiery sermons made him chaplain of the Continental Congress until a squabble with some of the Founding Fathers forced him to resign. A reader of Boehme and other Rosicrucian thinkers, Duche embraced Swedenborgianism practically upon reaching London, and at his study group some of the most interesting figures in London's esoteric underground could be found: the painter and stage designer Philip de Loutherberg, who had known Swedenborg personally and whose early "special effects" were put to use in David Garrick's Drury Lane Theatre; the Swedish alchemist and Freemason Augustus Nordensköld, who, among other extravagant ideas, proposed a balloon trip to Africa to start a free-love commune; the Marquis de Thomé, propagator of a Swedenborgian Rite of Freemasonry; and the artists John Flaxman and William Sharp. Another member was William Blake.

Much has been written about Blake's interest in esoteric and hermetic philosophy, research pioneered by the late poet and scholar Kathleen Raine.[25] But Blake was also a political poet, and he moved in radical political circles. As his biographer Peter Ackroyd remarks, "There is no doubt that his closest associations were with people who held advanced republican views."[26] He knew Mary Wollstonecraft, the early feminist and author of A *Vindication of the Rights of Women*. He also knew Thomas Paine, the British-born American revolutionary and author of *Common Sense* and the incendiary *The Rights of Man*, who, incidentally, at one time lived on Fetter Lane. Blake also worked for the political publisher Joseph Johnson and at one point was arrested for sedition, an experience that threw the nervous and often socially challenged poet into a crisis. (He was eventually acquitted.)

Blake's politics were, though, at bottom, very different from the skeptical, rational, Enlightenment brand that Paine and Wollstonecraft endorsed. Blake was much more apocalyptic, millennial, and spiritual—like Swedenborg, he looked forward to a New Jerusalem— and he famously rejected the Enlightenment reason that wanted to do away with religion, crying, "Mock on, Mock on, Voltaire, Rousseau." Yet like many of his contemporaries, Blake was thrilled by the American War of Independence, and in his long poem *America, A Prophecy* he blended his own mystical nationalism and mythological pantheon—symbolized by the giant Albion, the revolutionary Orc, the creative Urthona, and the repressive Urizen—into a story of the American Revolution seen as a "cosmic conflict" that involved "the lost regions of Atlantis" in the context of a "larger impulse towards spiritual rebirth and revelation."[27] Although Masonic emblems appear in some of his illustrations, it's unclear if Blake ever became a Mason. In his early years as an engraver, he lived near Freemason's Hall on Great Queen Street, and many of his friends were Masons. Blake was fascinated with antiquity and the ancient past and would have been interested in a society of members who "believed they had inherited a body of secret knowledge from before the flood."[28] He would also most likely have known that many of the people responsible for the great cosmic battle across the Atlantic belonged to this society themselves.

WARS OF INDEPENDENCE

That Freemasons were involved in the American War of Independence is by now a truism. Dozens of books have been written on the subject, some interesting, some not; some based on diligent research, some on wild speculation; and still others, not infrequently, on sheer fantasy. Earlier I pointed out how Masonic ideas were crucial to American politics from the start—how the Great Seal, for instance, with its eye in the pyramid emblem, is a clear Masonic icon. Perhaps even more obvious is the Washington Monument, an unavoidably Egyptian nod to the esoteric ideals embraced by the early Americans. And if writers like David Ovason are correct, the nation's capital itself is a kind of Masonic magical talisman, designed to attract the beneficial energies of the constellation Virgo, which, he argues, has a particular importance in Freemasonry.

In *The Secret Architecture of Our Nation's Capital: The Masons and the Building of Washington, D.C.*, Ovason speculates on the esoteric intent behind the design and organization of the capital, arguing that the city's layout embodies, quite literally, the beliefs and ideals of Freemasonry. It's a fascinating if debatable thesis. That when George Washington laid the cornerstone of the Capitol building in 1793, he wore a Masonic apron embroidered with occult and Masonic symbols, as well as a zodiac, is an intriguing, if no longer "hidden," fact. But that he and other Founding Fathers arranged the city's best-known landmarks, like the Capitol, the White House, and the Washington Monument, to mirror a triangle of stars in the constellation of Virgo, hence dedicating the city to its influence seems, for this writer at least, a bit of a stretch—and oddly reminiscent of the thesis put forth by Robert Bauval in *The Orion Mystery* that the layout of the pyramid complex at Giza likewise mirrors the "belt" of stars in the constellation Orion. Yet as less speculative accounts of Freemasonry and the American Revolution make clear, we needn't go to these perhaps extravagant lengths to see that Masonic ideas and philosophies informed the birth of this particular nation.

For one historian of Freemasonry, "the influence of the Freemasons in the American Revolution has been exaggerated,"[29] but we needn't conclude from this that the link was negligible. Baigent and Leigh argue that there's no evidence for the War of Independence being part of a "coherent, organized 'Freemasonic conspiracy,'" and that to see it as " a movement engineered, orchestrated and conducted by cabals of Freemasons in accordance with some carefully calculated grand design" is probably misguided.[30] They concede that Rosicrucian ideas may have made their way across the Atlantic as early as the Jamestown settlement; but the kind of deliberate foundation of a Rosicrucian-Masonic society in the New World that Manly P. Hall envisioned is doubtful. They're probably right. What seems to have been at work here is something even more enigmatic and subtle than the activities of secret societies or "silent bodies": the dissemination of ideas through the occult medium of the *zeitgeist*, the "spirit of the age." Even without the help of an esoteric cabal, Masonic ideals would have permeated the common consciousness the way that, say, ideas about "political correctness" did in the late 1980s and 1990s.

By the time of the War of Independence, Masonic ideals had spread throughout the colonies, primarily through military "field lodges." Masonry itself attracted men on all social levels; it was, in fact, this egalitarianism that linked Freemasonry with the radical politics that would soon erupt on the Continent and made it a threat to the aristocracy and the Church. Yet as any student of the time soon discovers, Freemasons were on both sides of the American conflict, just as they would be during the French Revolution. Indeed, although conspiracy theorists like the vociferous Abbé Barruel denounced the French Revolution as a Masonic plot, being a Freemason didn't save one from an appointment with the guillotine, as the Mason and revolutionarily named Philippe Egalité, who cast the deciding vote to behead Louis XVI, found to his dismay when he himself was guillotined not long after Marie Antoinette. The idea that Freemasons were "responsible" for the American and French revolutions is, anti-illuminist propaganda notwithstanding, not true. That they were involved in them is. Given Freemasonry's popularity then, it would have been surprising if they weren't.

When the Founding Fathers drew up the Constitution, it was almost inevitable that the progressive notions of liberty, equality, brotherhood, tolerance, and the "rights of man" that were tenets of Freemasonry would be prominent. These beliefs, which characterized much Enlightenment thinking, were not somehow "fed" into the zeitgeist through the Masons—they were "in the air." But Freemasonry was one of the avenues through which they reached a wide audience, many of whom had probably never read David Hume, John Locke, or Voltaire, names associated with the Enlightenment ideals.

The ideals held sacred by Freemasons, which many saw coming to a remarkable fruition in the founding of the United States, may even have been responsible for the colonies winning the war—or, as Baigent and Leigh suggest, for the British purposely losing it. Some British generals, Freemasons themselves, recognizing the sentiments behind the American bid for independence, deliberately fulfilled their duties with something less than zeal and on more than one occasion allowed the Americans to escape, fall back, or regroup when they could easily have crushed them. One case in point was the disastrous attempt in 1777 by the British General Sir John Burgoyne—not a Freemason—to cut the colonies in half by marching his army south from Canada to combine with that of Sir William Howe, who, Burgoyne mistakenly assumed, would lead his army north to Albany. That Burgoyne wasn't liked by the British officers serving in America certainly didn't help, but it can't account for the reluctance Howe and others showed to do no more than was absolutely required of them. This led, along with Burgoyne's own incompetence, to his surrender at Saratoga, the most decisive victory for the Revolution; on the strength of it, the French entered the war on the American side. Eventually, as Baigent and Leigh argue, the lackadaisical, half-hearted campaign convinced Britain it wasn't worth continuing.

This isn't to say no American Freemasons were loyal to the king. According to one source, "of the 7 Provincial Grand Masters, 5 supported George III, and condemned revolutionary agitation against the established authority."[31] Masons had displayed a conservative agenda before; as we've seen, the Jacobite scare led the Grand Lodge to affirm its loyalty to the "establishment." One American Mason, Reverend Duche—who started the London Theosophical Society—left the colonies precisely because he was against breaking ties with Britain. Duche even wrote a letter to George Washington while the president-to-be was enduring that winter at Valley Forge, entreating him to abandon the battle and negotiate peace with the British. As chaplain to the Continental Congress, Duche was very close to the Founding Fathers; his wife, Elizabeth Hopkinson, was the sister of Francis Hopkinson, one of the signers of the Declaration of Independence. A Mason, Francis Hopkinson was on the committee responsible for the design of the American flag and the Great Seal.

Masons, it seems, stood on both sides of the American revolutionary fence, although the esoteric reasons behind the British resistance to the colonies' calls for independence have received little attention so far. But if the American Revolution had more than one link to Freemasonry and its ideals, the one her ally France would face little more than a decade later was, for many, illuminated through and through.

5

ILLUMINATIONS

Arguably, the period in France leading up to the French Revolution (1789–1799) was the most charged with occult politics of modern times, rivaled perhaps only by the apocalyptic, mystical decades that preceded the Bolshevik rise to power in Russia little more than a century later. As the Baroness d'Oberkirch, a contemporary observer and a participant in occult crazes in centers from Paris to Strasbourg, remarked, "Never, certainly, were Rosicrucians, alchemists, prophets, and everything related to them so numerous and so influential. . . . Looking around us, we see only sorcerers, initiates, necromancers and prophets."[1]

The late eighteenth century is usually regarded as an "age of reason," but as historians like Robert Darnton and Christopher McIntosh make clear, this was only its "daylight" character. Its "night" side had a different face, one, as is often the case, best seen in the popular culture of the time. As today, the tabloids and popular press in Paris and other major French cities were filled with stories of the bizarre, the magical, and the unearthly. Most of these would barely rate an episode of *The X-Files*, but that they occupied the minds of thousands of readers indicates a "dissatisfaction with the world as given" and what I have elsewhere called an "instinctive yearning for some kind of beyond, for *something more*."[2] This need for "something more" was satisfied, in a perhaps vulgar way, by the numerous magical potions and nostrums sold by busy Parisian street hawkers, who did a lucrative trade. Greater in some periods than in others, when this need reaches a certain intensity, occult expectations spill over into the social and political sphere.

In pre-Revolutionary France, occult desires met growing social and political unrest as well as the new skeptical philosophies to create a heady belief in an imminent shift in the nature of things. Enlightenment skepticism weakened the Church, but it also produced a hunger for more satisfying spiritual beliefs, for mystery and the unknown. One way this hunger was met was through Freemasonry and other occult philosophies that blended with the very skeptical systems of thought they rose up to complement. This isn't surprising. The history of Western consciousness in the last three centuries has seen an oscillation between extreme rationality and extreme irrationality, with the occasional brief balance between the two getting it "just right," in what I have elsewhere called "the Goldilocks syndrome."[3] Whether this oscillation will continue or whether, through means still unknown, we will arrive at what the philosopher Jean Gebser calls "the integral structure of consciousness"—a fruitful balance between rationality and what Gebser sees as older, more primitive forms of consciousness—remains to be seen.[4]

ROMANTIC AND CLASSIC

This oscillation in Western consciousness resembles a polarity in Western temperament that in crucial ways, I think, informs the manifestations of occult politics to come. That its most concise expression comes from a poet and philosophical essayist with no interest in esotericism, and whose interest in politics was really an adjunct to his concern with aesthetics and forms of religious belief, may be an advantage.

T. E. Hulme is little read today. When he died in World War I, he was known mostly as a kind of philosophical journalist, contributing to magazines like A. R. Orage's *New Age*, a remarkable clearinghouse for "alternative" ideas.[5] In his essay "Romanticism and Classicism,"— discovered after his death in a collection of notebooks—Hulme argues that the "positive principle" behind the French Revolution was strongly linked to the rise of Romanticism. People who were "for" the Revolution and saw it as a kind of "new religion" had been "taught by Rousseau that man was by nature good, that it was only bad laws and customs that had suppressed him. Remove all these and the infinite possibilities of man would have a chance." For the Romantics, Hulme argues, man was "an infinite reservoir of possibilities," and if you can get rid of "oppressive order," "you will get Progress."

Against this optimistic view, Hulme presents what he calls the Classical view, which is not distant from the religious view, at least that of the Church. For it, "man is an extraordinarily fixed and limited animal whose nature is absolutely constant. It is only by tradition and organization that anything decent can be got out of him."[6] The Church had a handy formula to express this concept: man, it taught, was guilty of original sin. Far from "infinite reservoirs," we are fallen creatures in need of salvation. The Enlightenment and the Romantic movement, although opposite in many ways, agreed on one thing: the need to jettison this idea, which both believed suppressed our potential for growth and evolution, in a word, for "progress."

These radically opposing views seem to fit into the distinction made in the introduction between progressive and traditional politics. For Hulme, Romanticism is "spilt religion." "You don't believe in a God," he writes, "so you begin to believe that man is a god. You don't believe in Heaven, so you begin to believe in a heaven on earth." This confusion comes about, Hulme argues, because what he, along with the Church, sees as the given hierarchy of things—the divine at the top and the human and natural somewhere below—becomes mixed up. "The concepts that are right and proper in their own sphere," he writes, "are spread over, and so mess up, falsify and blur the clear outlines of the human experience."[7]

Eric Vogelin's Gnosis

The necessity for hierarchy and tradition in order to get "anything decent" out of us would inform the esotericism of the Traditionalist school, which we will look at later. And the idea that because "you don't believe in Heaven, you begin to believe in a heaven on earth" is a concise formulation of the political philosopher Eric Vogelin's argument against what he calls forms of Gnosticism in politics—albeit a Gnosticism colored by his peculiar use of the word. As Richard Smoley cautions, "For Vogelin, Gnosticism becomes a catchall term that embraces everything in Western civilization that he hates and fears."[8]

As a defender of Christianity and of a very conservative view of Western values, Vogelin saw all attempts to have "a heaven on earth" as evidence of what he called "the immanentization of the eschaton"— the overthrow of the fixed conditions of life, including original sin, and the heralding of the Last Judgment. (Readers of Robert Anton Wilson and Bob Shea's *Illuminatus!* trilogy will recall their comic use of this unwieldy phrase.) There is some value in his view, and Vogelin is right to point out the dangers inherent in millenarian beliefs. That the road to various future utopias has been paved with present human bloodshed is clear to any student of modern history, but Vogelin mislabels as "Gnostic" what is really an apocalyptic vision. Yet the notion that mankind should simply accept things as they are not only goes against our inherent appetite for "something more" but argues for a colossal indifference toward human suffering, political, social, and economic. Reading Vogelin's difficult, knotty prose, I get the impression that behind it he is saying, "How *dare* these limited, sinful creatures believe that they can create a better world?"—a project, we know, that the Rosicrucians supported.

AN UNCONDITIONED LIFE

Vogelin's fear of the "the immanentization of the eschaton" (and Hulme's criticism of "spilt religion") aren't simply the prejudices of stuffy right-wing authoritarians; with Leo Strauss (whose ideas on "esoteric writing" we looked at in chapter 2), Vogelin is a powerful influence on modern conservative thought. And looking at the French Revolution and its descent into the Reign of Terror, or the Bolshevik Revolution's contribution to what P. D. Ouspensky called "the history of crime," we can see that Vogelin and Hulme have a point. Recalling the "holy sinning" in chapter 4, we see a need to "curb one's enthusiasm." Absolute freedom, in the sense of, say, a Marquis de Sade or the notorious twentieth-century magician Aleister Crowley—known more for his wildly indulgent lifestyle than for his esoteric acumen—often degenerates into mere license and what we can call "negative freedom." This is merely being "free from" something and not, as Nietzsche valued, being "free for" something, some purpose higher than mere self-gratification—an idea that relates to the "transcendental scale of values" mentioned in the introduction.

That the "liberation philosophy" Hulme and Vogelin associate with Romanticism and Gnosticism is of more than historical interest can be seen in the course of art in the last two centuries. In *The Use and Abuse of Art*, the cultural historian Jacques Barzun argues that much art, certainly from the Romantic period on, has been motivated by a rejection of so-called bourgeois life—which it sees as a "a collective infamy deserving opprobrium and death"—in favor of what he calls "a wholly unconditioned life."[9] This isn't the desire to reform, renew, and regenerate that motivated the Rosicrucians and later some forms of Freemasonry but an urge to throw off any restrictions whatsoever. We can see this in many "cultural heroes" of the last two centuries: the poet Arthur Rimbaud, the Dadaists, the Surrealists, Henry Miller, the Beats, the hippies, the Situationists, the punks. One call for an "unconditioned life" emerged in the counter-culture of the 1960s, when it adopted Aleister Crowley's maxim, "Do what thou wilt shall be the whole of the law," popular today with heavy metallers and goths. More succinct and immediate was Jim Morrison, lead singer of the rock group The Doors, who declared, "We want the world and we want it now," an adolescent request the world over. In the unconditioned world, immediate gratification is paramount, and as history shows, it is at least some of what fueled the French Revolution.

MASONIC RIGHT

One figure from the French Revolutionary days who would have embraced both Hulme and Vogelin, and was himself embraced by right-wing esotericists like Julius Evola, was the Savoyard counter-revolutionary and authoritarian philosopher Joseph de Maistre. Brilliant, incisive, and possessed of a misanthropy reminiscent of Fyodor Dostoyevsky's Grand Inquisitor, de Maistre was a Freemason radically opposed to the ideals of the French Revolution. Initiated into an esoteric Scottish Rite Lodge in Lyon, an esoteric center at the time, and influenced by the works of the illuminists Martines de Pasqually, Louis-Claude de Saint-Martin, and Jean-Baptiste Willermoz, de Maistre nevertheless had no patience with what he saw as woolly minded liberal ideas about universal brotherhood and religious tolerance. As Isaiah Berlin comments, de Maistre believed that "man can only be saved by being hemmed in by the terror of authority."[10]

At first sympathetic to the need for reform, aware of the corruption in Louis XVI's court, de Maistre was soon repelled by the Revolution's savage "leveling" and warned that only a government rooted in religion could avoid the chaos and bloodshed it had unleashed. The philosophical defender of established authority, in the state and in religion, he would have been brought to the guillotine, had the Committee for Public Safety got its hands on him. Along with the divine right of kings—a spiritual dispensation that for him included nations' constitutions, which, he believed, were "written" by God—he championed papal infallibility and argued that the Pope was, in the end, the final authority in temporal, as well as spiritual, matters. One of his epigrams sums up his belief: "Wherever an altar is found, there civilization exists." No wonder that among his modern-day readers we find the conservative political analyst Pat Buchanan. Yet we can't dismiss de Maistre as merely a predecessor of the neoconservatives. Another of his great readers was the French "decadent" poet Charles Baudelaire, who, along with many others in 1848, spent time on the revolutionary barricades in Paris.

De Maistre's ideas were echoed across the English Channel by the conservative thinker Edmund Burke, a more congenial intellect, whose work lacks the obsessive drive of de Maistre's. Like Burke, de Maistre opposed the shallow rationalism of the Enlightenment, one reason for his lifelong support of esoteric Freemasonry, even though it was outlawed by the Church he embraced. But de Maistre's opposition to naïve rationalism wasn't limited to his mystical, religious belief. He scorned the "back to nature" ideology associated with Rousseau, arguing that the idea that man was "naturally good" was sheer fantasy. "Man in general," de Maistre wrote, "if reduced to himself, is too wicked to be free," and when Rousseau asked rhetorically why, if man is born free, he is everywhere in chains (provided by the Church, the state, and other agents of civilization), de Maistre replied by asking why, if born carnivorous, sheep only nibble grass? (The answer is because they are made that way, and there seem few calls for sheep to throw off their vegetarian shackles and express their "true" nature.) De Maistre's point is that we shouldn't ask how man, or anything else in nature, *should* be, but should look at how he *is*. And what de Maistre saw was that man, like everything else in nature, was a killer. Rather than the placid stream by which poets lingered and calmly meditated, nature was instead "an enormous slaughterhouse," and, as Isaiah Berlin points out, the hangman plays a central role in de Maistre's philosophy.[11]

ILLUMINATI!

De Maistre wasn't the only Freemason to find a place on the right. The Golden and Rosy Cross Order, a German Masonic-Rosicrucian society, was founded in 1710 and seems to have continued until 1793, by which time it splintered into other groups: the Knights of Light, the Brothers of Light, and the Asiatic Brethren, all of whom incorporated elements of Sabbatai Zevi's teachings.[12] According to Christopher McIntosh, the Golden and Rosy Cross "upheld faith against scepticism, revelation against reason, Christian doctrine against deism or paganism, monarchy and established hierarchy against democracy, tradition and stability against change and progress"[13]—all values de Maistre and others on the occult right would support. But generally, Freemasonry was regarded by both the Church, which had outlawed it in 1738, and by secular authorities, which took similar steps some years later, as an agent of dissent and social disorder. And although, as Jasper Ridley makes clear, there were both loyalist and revolutionary Freemasons,[14] as the Grand Lodge had done years before, conservative Freemasons had to work hard to avoid being tarred with the radical brush. One group that made this difficult was the Bavarian Illuminati.

Much has been written about the Illuminati, most of it prompted by hysterically paranoid fantasies, and elsewhere I have explored their history at some length.[15] The two authors most responsible for forging the conspiratorial link between the Illuminati and the French Revolution were the ex-Mason and priest Abbé Barruel and John Robison, a professor of natural philosophy and secretary of the Royal Society of Edinburgh. Robison's scientific credentials are impressive: he collaborated with James Watt on an early steam car, contributed to the 1797 Encylopaedia Britannica, and invented the siren. Barruel's rollicking four-volume account *Memoirs Illustrating the History of Jacobinism* (1797), and Robison's slightly more sober but equally paranoid work *Proofs of a Conspiracy Against All the Religions and Governments of Europe Carried on in the Secret Meetings of Freemasons, Illuminati and Reading Societies* (1797), provided the foundation for a conspiracy consciousness that continues today.[16]

Founded by Adam Weishaupt, a professor of canonical law at the University of Ingolstadt, on May 1, 1776—two months before the signing of the American Declaration of Independence—the Illuminati was really a gigantic oxymoron. Regarded as an occult secret society, the Illuminati was actually a rabidly rationalist group opposed to mysticism and occultism. An extreme exponent of the Enlightenment ideals of science, atheism, and egalitarianism, to achieve its ends it nevertheless employed occultism, religious belief, and hierarchy. Like the Moravians, the Illuminati infiltrated other Masonic groups to bring them over to its cause, which was, as Weishaupt declared, a world in which "princes and nations shall disappear from the face of the earth without violence" so that "the human race should attain to its highest perfection, the capacity to judge itself."[17]

In another curious meeting between extreme right and left, Weishaupt, founder of an organization antithetical to all authority (except perhaps his own), was educated by the Jesuits, a Catholic "secret society" that also gave birth to his ideological opposite, de Maistre. It's likely that Jesuit casuistry facilitated Weishaupt's plan to dominate Continental Freemasonry. (Even Barruel and Robison admitted that the English Grand Lodge was innocent of this diabolical illuminist plot.) Freemasonry provided a ready-made network of communication, a system of hierarchical organization, and an ethos that shared, in different degrees, many of the ideals Weishaupt wished to disseminate. He would use it, absorbing its mystically egalitarian followers, until the time was ripe to present them with the true illumination.

Weishaupt's first gambits were faltering; only on his second try did he enter a Strict Observance Lodge (earlier he couldn't afford the fees). But soon things went smoothly. Illuminated Freemasonry spread quickly, mostly in German-speaking countries. Oddly, France, believed to be targeted for much illumination, resisted it—understandably, as it already had enough Masonic societies to deal with; by one estimate, by 1789 there were at least thirty thousand Freemasons in France. Eventually, figures as luminous as Goethe, Mozart, and Schiller, as well as the mysterious Count Cagliostro, entered Weishaupt's new, even more secret lodge. Yet only Weishaupt's closest initiates knew his true plan: to overthrow the established authorities, papal and secular, of Europe.

For all their paranoia, Barruel and Robison were right to recognize that Weishaupt, who originally only wanted to break the Jesuits' hold on his native Bavaria, had grandiose revolutionary designs. They went wrong in saddling the Illuminati with the sole responsibility for the Revolution. Weishaupt may have dreamed of a Europe free from Pope and king, but as one commentator remarked, he was "barely able to organize a picnic, let alone the Terror."[18] Yet this mattered little when the truth behind the Illuminati emerged.

This happened because of a quarrel between Weishaupt and one of his lieutenants, the Baron von Knigge. Knigge was more mystically minded than Weishaupt, and he joined the Illuminati after being rejected by a Rosicrucian group. Knigge's zeal brought in many new members, and he expected to advance along the esoteric path accordingly. But when his progress was oddly halted, he confronted Weishaupt. Not wishing to lose Knigge, Weishaupt revealed his true plan. Knigge agreed to keep mum, but only if Weishaupt agreed to make the Illuminati a *real* esoteric society. Knigge introduced more and more mystical initiations, countering Weishaupt's designs.

81

Weishaupt eventually decided that Knigge would have to go. He did, but not before he blew the whistle.

Other Masons who suspected Weishaupt's goals spoke against the Illuminati. When the "media" got wind of the business, damaging exposés appeared in the press, corroborating rumors spread by disaffected members. Fears that the government had been infiltrated—reminiscent of McCarthyite America—awakened public anxiety. Things came to a head on June 23, 1784, when the Bavarian government outlawed all secret societies, regardless of whether they were illuminated or not. Non-illuminated Freemasons distanced themselves from Weishaupt's cabal, but in the hysteria few bothered with such subtle distinctions. Freemasonry, esotericism, and occult orders of any stamp were lumped together as threats to "national security," a maneuver governments often employ to facilitate a wave of repression. The rest of the Continent soon followed. The outlook that spawned Barruel, Robison, and later Nesta Webster and the authors of *The Protocols of the Elders of Zion* took root and has never really disappeared. A few years later, when not only the Bastille but also many heads fell, it was obvious to many that the path to illumination led through the destruction of civilization and mob rule.

SOCIETIES HARMONIOUS . . . OR NOT

The year 1784 saw the beginning of a dark time for esoteric orders, but it was also the year that a general Convention of Freemasons, called by the lodge *Les Amis Reunis*, also known as the *Philalethes* (Lovers of Truth), was held in Paris. The convention didn't go that well; one sour note was hit by the flamboyant Count Cagliostro, initiate of the Strict Observance Lodge and the Illuminati, and hierophant of his own brand of Egyptian Masonry, which some scholars believe he learned from Rabbi Falk but the details of which Cagliostro himself claimed to have discovered on a London bookstall. (For what it's worth, the immortal Comte de Saint-Germain claimed to have learned the rite in ancient Egypt itself and later passed it on to the count.) Cagliostro saw his own work as the regeneration of mankind, and his tolerant lodges initiated women as well as Jews; he demanded that the other lodges destroy all their records and come under his direction. Not surprisingly, they passed on his offer. This particular clash among Masonic brethren highlights the schisms and dissension endemic to the occult groups jostling for position in the early dawn of the Revolution. Like many at the time, esotericists and occultists who would soon be revolted by the Revolution's mass murders initially embraced the heady sense of radical change. In *The Prelude*, the poet William Wordsworth, along with Rousseau a great lover of nature, famously declared that then it was "bliss to be alive, and to be young very heaven." After the blades fell, Wordsworth and his fellow Romantic Samuel Taylor Coleridge were appalled, and both moved toward more conservative political beliefs. A similar sea change occurred among the occultists.

One of the earliest occult groups presaging the Revolution was the Order of the Elect Cohens, inaugurated in 1754 by the Swedenborgian, Rosicrucian, and Freemason Martines de Pasqually. (*Cohen* means "priest" in Hebrew.) Incorporating Masonic elements, the order focused on theurgy and "operative," ceremonial magic, in which the "operative magician" calls down a visible embodiment of a god, a practice associated with the Neoplatonic philosopher Iamblichus and later with the Hermetic Order of the Golden Dawn. Pasqually's mystical philosophy also embraced cabalism and a form of number magic, "arithmosophy," and it's said he was initiated into a Écossais (Scottish) Masonic lodge by Baron Hund's supposed "unknown superior," Charles Edward Stuart. Pasqually's work came to be called Martinism—confusingly, the teaching of his most important disciple, Louis Claude de Saint-Martin, was given the same name—and is somewhat similar to that of the Benedictine Antoine-Joseph Pernety, who led a group devoted to oracular experiments with what they called "the Holy Word," a kind of eighteenth-century channeling. The entity in question was referred to as *la chose*, "the thing."

Pernety's group met in Avignon, home to many Jacobite émigrés, and it's thought he came into contact with the Golden and Rosy Cross Order in Berlin. Pernety was for a time librarian for Frederick William II, King of Prussia, and in 1781 Frederick William was initiated into the order by Johann Rudolf von Bischoffswerder.[19] As Christopher McIntosh argues, this had far-reaching consequences. Pernety believed that he and his followers were chosen as the leaders of a new society, the new "people of God." After Frederick William ascended the throne in 1786, following Frederick the Great, Bischoffswerder "exercised a strong influence over Prussian foreign policy and promoted a counter-revolutionary crusade against French Jacobinism" (the Jacobins were the extreme radicals of the Revolution).[20] Another member of the order, Johann Christoph Wöllner, had even greater influence over the new king, becoming his economic adviser, speech writer, and later the Minister of Ecclesiastical Affairs. Wöllner's policies illustrate the ironic truth that "Rosicrucianism in the late 18th century became a rallying point for those who were of conservative outlook and were opposed to the socially radical, rationalistic and anti-religious tendencies which were becoming a serious challenge in Germany."[21] In an example of what C. G. Jung called an "enantiodromia"—when something becomes its opposite—Wöllner created a kind of Rosicrucian Protestant inquisition, an "ecclesiastical secret police" who reported on dissident teachers, preachers, and professors, a far cry from the original Rosicrucian impulse. In France, this conservative turn would have to wait until the initial enthusiasm for the Revolution had faded.

MESMERIZED MASONS

As mentioned, the work of the Austrian scientist Franz Anton Mesmer added to the pre-Revolutionary esoteric currents. Even though Mesmer wasn't particularly political (nor was he a true occultist) and was largely dependent on upper-class patronage, his ideas were nevertheless adopted by radical individuals and blended with Rousseau's to form a mesmeric version of the "noble savage." For Rousseau, decadent civilization was responsible for mankind's ills. A "return to nature" was needed, a step back to our primal, pre-fallen state; thus man would become regenerated and usher in a new age, a theme sounded in different ways by Rosicrucians, Masons, and Swedenborgians. Mesmer believed that "animal magnetism" was a revolutionary new insight into an ancient truth and that only vested interests prevented it from being acknowledged as a remedy for a variety of physical and social ills. As today, his form of "alternative medicine" was scorned by the establishment, but its opponents weren't only of a conservative bent. Among the scientists who rejected his claims at an examination commissioned by the French Academy of Science was the Mason and revolutionary Benjamin Franklin. Yet the Marquis de Lafayette, the French hero of the American Revolution, informed George Washington that he was considered one of Mesmer's most enthusiastic students and that there was a strong connection between his dedication to the American republic and his devotion to mesmerism.[22]

Many believed in a conspiracy that prevented "the people" from benefiting from Mesmer's discoveries and that also aimed at thwarting other "radical" scientists' efforts to broaden the fields of knowledge. As Robert Darnton argues, "Some mesmerist works developed political overtones; they showed that privileged bodies, supported by the government, were attempting to suppress a movement to improve the lot of the common people."[23] Although the French Parlement took no action against Mesmer and his success rate ensured no lack of patients, an unseemly smell clung to his practice, no doubt encouraged by reports of the orgy-like atmosphere accompanying the mesmeric "baths" central to his cure. The frequent dishabille and orgasm-like "crisis" that followed the successful treatment of Mesmer's attractive female patients no doubt added to suspicions about the animal element in his magnetism.

Mesmer himself courted aristocracy and exhibited a haughty, regal manner, and would have made an easy target for the growing resentment against the upper classes; predictably, when the revolutionary underground became the new establishment, mesmerism was outlawed as just another upper-class fad. Some feared that counter-revolutionaries could use animal magnetism to communicate secret plans.[24] But Mesmer's ideas percolated down to the radical consciousness by way of the Societies of Harmony he started in 1783, whose aim was to help in the coming regeneration of mankind. Two not-so-harmonious members, Nicolas Bergasse and Jacques-Pierre Brissot, injected considerable radicalism into Mesmer's system. Bergasse, Mesmer's pro-tégé, declared that in "raising an altar to mesmerism" he was really raising one to "liberty," and he eventually accused Mesmer of selling out to high society. Out of Bergasse's own mesmerist group, two leading Girondists—moderate revolutionaries who would fall to the Jacobins' blade—emerged, Etienne Clavière and Antoine-Joseph Gorsas.[25]

Brissot, a writer and another leading Girondist, was equally elo-quent on the links between Mesmer and liberty. He added an element of secrecy that seemed to confirm the worse suspicions of the good Abbé Barruel. "The time has now come for the revolution that France needs," Brissot argued, "but to attempt to produce one openly is to doom it to failure. To succeed it is necessary to wrap oneself in mys-tery; it is necessary to unite men under the pretext of experiments in physics but, in reality, for the overthrow of despotism."[26] Just as a patient would recover her "natural" health following the "crisis" that freed her blocked magnetic energies, so too French society would be re-stored to its pristine state once the Revolution cast out its impurities.

Yet Brissot, who fell to the blade in 1793, was equally motivated by his failure to make a name for himself in the Parisian salons; de-termined to show himself the equal of any urban *philosophe*, as the son of a provincial tavern keeper, he couldn't compete in the fashion-able Parisian cafés. He detested the world of the literary "bon ton" and argued that the government and the academies were determined to stifle new thought, particularly his.[27] "The domain of the sciences must be free from despots, aristocrats, and electors," he declared. Bris-sot wasn't alone in his contempt, and he can serve as an example of how base motives often blend with high ideals when the revolutionary kindling ignites. Another revolutionary who espoused ideas similar to Mesmer's was Jean-Paul Marat, who wrote on the secrets of electric-ity, light, and fire and who was equally snubbed by the Academy, a re-buff that bore a persecution complex. It could be argued that in some ways the French Revolution was linked to frustrated *philosophes* in the way World War II was linked to a frustrated artist, the third-rate painter Adolf Hitler.

But if Bergasse and Brissot bonded Mesmer's ideas to a primitive, "natural" humanity, others forged more angelic links. Jean-Baptiste

Willermoz of Lyons, a Strict Observance Freemason since the age of twenty—and possible holder of the Guinness record for the number of mystical societies he belonged to—was initiated into Martines de Pasqually's Elect Cohens in 1767. After his master's death in 1774, Willermoz developed Pasqually's theurgic magic, but he was also concerned about the order's growing lack of direction. To counter this he initiated what was effectively a new Masonic rite. The Order of Beneficent Knights of the Holy City included six grades of what became known as the Rectified Scottish Rite, an outgrowth of Strict Observance. At a grand Masonic conference in the late 1770s organized by Duke Ferdinand of Brunswick and Prince Charles of Hesse-Cassel, two leading figures in Strict Observance, Willermoz persuaded the Rectified Scottish Rite to abandon its Templar myth, instituted by Baron Hund, and to adopt his new Martinist system.

Yet Willermoz was also an ardent mesmerist and a member of a Society of Harmony, where he seemed to combine mesmerism and Pasqually's theurgy in a pursuit reminiscent of the Benedictine Antoine Pernety. At gatherings, Willermoz recorded the pronouncements of women experiencing a "magnetic trance." These were known as *crisiacs*, somnambulists who acted as oracles and whose communications from the "spirit world"—adding a touch of Swedenborg to the heady brew—Willermoz would try to decipher. As with today's channelers, Willermoz's *crisiacs* often voiced rather general revelations about the coming new dawn and the return of the ancient religion, but they occasionally produced something unusual, and Willermoz felt he needed help in decoding it. For this he turned to one of the most profound figures of the period, Louis Claude de Saint-Martin, the "Unknown Philosopher."

THE UNKNOWN PHILOSOPHER

Unlike many habitués of esoteric circles in this time, Saint-Martin was a true hermetic philosopher; like Swedenborg he was deeply concerned with mankind's spiritual destiny. He knew that for any political or social revolution to be worthwhile, it had to be based on an inner transformation. Like Wordsworth and Coleridge, he initially felt sympathy for the Revolution's ideals, but its horror soon repelled him. He was a victim of the upheaval himself; of a noble family, the Revolution made him penniless. He wrote that in Paris in 1792, "the streets near the house I was in were a field of battle; the house itself a hospital where the wounded were brought."[28] In 1794 an edict banning the nobility from Paris forced him to return to Amboise, the place of his birth. To protect himself, he wrote under the name "the Unknown Philosopher."

Saint-Martin's vision is one of profound responsibility; among his "counsels of the exile" he writes: "The function of man differs from that of other physical beings, for it is the reparation of the disorders of the universe."[29] The only sign that we are "regenerated," he tells us, is that "we regenerate everything around us."[30] In a time when the rights of men—and women also, to give Mary Wollstonecraft her due—were being demanded, Saint-Martin instead burdened his readers with a metaphysical obligation that the cabala calls *tikkun*, which means to repair the damage done by the overflowing of the *sephiroth*, the "vessels" of the Tree of Life. Instead of expecting life, society, or the government to guarantee our happiness, and complaining loudly when it doesn't, Saint-Martin demands from us the opposite: that we dedicate our lives to making the world a better place—a banal chore on the face of it, but in practice very difficult. Like Jean Baptiste Willermoz, Saint-Martin was a follower of Martines de Pasqually, but he eventually broke with Pasqually's theurgic teachings to follow his own more meditative path.

Saint-Martin was initally attracted to mesmerism but eventually rejected it also as too materialistic and in danger of attracting unwanted astral spirits. One particular "unwanted astral spirit" seems to have disturbed Saint-Martin profoundly. Willermoz informed him that one of his *crisiacs* had contacted an "entity" that Willermoz called the "Unknown Agent," a variant of Baron Hund's "unknown superiors." An equally unknown representative of this supernatural source gave Willermoz some notebooks containing messages from the Unknown Agent, directing Willermoz to establish an esoteric group within his Rectified Scottish Rite that would receive word from the

Unknown Agent directly. Exactly who or what the Unknown Agent was remains a mystery, and for a few years, Willermoz and his group struggled to decipher its strange communiqués. Saint-Martin and Willermoz had by this time followed their separate paths, but when Willermoz informed Saint-Martin about the Unknown Agent, the Unknown Philosopher rushed to Lyon to confer with him. Yet something about these directives from beyond disturbed Saint-Martin, and not long afterward, he abandoned attempts to decode the Unknown Agent's messages.[31]

With Swedenborg, Saint-Martin believed that the "material world was subordinate to a more real spiritual realm in which primitive man had once ruled and into which modern man needed to be reintegrated."[32] He believed in an "ideal society based on a natural and spiritual theocracy, governed by men who would be chosen by God and who would regard themselves as 'divine commissioners' to guide the people."[33] Like many esoteric thinkers, Saint-Martin saw human misery as a consequence of the Fall, our descent from higher realms through some "crime" that imprisoned us in a universe of space, time, and matter. Saint-Martin in a way typifies the shift in mesmerism in the last days of the *ancien régime*. More and more mesmerists abandoned treating sick individuals to focus on prescribing for a sick society. The *crisiacs* communiqués that Saint-Martin helped Willermoz decode would, they believed, trigger the crisis that would return the state to its primitive innocence.

CAGLIOSTRO

One Freemason who arguably helped bring on the Revolution was the enigmatic Sicilian magician Count Cagliostro. As mentioned, Cagliostro, whose real name may have been Giuseppe Balsamo, was a student of Rabbi Falk. In 1787, while in London, Cagliostro, along with Saint-Martin, may have met William Blake at Jacob Duche's Theosophical Society; we know that the painter Philip de Loutherbourg, a member of the society, was a friend of the "Great Copt" (a title Cagliostro took from Rabbi Falk) and that Cagliostro stayed at

Loutherbourg's Hammersmith house more than once. Saint-Martin was happy to remain a semi-obscure figure, wrapped in the cloak of the Unknown Philosopher, but Cagliostro's sensational life is an object lesson in the dangers of notoriety.

It's untrue that Cagliostro used his brand of "Egyptian Freemasonry to undermine legitimate governments and religion" and that he had planned to mount a "Masonic war" against Rome,[34] an accusation used to justify the Great Copt's cruel imprisonment and eventual execution at the hands of the Church. But his sincere belief in the regeneration of mankind and his tolerant, inclusive Freemasonry offered a powerful substitute for Rome's rigid authoritarianism in the last days of the Inquisition. Although he was drawn to the Illuminati, the free-wheeling Cagliostro no doubt saw Weishaupt's group as just another order; like Willermoz, he collected initiations as others might do stamps. His great appeal to the common people was a threat to the establishment. Like the Rosicrucians, he treated the sick across Europe gratis, and often his was the only treatment available to the poor. Born in a Palermo slum, Cagliostro knew poverty at firsthand and did what he could to alleviate it.

Although on occasion Cagliostro was, like other great esoteric figures, something of a con man (one thinks of Madame Blavatsky, Aleister Crowley, and Gurdjieff), when he was initiated into the Esperance Strict Observance Lodge at the King's Head Pub in Gerrard Street in Soho, London on April 12, 1777, he was literally transformed. If Freemasonry's aim was regeneration, with Cagliostro it succeeded. It became his life's mission; for the rest of his days he spread the Masonic message across Europe, rattling through Venice, Berlin, Paris, and St. Petersburg in his black coach emblazoned with cabalistic symbols. He wasn't always successful; his attempt to initiate Catherine the Great of Russia into his Egyptian Masonic rite was a complete failure. Catherine was an utter rationalist, a student of Voltaire, and mysticism of any kind disgusted her, but she also feared that Cagliostro's tolerant lodges would breed dangerously democratic ideas. Cagliostro had more luck with the Duke of Orléans, otherwise known as Philippe Egalité, brother to Louis XVI, who hated Marie Antoinette and had designs on the throne. The duke was an inveterate Mason and had been a student of Falk's. But it was Cagliostro's unfortunate encounter with Marie Antoinette in the "Diamond Necklace Affair" that precipitated his downfall.

In 1781, Cardinal Rohan, a member of a powerful noble family, was duped by the adventuress Jeanne de la Motte into thinking that Marie Antoinette wanted him to act as her agent in purchasing a fabulously expensive necklace, originally made for Madame du Barry, Louis XV's mistress. Although for years Rohan had sought Marie Antoinette's favors, both political and sexual, she detested him and had frequently blocked his attempts to advance his career. Cardinal Rohan saw Cagliostro as a spiritual advisor, and when he learned from Jeanne de la Motte, who convinced him that she was an intimate of the queen, that Marie Antoinette wanted him to make the purchase for her, he was ecstatic and asked Cagliostro for advice. Seeing the Cardinal's happiness, Cagliostro advised him to trust his feelings. This innocent remark, which Cagliostro no doubt immediately forgot, led to several months in the Bastille. Rohan secured the necklace, and at a clandestine meeting during which a courtesan Jeanne de la Motte had hired to impersonate Marie Antoinette accepted it, Rohan believed he was on the way to enjoying the queen's intimacies.

The affair turned nasty when the jewelers approached Rohan for the first part of the payment. Jeanne de la Motte believed Rohan was wealthy and would simply pay up to avoid scandal, but he refused, and eventually the jewelers approached the queen. When she heard of the plot, she was furious and accused Rohan and Cagliostro of masterminding it. Louis XVI had them arrested, and although both Rohan and Cagliostro were eventually acquitted and Jeanne de la Motte imprisoned, the accusations stuck.

Cagliostro's part in the affair was practically nonexistent, but it was sufficient to ruin his already checkered reputation. Henceforth he lived as a perpetual "ignoble traveler," thrown out of country after country because of the scandal. But the real victim was the queen. Her abuse of Cagliostro and her role in a debacle over an enormously expensive necklace while her people were starving—when told that they had no bread, she famously replied, "Then let them eat cake"—enraged her subjects. Goethe, an illuminated Mason of a conservative political bent, followed the case in Germany and was appalled. "The intrigue is utterly destructive to royal dignity," he wrote. "The Necklace Case is the prelude to revolution."[35] He was right.

Exiled from France, Cagliostro found himself in London, where his Egyptian Rite drew few initiates. He wrote a strangely prophetic *Letter to the French People* that sold well in Paris and seemed to predict the coming catastrophe. Cagliostro wouldn't return to France, he declared, until the Bastille was torn down and made into a public promenade; the time was right, he said, for a new vision to rule the governments of the world. Calls for a new vision were fairly commonplace, but Cagliostro hit the bull's eye with the Bastille. His case against the king for false imprisonment was argued by anti-Bourbon lawyers, who looked to the Duke of Orléans as a possible substitute and who attacked the policy of the hated *lettres de cachet*, edicts from Louis XVI basically allowing arrest without explanation, an eighteenth-century version of some current antiterrorism legislation. All this provided sufficient circumstantial evidence for Europe's aristocracy to turn a wary eye on the Great Copt. Becoming friends with the notorious English Jewish convert Lord George Gordon, responsible for a wave of anti-Catholic riots in 1780, didn't help Cagliostro's reputation. The Vatican put him on their "most wanted" list and pondered how to end his troublesome career.

Sadly, Cagliostro made the mistake of ceding to his wife's wishes and took her to Rome to see her family. She had been with Cagliostro for twenty years and had grown tired of the life. Unaware of how seriously the Church was gunning for him, she agreed to testify against her husband, in order, she thought, to make a clean break. Cagliostro was oblivious to this and, never one to think small, had designs to initiate the Pope and win Catholicism over to his Egyptian Freemasonry. The gods had other plans. In 1789, Cagliostro was arrested and thrown into Rome's infamous San Leo prison. Sentenced to death for heresy and Freemasonry, the Church in its mercy commuted this to life imprisonment. Cagliostro spent his last years in a cold, tiny cell, his only illumination a small skylight. He was undoubtedly tortured. "I do not believe," he wrote, "that God punishes sinners in Hell as cruelly as this." Among his several accomplishments, the Great Copt enjoys the distinction of being the last prisoner executed by the Inquisition—ignoring his sentence's commutation—probably strangled by his guard. His death wasn't believed, and when French soldiers captured the prison in 1797, they searched for him, a hero of the Revolution.

Yet Cagliostro had the last laugh. On July 14, 1789, a mob stormed and captured the Bastille, releasing its prisoners. Ironically, one of them had recently been the Marquis de Sade, who is reported to have addressed a crowd in the street from his window only a few days before, shouting, "They are killing the prisoners in here!" and starting something of a riot. He was transferred to the insane asylum at Charenton two days later and missed being liberated. The Revolution had started, and soon after the building was demolished. Today, just as Cagliostro predicted, it is a public promenade, easily accessible on the Paris Metro.

6

Spirits Rebellious

Cagliostro's wasn't the only prediction about the French Revolution. Catherine Théot, an "old and nearly blind woman" who had gathered a band of followers, "prophesied, and her predictions were realized." One in particular concerned Robespierre, whom she spoke of as "the king of bloody sacrifices," remarking that "the head of Louis XVI is heavy" and that only Robespierre's "can be its counterpoise."[1] Such regal premonitions, suggesting that Robespierre should crown himself king, later led to his downfall when his rivals accused him of messianic pretensions. She also announced that she would trigger the apocalypse by giving birth to God, for which claim she became known as "the Mother of God." She was eighty-three at the time. Suzette Labrouse likewise made sensational predictions about the fate of the Church and the aristocracy. She made a pilgrimage to Rome where, like Cagliostro, she hoped to convert the Pope. Like Cagliostro, she spent her remaining days in prison.

Perhaps the most famous predictions about the Revolution were made by the writer Jacques Cazotte. At a dinner party in Paris in 1788, Cazotte, the author of the delightful occult comedy *The Devil in Love* and, like Saint-Martin and Willermoz, an initiate of Martinez de Pasqually's order, accurately prophesied the fates of several people attending. One guest, Guillaume de Malesherbes, proposed a toast "to the day when reason will be triumphant in the affairs of men," a day, he added, "which I will never live to see." Cazotte disagreed: Malesherbes would live to see that day, and it would arrive in six years. A revolution was approaching, Cazotte informed the startled guests, and it would affect everyone in the room.

Jean de La Harpe, a skeptic and atheist, was amused by Cazotte's confidence and recorded his predictions in order later to prove that all prophecy is mere superstition. Ironically, La Harpe's notes are the best evidence for Cazotte's accuracy. Cazotte told the Marquis de Condorcet, the famous philosopher and apostle of progress, that he would die in prison, from poison taken to avoid execution. He also said that Chamfort, a favorite of Louis XVI, would try to kill himself by cutting his veins but would only die some months later. But Dr. Vicq d'Azyr would be successful, assisted by another in his gruesome pursuit. The astronomer Jean Bailly would die on the scaffold, as would Messieurs Nicolai, Roucher, and Malesherbes himself, all victims of the mob. Cazotte's host, the Duchesse de Gramont, would meet the same fate, as would the other ladies present.

The skeptical La Harpe asked about his own future. Would he die too? No, Cazotte replied, he would convert to Christianity—for a committed atheist, a fate perhaps worse than death. And Cazotte himself? Here the novelist was somewhat vague, likening his destiny to that of the man who during the siege of Jerusalem walked around its walls crying "woe to Jerusalem" until he was crushed by a stone from a Roman catapult. In 1792, after his plans for a counter-revolution fell into the wrong hands, Cazotte was executed by the Paris tribunal.

Cazotte's other predictions proved equally correct. Condorcet did poison himself in a prison cell. Chamfort did try to slit his wrists but failed and died months later at the hands of a doctor treating his wounds. Dr. Vicq d'Azyr fared better, receiving the services of a fellow prisoner, who opened his veins so he could avoid the blade. The others were guillotined. La Harpe, horrified by the bloodbath, retreated to a monastery and became a devout Catholic. And as Christopher McIntosh makes clear, the triumph of reason that Malesherbes despaired of was by the time of his death in full force.

In a macabre example of historical irony, in the midst of the insane Terror, several "cults of reason" sprang up, designed to take the place of the hated Church. One such, the Théophilantropes, offered "no rites, no priests, nothing that could cause offence to any sect,"[2] evidence that political correctness isn't limited to our own time. Robespierre had his own religion, the Cult of the Supreme Being, whose devotees baptized their children in the name of "liberty, equality, and fraternity." After the Thermidorian Reaction in 1794 relieved Robespierre of power, aided by the Mother of God's injudicious predictions, his cult was aborted. Robespierre was executed the same year, a victim of the Reign of Terror he helped perpetuate, but by then the Revolution had been eating its own for some time. The same year saw another martyr to reason, the wonderfully named Anaxagoras Chaumette, whose "cult of reason" included rituals in Notre Dame with a procession of maidens paying homage to a white-robed goddess. The notion of a Supreme Being is a mainstay of Freemasonry, but "the dreadful terror that had reached its peak in the execution of the King was abhorrent to the civilized creed of the majority of masons."[3] As the guillotine fell with a sickening monotony, the Masonic minded did well to be discreet.

Yet for those partial to the Templar myth of Masonic roots, Louis XVI's execution in 1793 was in fact an act of revenge against the aristocracy that sent Jacques de Molay to the flames. Legend has it that as Louis' head hit the basket, someone in the crowd leaped up and, dipping his fingers in the blood, flung it over the cheering mob, shouting, "Jacques de Molay, you are avenged!" showing that the good Abbé Barruel was right to anchor the agents of the Revolution among the Masonic flock.

ENTER THE *EGREGORE*

Cazotte himself was aware of the dangerous energies unleashed by the Revolution. He even broke with his good friend Saint-Martin when the gentle mystic voiced some sympathy with the aims of the radicals. Although Cazotte didn't use the term, he would no doubt have agreed that, whatever started it, the Revolution soon took on a life of its own, coming under the power of an *egregore*, Greek for "watcher," a kind of immaterial entity that is created by and presides over a human activity or collective. According to the anonymous author of the fascinating *Meditations on the Tarot*, there are no "good" *egregores*, only "negative" ones. "One cannot engender positive *egregores*," this modern unknown philosopher declares. True or not, *egregores* can nevertheless be "engendered by the collective will and imagination of nations."[4] As Joscelyn Godwin points out, "an *egregore* is augmented by human belief, ritual and especially by sacrifice. If it is sufficiently nourished by such energies, the *egregore* can take on a life of its own and appear to be an independent, personal divinity, with a limited power on behalf of its devotees and an unlimited appetite for their future devotion."[5] If, as some esotericists believe, human conflicts are the result of spiritual forces for spiritual ends, and these forces are not all "good," then collective catastrophes like the French Revolution take on a different significance.

Even if occult forces aren't responsible, an *egregore* nevertheless seems an expression of what the philosopher Jean Gebser calls "the magical structure of consciousness," which he associates with "group consciousness" and the "vegetative intertwining of all living things." Gebser observed this intertwining firsthand in the Nazi Brown Shirts in Munich in the late 1920s. A decade later their kind of group consciousness spread across Europe, setting it ablaze. Mass movements like Nazism embrace the power of the magical structure of consciousness to overrule critical discernment and bind people into a whole, the *volk*. Morris Berman, again writing of the Nazis, makes a Gebserian remark that seems to resonate with the notion of the *egregore*: "An entire culture can eventually undergo very serious changes as the result of the slow accumulation of enough psychic and somatic changes on an invisible level."[6] Many New Age advocates who celebrate "group consciousness" might profit from reading Gebser and from considering the possible existence of *egregores*.

ZANONI

One work of occult fiction that recognizes the negative forces fueling the French Revolution is the remarkable Rosicrucian novel *Zanoni*, by the nineteenth-century writer, occultist, and politician Edward Bulwer-Lytton. Sadly, Bulwer-Lytton is little read today and is remembered, if at all, for one of the most clichéd openings lines in literature, "It was a dark and stormy night," from his novel *Paul Clifford*. (More to his credit, he is also the source of the saying, "The pen is mightier than the sword.") Lytton deserves better press. Along with *Zanoni*, he is responsible for a fascinating work of political-occult science fiction, *The Coming Race*, about a society of highly evolved supermen who inhabit a subterranean kingdom. Regrettably, with its proto-fascist theme of an occult "master race," the novel has become a mainstay of the strange genre of occult Nazi literature. Lytton was one of the first scientific investigators of the paranormal, and his disturbing ghost story, *The Haunter and the Haunted*, remains a classic; another occult work, the alchemical *A Strange Story*, centers on reincarnation and the quest for the elixir of life.

Zanoni's vast plot surrounds the adventures of its eponymous immortal Rosicrucian adept, his love for a mortal woman, and his relationship with his teacher, the grim master Mejnour, told against the backdrop of the Reign of Terror. One section, "The Dweller of the Threshold," an encounter with a frightening spiritual presence, was adopted by Rudolf Steiner for his own vision of spiritual evolution in his influential *Knowledge of the Higher Worlds and Its Attainment*. In this initiatory trial, the neophyte confronts a personification of his or her "shadow," or unredeemed "dark side." In *Zanoni*, as the Terror takes root, the shadow or *egregore* of an entire society rises up, embodied by Lytton in the character of the painter Nicot, a repellent figure who sells his services to the highest bidder and desires the downfall of everything superior to him. This is Lytton's take on the "savage leveling" of the bloodthirsty Jacobins, but it's also his view of the talented but opportunistic artist driven by greed rather than by dedication to his art. In *Zanoni*, Lytton redirects occult science from the minutiae of cabalistic ritual to the will and imagination of the magician himself.

This theme, rooted in Renaissance adepts like Pico della Mirandola and Paracelsus, struck home with the Romantic consciousness and its celebration of the imagination. It found popular expression in the work of Lytton's friend and fellow occultist Eliphas Lévi. Perhaps more than anyone else, Lévi is responsible for the image of the magician and occultist as we know it today, and he emerged from a fascination with popular occultism that had its start in the years leading up to the Revolution.

POPULAR OCCULTISM: A DIGRESSION

The Terror was a bad time for esotericists, but as we've seen, the preceding years saw the spread of a robust genre of popular culture, what we call "occultism." Much of our contemporary mystical interest stems from the occult revival of the 1960s, but the '60s fascination with the occult was itself part of a popular attraction that began in France in the 1770s. Beginnings are notoriously elusive, but the appearance in 1773 of the first volume of an ambitious work entitled *Le Monde primitif* (The Primitive, or Primal, World) by the eccentric Court de Gébelin may serve our purpose. A Protestant theologian from the Languedoc and later president of a Masonic lodge, Court de Gébelin was one of Mesmer's most celebrated patients, being cured of a swollen leg and jaundiced face by the Austrian's magnetic passes. Court de Gébelin's enormous work, which the encyclopedist d'Alembert remarked would require forty men to finish, was a bestseller—even Louis XVI was one of its readers—and he became famous, lecturing to packed houses at his own museum. His theme—that ancient languages revealed the trace of a lost "primitive" science, similar to the *prisca theologia*—was welcomed by the mesmerists, who believed their work revived the lost "natural" health of ancient man. Less welcome was the fact that Court de Gébelin died at a mesmeric tub or *banquet* in 1784.[7]

Gébelin's belief that ancient languages carried echoes of a primitive, natural society that had enjoyed an enviable health and harmony was perhaps most effectively conveyed in his remarks about the Tarot. He hit the still-popular esoteric note when he remarked that the cards were a work of the ancient Egyptians, "one of the books saved from the flames that destroyed their superb libraries." Regarded innocently since the fifteenth century as merely "a mass of extravagant figures which are of no significance in themselves," the Tarot, Gébelin announced, was really a repository of ancient lost knowledge.

One figure profited from Court de Gébelin's tantalizing remarks and may be more responsible than anyone else for the "occult roots" of the Tarot: a curious character named Alliette, who wrote under the pseudonym "Etteilla," his own name written backwards, a familiar magical trope. Starting out as a common fortune teller, Etteilla added to Court de Gébelin's remarkable claims, stating that the Tarot had been devised 171 years after the Flood, that a committee of magi spent four years producing it, and that it was initially conceived by Hermes Trismegistus himself. Henceforth the Tarot was also known as "The Book of Thoth," Thoth being the Egyptian god associated with magic and Hermes. Etteilla ran a lucrative occult business making talismans, casting horoscopes, tutoring in "practical magic," making house calls as a "spiritual doctor" and "perpetual soothsayer," and giving Tarot readings. His success came from using cabalistic devices in a way the new popular occult audience could easily grasp, rather as some current New Age authors spoon-feed their readers mystic insights.

Another explorer in Court de Gébelin's "primitive world" was the Hebraic scholar Antoine Fabre d'Olivet. Following the encyclopedic turn of the time, he planned to synthesize every fact then known. For twenty years he studied ancient Greek and Latin as well as contemporary works and plunged into a deep reading of Egyptology, a new science at the time, based more on textual interpretation than spade work. He believed that ancient Egyptian wisdom lay hidden in the Book of Genesis. The Bible had suffered from execrable translations, and Fabre decided to restore the Hebrew language to its origins. To that end he studied Arabic, Syrian, Chaldean, Samaritan, Chinese, and again Greek. He had, he thought, found the true ur-Hebrew and believed it was composed of three different levels, or senses—an idea Swedenborg hit upon in his own deep reading of scripture.

Popular occultism reached an audience in the years following the Revolution in the work of the French Romantics, especially in the fantastic tales of Théophile Gautier and the unclassifiable work of the eccentric poet and essayist Gérard de Nerval.[8] In Les Illuminés, which includes accounts of Cagliostro, Jacques Cazotte, and other figures from the occult Enlightenment, de Nerval shares Abbé Barruel's suspicions about the insidious Adam Weishaupt. De Nerval also provides a poetic account of the origins of Freemasonry in his exotic *Voyage in the Orient*. To this brief mention of Romantic writers we can add Charles Nodier, who wrote darkly of secret societies plotting political *coups*. Readers of *Holy Blood, Holy Grail* may recall that Nodier appears as one of the Priory of Sion's Grand Masters.

THE NEW PRETENDERS

After the Revolution's self-destruction in 1799, Napoléon Bonaparte seized power, and between then and his final defeat in 1815, all of Europe was drawn into war. It was an apt beginning to a century that would bring new revolutions to France, in 1830 and in 1848, and also new political intrigues. As with the Jacobites, these involved a "pretender" to the throne. The romance surrounding these pretenders soon metamorphosed into a semi-mystical movement, similar to that around the Stuarts. Perhaps most esoteric was the legend of the Dauphin, the alleged son of Louis XVI, who was believed to have escaped his parents' fate; as Louis XVII, he would, like the Stuart pretenders, have a legitimate claim to the throne. A similar situation followed the execution of the Russian royal family at the start of the twentieth century, with the Romanovs' daughter Anastasia supposedly escaping the murder. Recent DNA data seems to have ended speculation in both cases, showing that the Dauphin died in prison in 1795 and that all the Romanovs were murdered.[9]

In 1814, Louis XVIII, the beheaded king's brother, a reactionary oblivious to his nation's aimlessness, took the throne. (He had to give it up briefly in 1815 when Napoléon returned for his "hundred days.") Two successive catastrophes had left France with an identity crisis. After decades of madness and war, it's understandable that a hunger arose for some kind of certainty anchored in the monarchy, whose continuity had been broken by the Revolution and the usurper Napoléon. A royalist movement known as the "Saviors of Louis XVII" drew many supporters; its most radical embraced the myth that Louis

XVI's execution was, as mentioned, an act of revenge perpetrated by latter-day Templars. Abbé Barruel's sensational but for the most part fictional work bolstered this idea.

One candidate for the role of Dauphin was Charles Edouard Naundorff, who called himself the Duc de Normandie and arrived in France from Prussia in the early 1830s, bearing a striking resemblance to the murdered king. He wasn't welcomed by the present ruler, Louis Philippe, and was banished in 1836. Naundorff lived in London for many years and died in 1845 in Delft, Holland, where he was buried as Louis XVII. Naundorff seems to have been something of a visionary; among his many books, which he claimed were divinely inspired, was *The Heavenly Doctrine of the Lord Jesus Christ*. Naundorff's son, Charles Guillaume, like Charles Edward Stuart, carried on the claim and was supported by some newspapers.

THE WORK OF MERCY

Behind the Naundorffist movement, however, lay deeper motives than merely securing the legitimate line of regal descent. The excesses of the Revolution swung the political pendulum toward the right, and the Naundorffists saw France as the seat of a new world order rooted in the monarchy and decreed by providence. One such royalist prophet was a bizarre character called Ganneau, an aged man also known as "the Mapah," who wore women's clothing while preaching of man's fall from divine grace. "Mapah," one assumes, is a title denoting androgyny, comprised of "Ma" and "Pa." Another figure who preached the return of a golden age was the strange visionary Eugène Vintras.

In 1839, Vintras, the manager of a small cardboard box factory, met Ferdinand Geoffroi, a notary and fervent Naundorffist. The meeting would change Vintras' life. His already mystically inclined temperament was excited by Geoffroi's extravagant claims for the coming Naundorff regime, which he saw as presaging the millennium. Vintras embraced the Naundorff cause, too, and went Geoffroi one better when he reported that he had received divine messages from the Archangel Michael—confirmed by the Virgin Mary and St. Joseph—that he was to become its leader. The new gospel would be called the "Work of Mercy," and Vintras' first task was to gather disciples to share the work of redeeming the world by establishing a new heavenly kingdom centered in France. The idea of a nation having a divine mission emerged elsewhere during the nineteenth century, in an apocalyptic sense in pre-Revolutionary Russia and as the doctrine of Manifest Destiny in the United States. Pragmatic England would root its own empire in the more banal cause of commerce.

At his cardboard box factory in Tilly, Vintras set up an oratory, where he kept communion hosts that he claimed were sent to him by people who feared they would be profaned by unholy individuals. Their fears were warranted, Vintras believed, because the hosts had produced real blood. These bloody hosts were to prove something of a problem for the prophet. By this time Vintras had amassed a large following, including some clergymen. One in particular, the Abbé Charvoz, became an energetic publicist for the cause. Vintras was inclined not to publicize the business of the communion hosts, but for Charvoz they were an excellent public relations opportunity. He gathered sworn statements about the blood's authenticity from a number of distinguished persons, including several doctors. With these endorsements, Charvoz printed thousands of copies of a pamphlet, celebrating Vintras and his miracles. The pamphlets sold well, and when one reached the Bishop of Bayeux, he was appalled, and he declared that the miracles were fakes and that Vintras' teaching was contrary to that of the Church. By this time the government was also troubled that the Naundorffists were gaining the support of a popular mystical religious sect, and thinking to nip this threat in the bud, they leveled trumped-up charges against Vintras and Geoffroi, accusing them of defrauding followers of money. The public was outraged, and although the supposed victims actually testified in Vintras' favor, the two were nevertheless sent to prison. While serving his five-year sentence, Vintras discovered that Pope Gregory XVI had condemned his work.

It was the beginning of a wave of persecution. A disgruntled ex-worker of mercy published a pamphlet accusing Vintras of sexual perversions, reprising the Templar smear campaign. Although false, the allegations stuck, and in 1848, the Church declared Vintras a heretic.

Vintras countered by excommunicating the Pope and declaring himself the pontiff of his own church, whose priesthood included women. He also announced his role in a cosmic battle against the agents of black magic. Whether black magicians were responsible or not, other allegations compelled Vintras to leave France and relocate to London, where he carried on his struggle against the forces of evil from the respectable neighborhood of Marylebone Road.

In 1863, Vintras returned to France. The Work of Mercy had started in England by then and had spread to Italy and Spain; in 1867 Vintras opened the Center of the White Carmel in Florence. He spent his last years in Lyons, a home to many mystics. Vintras died in 1875, and the Work of Mercy passed on to a rather different character, the Abbé Boullan, who appears as Dr. Johannès in J. K. Huysmans' satanic novel *Là-Bas*, a classic of *fin-de-siècle* decadence. Huysmans portrays Boullan as a white magician, but less fictional accounts suggest he was a mage of a different color.[10]

The Professor of Transcendental Magic

The year 1875 also marked the death of an occultist known to his disciples as the Professor of Transcendental Magic, one of many titles this eccentric character had enjoyed. Born Alphonse Louis Constant in 1810, by 1855, with the publication of his *Dogme et ritual de la haute magie* (translated by A. E. Waite in 1896 as *Transcendental Magic*), he had been reborn as Éliphas Lévi, adopting what he claimed was the Hebrew equivalent of his two given names.[11] Prior to emerging as a cabalist and occultist of doubtful erudition but effective literary powers, Lévi had planned to become a priest but left the seminary because he couldn't ignore the fairer sex. Before he gained a wide readership, which continues today, through his often erroneous but exciting accounts of the cabala, Tarot, and history of the occult, Lévi had acquired a much smaller audience as the author of impassioned but ill-argued political tracts, voicing a strident socialism peppered with revolutionary rhetoric. If there is doubt that all occult politicians are not of the right, a look at Lévi's career helps to dispel it.

Before creating occultism as we know it, Lévi haunted the Paris literary scene, eking out a living by writing and illustrating; many students of the occult know Lévi's striking and often-reproduced illustrations of the Goat of Mendes, or the Templars' alleged deity Baphomet, without knowing their author. After leaving the priesthood, he taught at a boarding school for a year, then worked as a traveling actor. He became friends with the militant feminist and socialist Flora Tristan, described by her grandson the painter Paul Gauguin as "a blue stocking, a socialist and an anarchist" who "spent all her money to further the workers' cause." The workers were apparently fond of Flora, as they erected a monument in her honor at her grave in Bordeaux.

Many of the radical views that would cause Lévi much trouble came to him through Flora Tristan, and he would later edit her posthumously published book, *L'Emancipation de la femme* (The Emancipation of Women). While his ideas on woman as the "savior" of man—a constant theme in his career—were often moving, they frequently smacked more of inexperience than insight. Monsignor Olivier, the Bishop of Evreux, who befriended Lévi, thought his work of Mariolatry, *La mère de Dieu* (The Mother of God), more naïve than shocking. "If you knew women better," the Monsignor wrote, "you would not adore Woman so unreservedly," an insight Lévi could have profited by.[12]

At the same time as he absorbed radical ideas, Lévi also first encountered the peculiarly French version of monarchical mysticism. In his highly readable *History of Magic*, Lévi recounts his meeting with the "Mapah," also known as Ganneau. In 1839, with a friend, the occult novelist Alphonse Esquiros, Lévi visited the weird prophet in a squalid Parisian garret. Ganneau, a "bearded man of majestic demeanour," wore a tattered woman's cloak that gave him the appearance of a "destitute dervish." His followers seemed mesmerized by his words, and Ganneau told Lévi that he, not Charles Edouard Naundorff, was really Louis XVII and had returned to earth to accomplish the work of regeneration; where he had been in the interim is unclear. The woman who shared Ganneau's beliefs, and who appeared to be a somnambulist, was really Marie Antoinette. Lévi claimed that the incendiary power of the Mapah's words was demonstrated a decade later, when one of his disciples started the revolution of 1848. The young man announced that he was destined to "save the world by provoking the supreme crisis of universal revolution." Joined by two young boys, one bearing a torch and the other beating a drum, he gathered a crowd and marched toward the Boulevard des Capucines to "acquaint the ministry with the will of the people." Haranguing the crowd, which had turned into a mob, the Mapah's disciple entered a trance and somehow wound up carrying a pistol in each hand. A rush of people surged into the Boulevard des Italiens. The Mapaist had disappeared, but a shot was fired, and the revolution was ignited. The next day "all Paris was barricaded."[13]

Whether or not the Mapah's disciple actually started the revolution, Lévi threw himself into it, writing revolutionary songs, campaigning for workers' rights, and contributing to the left-wing press. Esquiros was elected to the National Assembly the next year, and Lévi's wife, Noémie Cadot (twenty years younger than he), became a feminist. Lévi's own incendiary works landed him more than one prison sentence. In 1841, after coming under the Mapah's spell, he served eight months for his book *La bible de la liberté* (The Bible of Liberty), a work "of questionable orthodoxy in matters of religion and of revolutionary intent in politics."[14] As "a passionate railing against the misuse of authority,"[15] the work was one of many, and its effectiveness was limited to getting its author arrested: an hour after the book went on sale it was confiscated. Like others before him, Lévi predicted that "mankind was on the threshold of a wonderful new age" when "sacred liberty" would no longer be rare among governments.

At his trial, Lévi claimed he was "a child of the people" who suffered with them and dared to speak in their name, well aware that he was attacking the "form and basis of the present social order." He abhorred violence, and his only crime was "a deep love of mankind." His eloquence worked against him. When bringing his defense to a close, he sought solidarity with those who judged him. "If the jury finds me innocent," he declaimed, " it will by that fact protest with me against the form of today's society."[16]

They weren't with him then, or on the other occasions he was arrested. In 1847, he was convicted of promoting class war by publishing his tract *Le voix de la famine* (The Voice of Famine), and served six months. The leftist press made him a *cause célèbre*, while Lévi himself did his time reading Swedenborg, who didn't make a good impression on him.[17]

Lévi's wife's association with a left-wing newspaper triggered his metamorphosis from radical to occultist. Lévi wrote for the leftist *Revue Progressive*, and its owner, the Marquis Montferrier, asked Lévi's wife to contribute as well. By this time Lévi had met the eccentric Polish émigré Jósef Maria Hoene Wronski, who had developed a theory of universal knowledge, Messianisme, uniting philosophy and religion. A soldier in the Russian and Polish armies, Wronksi was a brilliant astronomer who had worked at the observatory in Marseilles. His cosmological theories were so radical that he was asked to leave; henceforth he remained an intellectual wanderer, his poverty lightened only by the unflinching support of his wife. Alas, poor Lévi could have used such steadfastness; while he became acquainted with Wronski's ideas, which led him to the cabala, his wife was becoming acquainted with the Marquis Montferrier, her feminist ideas including a good dose of what would soon be called "free love." When she left Lévi for the Marquis he was shattered, and only his new devotion to occultism helped him through the crisis.

Wronksi had his own brand of occult politics, and in 1851 he published the exhaustively titled *Secret letter to His Highness Prince Louis-Napoleon, President of the French Republic, on the destinies of France and of the civilized world in general*. Wronski argued that if certain spiritual laws, which he believed could be expressed mathematically, were followed, all strife between nations would end and their true aims be accomplished. It was the destiny of Louis-Napoleon, the great emperor's nephew and present leader of France, to rediscover this secret. There was one hitch, a general misunderstanding about the true nature of Christianity, and like Fabre d'Olivet, Wronski believed a return to the scriptures was in order. He spoke of a "superior science" that Christ promised with the "advent of the Paraclete," hearkening back to some of the Moravians' views. In years to come, Lévi would cleave to this belief, anticipating the Reign of the Paraclete and predicting that in 1879 "a universal empire will be founded and will secure peace to the world."[18] Lévi's Paraclete seems to have missed the date; nevertheless, 1879 is an important year in esoteric history, at least by some accounts. According to Rudolf Steiner, it saw the beginning of the reign of the archangel Michael, a significant event in Steiner's idiosyncratic vision of occult history.

By the time Lévi made his prediction, his radical days were far behind him, and like many who start out on the extreme left, he had drifted over to the other side. The triad of liberty, equality, and fraternity were now "three truths which, in coming together, form a triple lie."[19] Regarding the Church, the randy defrocked priest called for "the absolute and invariable affirmation of a dogma preserved by an authorized hierarchy," a sentiment that echoes Joseph de Maistre. Lévi indeed speaks highly, if awkwardly, of de Maistre, seeing in him a man "of high intuitions and great moral courage" who "called for that day when the . . . natural affinity . . . between science and faith should combine them in the mind of a single man of genius."[20] Too modest to claim this distinction, Lévi nonetheless believed one *could* unite science, the Church, and occultism into a single system, a synthesis that gave his translator A. E. Waite no end of headaches. Like his politics, Lévi's occultism is rife with contradictions; he both castigates and celebrates the Church without batting an eye, and his insistence on the identity between occult science and Catholic dogma is repeated by the mysterious author of *Meditations on the Tarot*. As with that anonymous savant, for Lévi, "the miraculous and lawful hierarchy of the Catholic Church . . . alone has preserved all traditions of science and faith,"[21] an assertion that Johann Valentin Andreae, among others, would question.

Lévi's last days were sad. Like Vintras, Wronski, and others, he saw France as the savior of the world, and its defeat in the Franco-Prussia War in 1870 was a blow. Life was difficult during the siege of Paris, and the old revolutionary, who wrote a bible of liberty, wasn't taken with the commune that followed. His fiery beliefs expressed an impassioned response to inequity, but they inspired neither concrete social change nor a coherent political philosophy.

Raps across the Water

While Lévi was hitting the barricades in 1848, across the Atlantic another kind of revolution was starting. In Hydesville, New York, two sisters had ignited controversy over their claims to be able to communicate with the spirit of a dead man. In March of that year, the family of Margaretta and Kate Fox had been troubled by the repeated sounds of "knocks" and "raps" seemingly coming from nowhere; a search of their house revealed no source of the noises. One evening, as the sounds returned, as a joke Kate said, "Mr. Splitfoot, do as I do," and snapped her fingers. Immediately a snapping sound answered. Margaret, her mother, joined in, saying, "Do as I do," and clapped. This too was repeated. Mrs. Fox then thought to test "Mr. Splitfoot" as the children were calling the sounds. She asked him to tap out her children's ages. Mr. Splitfoot obliged, and even included three taps indicating the age of one child who had died. Mrs. Fox then said, "If you are a spirit, then tap twice." Two enormous bangs exploded. Eventually it emerged that the spirit was that of a man who had been murdered in the house when it was occupied by the previous owner. Mr. Splitfoot, it seemed, was real, and the age of Spiritualism had started.

Soon mediums, table turning, ectoplasmic hands, and floating tambourines flooded séances on both sides of the Atlantic. Speaking with the dead and communicating with spirits were not, in fact, new. Journeys to the underworld and oracles like the famous one at Delphi were common features of the ancient world. The difference now was that this was happening not to mythological figures or high priests but to everyday people; in the case of the Fox sisters, children, in fact. And the sheer number of spiritual phenomena prompted one writer to speak of them as "the invasion of the spirit people."[22]

Exactly why this invasion took place remains unclear, but someone who had extensive experience in communicating with the dead offered an interesting theory. Rudolf Steiner first encountered the spiritual realms when, as young boy, he was visited by the spirit of a dead relative.[23] Steiner was later critical of Spiritualism, saying that the idea of shaking hands with a spirit, or even photographing one, was a kind of sacrilege. By trying to make spirits *measurable*, that is, susceptible to scientific detection, the spiritualists, he said, were being more material than the materialists. Yet in a series of fascinating lectures given in Dornach, Switzerland, in 1915, Steiner offered an explanation for the spirit invasion.[24] In the nineteenth century, Steiner said, mankind was in danger of sinking completely into materialism. To prevent this, there was a kind of conference among initiates. Some "left-wing" initiates argued that knowledge of the spiritual world should be made accessible to all. But the "right wing" thought that this would only cause more problems and that such knowledge should remain in the hands of the initiates. Compromising, they agreed on a method of demonstrating the reality of the spiritual world. "And so it came about," Steiner told his audience, "that *mediumship* was deliberately brought on the scene."[25]

How successful this plan was is debatable. But one curious fact is that most mediums were women. Some, of course, were male; perhaps the most famous was the remarkable Scotsman Daniel Dunglas Home, who could hold live coals and float through windows. The American Andrew Jackson Davis made medical diagnoses while in mesmeric trance, and in France, the educationalist Hippolyte-Leon Rivail would become world famous as the Spiritualist teacher Allan Kardec. The major psychical investigators, like Oliver Lodge, William James, Frederick Myers, and William Crookes, were, of course, men. But the psychics they investigated were mostly women, like Eusapia Palladino, Leonore Piper, and someone we will be meeting shortly, Madame Blavatsky. Traditional clichés suggested that women were more imaginative, receptive, and poetic—meaning less hard headed and rational—than men, and so more "open" to the spirits or, less generously, more susceptible to fantasy. Yet more recent historians suggest that, in the nineteenth century, mediumship allowed women a "voice" that would otherwise have gone unheard. It "empowered" women and coincided with "the developing controversy over sexual inequality and agitation for women's rights." In the context of "gender politics and a society in flux," mediumship "emerged contemporaneously with the consideration of women's proper role and sphere" and was clearly linked to what was known as "the woman question."[26]

Mrs. Satan

One medium who shed particular light on the woman question was the remarkable Victoria Woodhull, one of the nineteenth century's most fascinating women's rights advocates. Among her many distinctions, she was the second woman to address the U.S. Congress (on women's right to vote), the first to address the House Judiciary Committee, and in 1872, the first woman to run for president; her opponents were the incumbent Ulysses S. Grant and the newspaper giant Horace Greeley. Her running mate was the first black vice-presidential candidate, Frederick Douglass, an ex-slave, abolitionist, and author of the *Narrative of the Life of Frederick Douglass, an American Slave*. Douglass apparently wasn't happy about his candidacy and neither acknowledged it nor campaigned for it. One reason may have been the sordid reputation of his running mate. This, however, didn't stop Victoria, who tried to run again in 1884 and 1892.

Victoria Claflin Woodhull was born in Homer, Ohio, in 1837. According to her biographer, her father was a con man and thief; her mother, an illegitimate, illiterate religious fanatic.[27] Her early years were full of poverty, filth, and squalor. Victoria displayed mediumistic and paranormal powers early on, and her father put her to work in his traveling sideshow as a clairvoyant and fortune-teller. She made successful predictions, could find missing objects, received messages from "beyond," and possessed magnetic healing powers (by this time, mesmerism was a staple of American life). She also claimed sometimes to visit an idyllic spiritual world, a kind of celestial utopia reminiscent of Swedenborg's accounts of heaven that must have contrasted sharply with her earthly lot. Her "spirit guides" (one of whom was the ancient Greek orator Demosthenes, whom one suspects advised her on her future career as a public speaker) informed her that she was destined to become a "ruler of the nation," an early indication of her brave but ultimately unsuccessful political ambitions.

At fifteen, Victoria married Canning Woodhull, a Cincinnati doctor and snake oil salesman, whom she soon discovered was an alcoholic womanizer. His erotic irresponsibility led to her contempt for the sexual double standard men enjoyed then. Canning used Victoria's talents to sell his "elixir of life," and after having two children, they moved to San Francisco, where she worked as a cigar girl and actress. Canning eventually deserted her and their children, and with her sister "Tennie C" (Tennessee) Claflin, Victoria took their magnetic show on the road, going to New York, Chicago, and other cities. Victoria divorced Canning and married Colonel James Harvey Blood—like Victoria, a believer in free love—and the couple settled in New York City with Tennie. There they started a salon frequented by many radical thinkers and entrepreneurs, one of whom was the prominent millionaire Cornelius Vanderbilt.

Vanderbilt had just lost his wife, and after Victoria and Tennie "cured" him of low spirits, he set them up with their own highly successful brokerage firm (the first on Wall Street run by women) and magazine, *Woodhull and Claflin's Weekly*. (It may have helped that Tennie became the seventy-six-year-old Vanderbilt's lover.) Here, according to one account, Victoria "preached her doctrines of free love, attacked the rich (though not, of course, Vanderbilt), and espoused Marxism."[28] In fact, along with its advocacy of short skirts, spiritualism, women's suffrage, free love, vegetarianism, homeopathy, licensed prostitution, and birth control, the newspaper printed the first English translation of *The Communist Manifesto*. Victoria was also a member of the Marxist International Workingmen's Association. Adding her possible brief stint as a prostitute, this must rank as a particularly odd manifestation of "leftist" occultism.

The success of the brokerage firm and the newspaper (whose masthead read, with perhaps a slight innuendo, "The Organ of the Most Advanced Thought and Purpose in the World!") made Victoria famous. In April 1870, she announced her plans to run for president as candidate for the Equal Rights Party, whose membership included an unusual coalition of feminists, workers, spiritualists, communists, and free lovers. In January the next year she addressed Congress, pointing out that as U.S. citizens, women *already* had the right to vote; they merely needed to exercise it. Yet not all advocates of women's rights were taken with Victoria. Susan B. Anthony, in particular, had her reservations, and while many were willing to talk about free love in salons, fewer were willing to put theory into practice, a double standard that another free lover, Mary Wollstonecraft, had encountered almost a century earlier.[29] "Mrs. Satan," as her detractors began to call Victoria, not only advocated free love and kept company with prostitutes (at a time when only "low" women admitted to enjoying sex), she also preached an unholy belief in spirits. Some of Victoria's other ideas were apparently less offensive: she was against abortion and advocated eugenics.

Ironically, free love itself linked Victoria with the Beecher-Tilton affair, a scandal that, as the cliché goes, rocked the nation, generating as much publicity at the time as the Monica Lewinsky scandal did in the 1990s. The hugely successful preacher and "deafening foghorn of virtue"[30] Henry Ward Beecher (brother of Harriet Beecher Stowe, author of *Uncle Tom's Cabin*) had been caught in an adulterous affair with the wife of one of his closest disciples, Theodore Tilton. It wasn't Beecher's first offense; years earlier, he had cuckolded the Brooklyn businessman, Henry C. Bowen, another close friend and supporter, and got away with it. Both Tilton and his young wife, Elizabeth "Libby" Richards, adored and admired Beecher. At first transported by their liaison, which the eloquent Beecher assured her was blessed in God's eye, Libby soon had misgivings, and eventually she confessed to her husband. Although naturally furious, Tilton agreed to Libby's demand that he do nothing to Beecher, and in any case Tilton himself was no angel, having had more than one affair during their marriage. He also believed that Beecher had somehow hypnotized her into this sacrilege.

Libby agreed to tell Beecher she had confessed, but Tilton couldn't contain himself and mentioned the affair to the feminist Elizabeth Cady Stanton. Stanton then told Victoria (feminists or not, the women still gossiped), who became as furious as Tilton. Beecher had repeatedly denounced free love from the pulpit and had attacked Victoria personally. Victoria even believed that rumors started by Beecher and his sister Harriet had led to her being evicted from her home, and for a time the presidential hopeful and her family spent their nights on the street; no one would rent to "Wicked Woodhull." Victoria broke the story in her newspaper, announcing that America's most famous preacher privately engaged in the free love he publicly castigated. Although Beecher, guilty on two counts (Tilton, Bowen, and perhaps others), was exonerated—the public apparently couldn't accept that he could be a hypocrite—and for her sins, Elizabeth Tilton was excommunicated from the Church, Victoria, who did nothing but print the story, was arrested for sending "obscene material" through the mail. She spent Election Day, 1872 in jail and was arrested eight more times while the scandal raged. Most people were happy that "Mrs. Satan" was getting her comeuppance for slandering one of the nation's celebrities; apparently a woman telling the truth was worse than a preacher telling a lie. But after a time many also realized that defending free speech was more important than denouncing free love and came to her defense.

Although she was eventually acquitted, the battle ruined Victoria. She lost both the brokerage firm and the newspaper and received death threats. There were no legal grounds for Victoria's arrest, nor for that of Tennie or Colonel Blood, and in hindsight it seems clear that the government did what it could to teach "Mrs. Satan" a lesson. Weary and disillusioned, in 1876 Victoria divorced Colonel Blood. Less than a year later she moved to England, where she lectured and published a magazine, *The Humanitarian*. In 1883, she married John Biddulph Martin, her third husband. She died in Worcestershire, in the West Midlands in 1927 at the age of eighty-nine.

7

Journeys to the East

Around the time Victoria Woodhull retired from political life, an even more flamboyant firebrand was set to emerge from Spiritualism's bosom. Although Helena Petrovna Blavatsky didn't run for president—and being born Russian, she couldn't—it would not have been surprising if she had. By the time she and her Platonic "chum" Colonel Henry Steel Olcott started the Theosophical Society, HPB, as she is known, had already lived more lives than most people do in a dozen incarnations. After running away from her husband on their unconsummated honeymoon at the age of eighteen (Nikifor Blavatsky was the vice-governor of a province in Armenia and a much older man), Blavatsky began a series of travels that exceeded even those of Christian Rosencreutz, journeying through Europe, the Middle East, North America, India, and, most famously, Tibet, with frequent pit stops in Russia to visit her sister. Even if, as some commentators argue, there's little corroboration for some of her itineraries, those that seem fairly secure are remarkable enough. Along the way, among other activities, HPB worked as a circus bareback rider; was assistant to the medium Daniel Dunglas Home; directed the Serbian Royal Choir; owned an artificial flower factory; was a journalist, a short story writer, and a piano teacher; and conducted séances in Cairo.

In the middle of these adventures, she also found time to survive the wreck of the *Eumonia*, a sea disaster as famous in its day as that of the *Titanic*, and to be wounded while fighting with the Italian liberator Giuseppe Garibaldi against the Papal army and the French at the battle of Mentana in 1867. She was also friends with the Carbonaro and probable Freemason Giuseppe Mazzini, leader of the revolutionary organization Young Italy.

Mazzini had proclaimed the existence of the Roman Republic in 1849 and defended it, with Garibaldi, against the French, who fought in support of the Church. The French general, Charles Oudinot, was a Freemason, another indication that in the revolutionary struggles of the last two centuries, Freemasonry has frequently appeared on both sides of the political fence.[1] After he liberated Sicily in 1860, Garibaldi himself became a Masonic Grand Master of the Italian Grand Orient, serving from 1862 to 1868. Although the Traditionalist René Guénon had little good to say about Blavatsky and Theosophy, he corroborates her comments about her time on the barricades. In *Theosophy: History of a Pseudo-Religion*, Guénon remarks that John Yarker, a high-ranking Mason, was a friend of Garibaldi and Mazzini, and that Yarker once claimed to have seen HPB in their company.[2] Given that Guénon had as much respect for revolutionaries as he had for HPB, this association wouldn't have been to her credit.

In a way, Garibaldi was instrumental in the origins of the Theosophical Society, although his revolutionary politics were less responsible than the style of clothes they inspired. Colonel Olcott, who would eventually play an enthusiastic Watson to Blavatsky's mystic Holmes, had been an agriculturalist, part of the commission that investigated the assassination of President Lincoln, and an unsuccessful lawyer. His interest in Spiritualism had brought him to the farm of the Eddy family in Chittenden, Vermont, on October 14, 1874. When Blavatsky visited the farm with the express purpose of meeting Colonel Olcott, who had written newspaper articles about the phenomena taking place there, she seems to have worn her own version of a "power suit." Although one biographer, commenting on her typical eccentric attire, remarked that she looked like "a badly wrapped and glittering parcel,"[3] on that occasion at least her fashion sense worked. When the rotund and forthright Russian medium and fellow journalist approached the sedate, respectable Olcott, what first struck him was her Garibaldi shirt, a crimson blouse with military embroidery that had been the height of *haute couture* a season or so earlier. Even if it was not love at first sight, Blavatsky's fiery top and offhand manner certainly captivated Olcott and a year later the Theosophical Society was born.

BASEBALL, HIDDEN MASTERS, AND CHEEKY CREATURES

Whatever your opinion of her and her work, Blavatsky's influence informed practically every esoteric movement that followed her. Éliphas Lévi brought a grab bag of occult ideas together to form occultism, and Blavatsky made no attempt to hide her debt to his work or to that of Edward Bulwer-Lytton. Lévi's ideas reached a relatively contained audience, but Theosophy quickly mushroomed into a worldwide occult phenomenon, gathering under its wing an assortment of influential and important disciples that would be the envy of any movement, political or otherwise. The poet W. B. Yeats, the artists Wassily Kandinsky and Piet Mondrian, the composer Alexander Scriabin, the inventor Thomas Edison, and even the man allegedly responsible for baseball, Abner Doubleday, who was a Union hero at the Battle of Gettysburg: all were ardent Theosophists. Whether or not he actually invented baseball, Doubleday was a national hero, and in his last years, when Blavatsky and Olcott had moved to India, he became president of the American branch of the Theosophical Society. Few things are as American as baseball, and for a time at the turn of the nineteenth century, Theosophy seemed in that league, too.

Although a spiritual movement dedicated to uniting science and religion in the search for truth, in both its tenets and in the lives of some of its central figures Theosophy had political influence and in several ways added to the debate on both the right and the left. While they didn't originate with Theosophy, two themes central to the occult politics of the coming century gained a wide audience through it. One we have already seen: the concept of "hidden masters" or "unknown superiors." Blavatsky became notorious because she claimed that these Masters had chosen her as their emissary and guided her on her travels and encounters. Earlier I mentioned Rudolf Steiner's belief that certain initiates had introduced mediumship in order to halt the advance of materialism in human consciousness. When this failed and Spiritualism instead became a source of error regarding the spiritual worlds—or so Steiner believed—the initiates entered another debate. They concluded that through a "personality very specially adapted through certain subconscious parts to draw a great deal from the spiritual world,"[4] some of the damage could be undone. This "personality" was Blavatsky.

Commenting on her aptness for the job, Steiner describes her as "an electrically-charged Leyden jar," from whom "electric sparks—occult truths—could be produced."[5] Blavatsky was a "cheeky creature" who exhibited "a lack of consistency in external behaviour," which, to anyone aware of Blavatsky's character, is certainly an understatement. This is why Blavatsky found herself caught in a struggle between the left and right initiates, with some adepts imposing a kind of "occult imprisonment" on her to prevent her from "leaking" certain occult truths that certain American brotherhoods had allowed her to know.[6] Certain Indian occultists set her free, obliging her to them. Hence, according to Steiner, the Eastern influence on her thought.

Whatever we make of Steiner's remarks, Blavatsky's Masters or Mahatmas were crucial to her success, not the least because they fed the hunger many felt at the time for a deeper spiritual mystery than what the churches could provide. At the height of her notoriety, Blavatsky's Masters held from the Himalayas, but they originally resided in Egypt, and her Great White Brotherhood, later populated by Tibetans, had its roots in the European tradition of the Rosicrucians and Freemasons. HPB's great-grandfather, Prince Pavel Dolgorukov, whose vast occult library she devoured as a child, was initiated in the 1770s into a Strict Observance Rite, which, we know, was founded in the 1750s by Baron von Hund, who claimed its legitimacy was derived from "unknown superiors."[7] The scholar K. Paul Johnson has controversially claimed that he can identify Blavatsky's Masters as specific flesh-and-blood individuals, but it seems likely that the notion of these "unknown superiors" are an amalgam of Rosicrucian, Masonic, and Western esoteric ideas, filtered through the "Leyden jar" of Blavatsky's "specially adapted" personality.[8]

THE RACE QUESTION

Another theosophical contribution to occult politics is the question of race, a delicate issue that stretched back into the past to discover the unblemished origins of "noble" humanity and into the future with the idea of our evolution into some higher form, something like the society of super adepts portrayed in Bulwer-Lytton's *The Coming Race*. Blavatsky's ideas about "root" and "sub" races fed into the nineteenth-century obsession with the origins of European peoples and languages. By the time Theosophy arrived, the accepted notion was that both ancient European peoples and languages had their roots in the Sanskrit-speaking Aryans, the "pure," "noble" race (*Aryan* means "noble") that had migrated from India to Europe. William Jones, the early English authority on Sanskrit, proposed that there was a commonality between the high cultures of India, Egypt, Greece, and Italy. In 1808, the philosopher Friedrich Schlegel argued that Sanskrit was the source of German, Greek, and Latin and that its original speakers had somehow left India to colonize northern Europe. But having left their homeland, the Aryans lost their original purity through miscegenation with less pure races. When the great Oxford Orientalist Max Müller declared that the Anglo-Saxons, Teutons, and northern Indians (not, however, the southern Indian Dravidians) were all of Aryan stock, he unfortunately opened the door to the kind of racial pseudo-science that would have the Nazis filling their death camps with "racial inferiors" at the same time that they sent expeditions to Tibet in order to measure the locals' skulls.[9] By the early twentieth century, a search was on to find out who was closest to the Aryans—who, that is, was the most pure. For later scholars, Blavatsky's claim that the Aryans were the fifth root race to emerge from the Atlantean subrace seemed to participate in what Nietzsche, who is frequently and erroneously labeled a racist, called "the great race swindle." Sadly, it often goes unrecognized that Blavatsky's notions about root races and a coming new race were more subtle than those of the esoteric racists who appropriated her ideas.

HIGHER TYPES

The other end of the race problem, the idea of humanity evolving into some higher type, has its own difficulties. The philosopher, Theosophist, and critic of the Bolshevik Revolution P. D. Ouspensky could say that "a new type of man is being formed now and amongst us" and that "the selection goes on in all races and nations of the earth,"[10] a remark that seems to express a multi-racial evolutionary outlook. But Ouspensky also wrote of the benefits of the Laws of Manu, the foundation of the Hindu caste system, which argues against a pluralistic evolutionary view. Ouspensky, however, remarked that what has come down to us as the Laws of Manu is really a "Brahmin fabrication," and that the Laws are not legislation but a record of the laws of nature regarding "the fundamental types of men."[11] He also argued that the strictures prohibiting a person of a lower caste, like a Sudra, from entering a higher one weren't part of the original Laws, of which only a few fragments have survived, but were later spurious additions to "legalize the bondage of castes." So for Ouspensky the laws of Manu, while not exactly "democratic" or "egalitarian," in their original form at least recognized that people *can* evolve and are not "fixed" as T. E. Hulme believed, which meant that a social structure built on this limited view of human potential was false. Whether or not Ouspensky's sense of the Laws of Manu is correct is beside the point—scholars would no doubt take issue with it. What's important is that Ouspensky, who saw the Bolshevik Revolution as the start of "the dictatorship of the criminal element,"[12] recognized that notions of radical egalitarianism were as dangerous as those of radical hierarchy, and that it's naïve not to recognize that profound differences *do* exist between people, specifically, between people who are interested in evolving and those who aren't.[13] These differences, however, were a matter of inclination, not race, and may, as some theorists believe, have a biological basis.[14]

Secret Doctrines, Secret Agents

One arena in which Theosophy encountered the race question head-on was India. Here Blavatsky proved herself a "cheeky creature" indeed. She and Theosophy started the move east after a collaboration between the society and the Arya Samaj, a Hindu reform movement started in Bombay in 1875 by Swami Dayanand Sarasvati, who was eager to promote a return to the Vedic teachings. Never shy to speak her mind, when Blavatsky left New York with Colonel Olcott in 1879 to relocate on the subcontinent, she lost little time in making clear her disapproval of the British Raj. Her anti-British remarks were so frequent and acerbic, and her support for India Home Rule and the Hindu nationalist cause so passionate, not to mention her celebration of Indian culture, heritage, and beliefs, that Her Majesty's government suspected her of working for the Russians. Blavatsky's remarks favoring the Russian social policy over the British only confirmed their suspicions—rightfully it seems: at one point she did offer her services to the Tsar, but was declined. This was the time of the Great Game, the political chess match between Russia and Britain over who would have the greatest influence in Asia, which Rudyard Kipling, a fervent Mason, brought to fictional life in his novel *Kim*.

By this time, HPB had not only physically moved to India, she had also rooted her Masters there, and later Theosophists like Alice Bailey claimed that their authority derived from an invisible brotherhood who lived in Shambhala, a hidden city located beyond Tibet, somewhere in the Gobi Desert; Blavatsky herself spoke of Shambhala in both *Isis Unveiled* and *The Secret Doctrine*. That Blavatsky's invisible brotherhood had headed for points east had support from Heinrich Neuhaus, a Rosicrucian pamphleteer, who agreed with René Guénon that the reason the Rosicrucians couldn't be found in Europe was that they had decamped to Tibet.[15] Blavatsky also found support for her Masters' relocation in the works of the French writer Louis Jacolliot.

In books like *Occult Science in India*, Jacolliot claimed that a society of "unknown men" really did exist in India and secretly influenced world events.[16] Guénon and others, like Blavatsky's fellow Russian and Theosophist Nicholas Roerich, would also occupy themselves with Shambhala, whose dark sister city, Agartha, would intrigue the French occultist Saint-Yves d'Alveydre.

That Blavatsky was suspected of being a Russian spy had some comical results. Her disgruntled housekeeper, Emma Coulomb, whose questionable revelations about HPB's notorious Mahatma letters led to charges of fraud against Blavatsky, once stole some pages from her notebook that seemed to be written in some sort of code and sent them to a Christian missionary. As Blavatsky's remarks about Christians in India were as respectful as those about the Raj, the missionaries were happy to have evidence that she was involved in some sort of intelligence work and sent the pages to the Calcutta police. But the police couldn't make sense of the code and dropped their investigation. Understandably: the code was really the secret language Senzar, which Blavatsky claimed was the original tongue of the equally secret *Book of Dzyan*, which formed the basis of her magnum opus, *The Secret Doctrine*. Yet while HPB could laugh this fiasco off, she was furious when in his report on her for the Society for Psychical Research—which described her as "one of the most accomplished, ingenious, and interesting impostors of history"—Richard Hodgson casually suggested that she was working for the Russians.

Blavatsky wasn't the only esotericist accused of spying. G. I. Gurdjieff sought his own secret brotherhood in Central Asia and was also believed to have worked for the Russians. In a fascinating if unbelievable account, James Webb suggests that, in one of Gurdjieff's many guises, he may have been Ushe Narzunoff, an associate of Agwan Dordjieff, a Buriat Russian and tutor to the thirteenth Dalai Lama. Webb's equating Gurdjieff with Narzunoff is untenable, but Dordjieff did work to strengthen ties between Tibet and Russia and at one point lobbied to have a Buddhist temple erected in St. Petersburg.[17] He was successful, and after the Revolution, Dordjieff spent most of his time in it, until he was arrested during Stalin's purges. Webb places Gurdjieff in the strange world of Russian politics in the years preceding the Bolshevik Revolution, a time of "mystic imperialism," when the "White Tsar" Nicholas II had grand designs for a Russian Asia and his court was filled with characters like Zhamsaran Badmaieff, a practitioner of Tibetan medicine, Prince Esper Ukhtomsky, an Orientalist and practicing Buddhist familiar with Theosophy—sometimes identified as Gurdjieff's Prince Lubovedsky in *Meetings with Remarkable Men*[18]—and the infamous Rasputin, making it a "collective for seers, monks, and mystics."[19]

But the British took the Russian threat seriously, and in 1903, when they discovered that Agwan Dordjieff was in Lhasa, an expedition, led by Colonel Francis Younghusband, a spiritualist, effectively became an invasion. Younghusband slaughtered more than a thousand Tibetans and occupied "the place of the gods," as the capital was called. Legend has it that as Younghusband approached, Dordjieff fled to Mongolia with the Dalai Lama (in some versions, Dordjieff is Gurdjieff, but there's even less support for this claim than for his being Narzunoff). In 1938, according to Christopher Hale in *Himmler's Crusade*, Younghusband advised the Nazi SS explorer Ernst Schäfer, a member of Heinrich Himmler's *Ahnenerbe*, or Ancestral Heritage office, on how best to avoid the British in his own trek to Tibet. Schäfer was sent to the top of the world by Himmler in order, among other things, to validate Nazi claims that Tibet was the last refuge of the Aryan root race.[20]

GO EAST, YOUNG THEOSOPHIST

If HPB ruffled the Raj's feathers with her disrespectful remarks and the possibility that she was a Russian spy, her influence on important figures was even less welcome. A. P. Sinnett, the editor of *The Allahabad Pioneer*, the leading newspaper in India and whose most famous contributor was Kipling, became a Theosophical convert. *The Pioneer* promoted Theosophy throughout India, and Sinnett's books, *The Occult World* and *Esoteric Buddhism*, spread the teaching to a wider readership, among whom was an obscure Austrian Goethe scholar named Rudolf Steiner. A. O. Hume, a high-ranking civil servant, also joined the fold. "AO," as he was known, was a hero of the Sepoy Rebellion of 1857, the son of the wealthy Scottish parliamentarian Joseph Hume, and, like Blavatsky, a Hinduphile. In 1885, to secure a greater role for Indians in the British administration, Hume organized the first meeting of the Indian National Congress. Ranbir Singh, the Maharaja of Kashmir, sponsored Blavatsky and Olcott's sojourn in India, and Sirdar Thakar Singh Sandhanwalia, founder of the Sikh reform group Singh Sabha, was one of their strongest allies. Blavatsky's relations with the Sikhs were strong enough for the British to worry when rumors of a Sikh rebellion gathered around her formidable figure.

Blavatsky's political clout was really a by-product of her cheekiness, but this wasn't true of the second Theosophical firebrand to hit the subcontinent's shores. When the ex-Fabian socialist, Marxist, feminist, and free-thinker Annie Besant reached Colombo in 1893, she was met by Colonel Olcott and a bevy of high British officials and Buddhist notables, and her journeys around India on that trip were like a royal procession. Her speeches to the numerous Theosophical lodges Olcott introduced her to were reminiscent of the incendiary addresses she was famous for in London. By this time, the idea of a renascent Hindu spirituality was fused with that of Hindu nationalism, and if there was a slight problem in translation, Annie did little to rectify it. If her audience thought she was calling for political revolt, Annie wouldn't correct them. All her life she had lived for a cause, and now practically a whole nation was handing her one.

Annie Besant discovered Theosophy, Madame Blavatsky, and India in 1888 when she reviewed *The Secret Doctrine* for W. T. Stead's *Review of Reviews*. A spiritualist and one of the fatalities of the *Titanic*, Stead numbered Bernard Shaw and H. G. Wells among his friends. Shaw and Wells were leading members of the Fabian Society, an influential non-Marxist socialist reform group of the *fin de siècle*; another member was Annie Besant. Most reviews panned Blavatsky's massive tome, but Besant's was positive and led to a meeting with HPB at her home in Landsdowne Road; by this time, Blavatsky had left India under a cloud, thanks to slanderous attacks by her covetous housekeeper, and moved to London. A fellow socialist, who had turned to Theosophy out of a personal grief, brought Annie to Blavatsky. At the end of the interview, when Annie was about to leave, Blavatsky looked into her eyes and said, "Oh my dear Mrs. Besant, if you would only come among us." She did.

Besant's life before her nearly miraculous conversion from anti-religious secularist to the faith of the Masters was as impressive as Blavatsky's. She was an outspoken advocate of Irish Home Rule, a cause she would similarly embrace in India. Her recognition of inequality between the sexes led to the breakup of her marriage and the loss of her children; she was considered an unfit mother, and her ex-husband got custody. Secularism, women's rights, free thought, socialism, and workers' rights were only some of the banners she supported. One cause in particular made her a household name. In 1877, with her friend Charles Bradlaugh, a leading member of the National Secular Society, she published a book on birth control by the American family-planning campaigner Charles Knowlton. Knowlton argued that working-class families had the right to decide how large a family they wanted, and his book showed how to do this. The Church was outraged, and Besant and Bradlaugh were arrested. The case gained national attention, and Bradlaugh and Besant escaped jail sentences only on a technicality. It wouldn't be the only time Annie's name was in the news. (Ironically, her conversion to Theosophy in 1889 triggered echoes of the affair when Koot Hoomi, one of Blavatsky's Mahatmas, required her to publicly recant her endorsement of contraception. In the Theosophical view, birth control only facilitated the animal passions, which were an impediment on the spiritual path. That Blavatsky herself thought sex "beastly" couldn't have helped.)

Besant became a regular contributor to the *National Reformer*, the newspaper of the National Secular Society, and the society soon asked her to speak at public meetings. Bradlaugh was a popular speaker, and he coached Annie in her new career. She was a natural and soon was traveling across England, drawing large crowds eager to hear her radical ideas. She came to national notoriety again in 1887 as one of the speakers associated with the "Bloody Sunday" riots. On November 13, 1887, police tried to stop a demonstration against unemployment held in Trafalgar Square. The demonstrators resisted and a riot broke out. Troops came in, dozens of people were hurt, one man was killed, and hundreds were arrested. Besant, who, as one biographer remarked, was "filled with the longing to serve humanity by some sort of glorious martyrdom,"[21] offered herself up for arrest, but the police were canny enough to recognize that this would only add to the chaos and declined. The next year she led a successful campaign to improve the working conditions of London's "match girls," young women who worked for low pay under horrendous conditions in London's match factories. She stood for election on the London School Board, won, and improved the lives of thousands of school children. She promoted a dock workers' strike that led to better pay and working conditions. And along the way she had relationships with some of the most progressive figures around, like Bernard Shaw, who later immortalized her as the character Raina in his play *Arms and the Man*. Little wonder, then, that when the fiery activist reached India's already troubled shores, the Raj was concerned.

HOME RULE

Although during Besant's triumphant tour of India many nationalist papers saw her as the country's savior and called for her to lead a campaign against the colonial government, not all Indians shared this view. Some Hindu nationalists saw Theosophy as one more manifestation of white elitism. And some Theosophists were unhappy with her politicizing of Theosophy;[22] Olcott himself—who nevertheless campaigned for a union between northern and southern Buddhists[23] and who also worked to improve the lives of the "untouchables," those lowest in the caste system—had his misgivings. Others were unhappy with what looked like her appropriation of HPB's throne and questioned her authority within the society. (Blavatsky had died in 1891 of Bright's disease.) Yet Besant's karma seemed to be leading her on a path that had political consequences, whether Theosophists or nationalists liked it or not.

Back in England Annie had given speeches on reforming the Indian Empire, and now the colonial government had what looked like a white Home Rule crusader on its shores. That she was a member of the elite class and had friends in high places, like Viscount Haldane, a senior figure in the British Liberal Party, made things even more difficult. Most of her fellow expatriates, Theosophists included, were unquestioningly imperialist and were uncomfortable with Annie's "going native." She learned Sanskrit, and in Benares, where she set up the headquarters for the Indian Section in 1896 (distinct from Adyar, the society's international headquarters), she started the Central Hindu College, where students were taught science and practical skills along with meditation and Hindu scriptures. Annie's aim was to secure a new leadership for India's future, and her experience on the London School Board and in the Fabian educational experiments served her well. Yet she may have had a larger goal in view. In 1889, Blavatsky had said that the true purpose of the Theosophical Society was to prepare for the arrival of the "new world teacher." Annie repeated this idea in the same year that she founded the school. In 1907, after Olcott's death, she became president of the society. That same year, with C. W. Leadbeater, a high-ranking Theosophist, Annie announced that the world teacher had arrived, in the form of the boy Jiddu Krishnamurti, whom Leadbeater had found on a beach near Adyar. This discovery led to as much turbulence within the society as Annie's political activities did without; for one thing, it prompted Rudolf Steiner, head of the German branch, to break away and start his own movement.

While waiting for the world teacher to mature, Besant continued her efforts on the mundane front. She joined the Indian National Congress—started in 1885 by "AO" Hume—and designed its original banner. Through the Congress, Mohandas Gandhi would eventually lead India to independence. Gandhi had met HPB and Annie Besant in London in 1889, and in 1891 he joined the society. For him, Theosophy was "Hinduism at its best," promoting "the Brotherhood of Man," a nod to Theosophy's links to the progressive ideals of Freemasonry. In his book on Indian Home Rule, Gandhi praised Hume's efforts, and to his biographer he remarked that in the early days of the Congress all the top figures were Theosophists. Through Theosophy, Gandhi, then a young law student struggling to adopt Western ways, rediscovered his nation's cultural heritage and works like the Bhagavad Gita, which became the most important book in his life. Gandhi's interest in Theosophy continued during his years in South Africa, where he met with other Theosophists and sometimes spoke at their meetings.[24] Jawaharlal Nehru was introduced to Theosophy by his tutor, F. T. Brooks, and was initiated into the society by Annie herself when he was thirteen. He would become another important voice in the Congress as well, and the first Prime Minister of an independent India.

When World War I broke out and England needed her colonies' help, Annie borrowed a phrase from her Irish Home Rule campaign and declared that "England's need is India's opportunity," a remark that, during war time, approached treason. As editor of *New India*, she criticized British rule, and in 1916 she founded the Home Rule League, which organized demonstrations, protests, and strikes. With a war on, the British took no chances, and in 1917 Annie was ordered to leave India. She refused and was arrested. In the garden of the hill station where she was held, she flew a red and green flag, India's colors. There were massive protests and calls for her release, and Gandhi, who had returned to India from South Africa, was among the many who wrote letters to the government demanding her freedom. Unlike the police at Trafalgar Square on Bloody Sunday, the Raj had made the mistake of providing those unhappy with British rule with a powerful rallying point. Forced to back down, the British agreed to concessions and announced that an independent India was its ultimate aim. Four months after her arrest, Annie was released. It was a national event, and all India celebrated, and soon after she was made president of the National Congress. In a career replete with achievement and controversy, this was a particular honor. British rule finally came to an end in 1947.

BEGINNINGS AND ENDS

For the rest of her life, Annie campaigned for Indian independence, showing her solidarity by wearing Indian dress. But with the advent of the world teacher in the form of Krishnamurti, her politics took on a broader scope, a story I tell elsewhere.[25] Others, too, felt that things had changed. In the face of the World War, Indian independence was only one of many challenges confronting a Western civilization that seemed close to suicide. In Russia, Britain's rival in the Great Game, the expectation of some millenarian event had been brewing for some time, and the nihilism, anarchy, and existential anxiety informing the novels of Dostoyevsky blended with a craze for occultism that swept through Moscow and St. Petersburg. As in France a century earlier, this added to the revolutionary mood, wedding social and political unrest to the anticipation of a spiritual apocalypse.

In 1900, the Russian philosopher and visionary Vladimir Soloviev wrote a strange work, *War, Progress, and the End of History*, that included a short story, "The Antichrist." Soloviev's prophetic visions were shared by the members of the Russian intelligentsia known as the "God-seekers." These included people like the poet Zinaida Hippius and her husband, the novelist and occult historian Dimitri Merzhkovky, who blended speculations on the mysteries of sex and a coming God-Man with reflections on Atlantis. This peculiarly hysterical atmosphere was perhaps best captured by the Symbolist novelist Andrei Bely, a Theosophist and fervent follower of Rudolf Steiner. In *Petersburg*, Bely portrays a young radical's attempt to assassinate his father, a senator condemned to death by the revolutionary tribunal. Bely combines Steiner's pronouncements on the destiny of the Slavic soul, which was supposed to fulfill a balancing function between the East and the West, with his own paranoia about the "Mongol peril," meaning the invasion of Russia by "Asiatic hordes," a reversal of Prince Ukhtomsky's dream of a Russian Asia. The result is an hallucinatory evocation of a society in collapse.

Bely believed that "since 1900 an enormous change has taken place in the world and that sunsets have changed since that year."[26] He wasn't the only one who saw some great shift on the Russian horizon. The Marxist, existentialist, and Orthodox Christian philosopher Nicolai Berdyaev felt it, too. In *The Russian Idea*, written in exile during the dark days of World War II, Berdyaev remarks that "Russia has always been full of mystical and prophetic sects and among them there has always been a thirst for the transfiguration of life."[27] He poses the question, "What was the thought of the Creator about

Russia?"[28] Berdyaev was profoundly influenced by the thought of Jacob Boehme, and he depicted his own vision of the future in his book *The New Middle Ages*. This called for a return to the kind of stable, spiritually oriented society that Berdyaev and others believed existed before the rise of the modern period. Deeply committed to the cause of human freedom—it is, in fact, the central theme of his work and was the reason he was deported from Soviet Russia in 1922—Berdyaev saw the problems caused by the new world of mass society and forced egalitarianism. Like others, he believed it had created a kind of spiritual free fall, an existential weightlessness, and he felt that a corrective could be found in some return to tradition.

Berdyaev wasn't alone. In one of the curious ironies of history, at the beginning of the new century, with the triumphant arrival of modern times, one of the most influential currents of thought was the call for a return to the past.

8

KINGS OF THE WORLD ON
THE MOUNTAINS OF TRUTH

While Annie Besant worked to free India from British rule, other Theosophists took up the cause of reform in even more radical ways. One member of the Theosophical Society who questioned Besant's role as Madame Blavatsky's heir was the American Katherine Tingley, who succeeded William Quan Judge as the head of the American section. Like Besant, but without her early notoriety, before finding Theosophy Tingley threw herself into a number of philanthropic efforts. She had already done volunteer work in prisons and hospitals when she had discovered spiritualism, but it was while feeding striking workers in a Manhattan soup kitchen that she met Judge. He introduced her to Theosophy, and she was converted on the spot. Like Besant, Tingley had always felt destined for some great work, and now the ailing Judge seemed to deliver it to her, if not on a platter, then in a tureen.

Judge had his own misgivings about the goings-on in India, and he seceded from Adyar in 1895, bringing several thousand Theosophists with him. He died the next year, and control of the American Society fell to Katherine. Not everyone was happy with this, and to calm fears and, more likely, to secure her position, she claimed that she had communicated with the dead Judge and that he called on his followers to accept her as their new leader. She also made a pilgrimage to India in order to make converts and to have her own meeting with one of the Hidden Masters. Not surprisingly, Koot Hoomi concurred with the etheric Judge and declared that Tingley was the new head of Theosophy in the new world.

Tingley and Besant kept up a rivalry for the next decade, showing that even in the esoteric community, bitterness and triviality often triumph over good sense. Tingley's Universal Brotherhood and Theosophical Society (as she renamed her new version of Theosophy) attracted far fewer seekers in India than Annie Besant's lectures did in the United States. But while both women combined a belief in Theosophy with a commitment to social reform, Tingley's approach seemed modeled on a more radical Rosicrucian theme. Rather than change existing institutions, Tingley's aim was to create an alternative society.

Such ideas weren't new. Around the time the "spirit people" invaded in the mid-nineteenth century, people like Robert Owen—who became a spiritualist—were already involved in the creation of alternative societies in England. While not establishing an alternative society, Henry David Thoreau's experiment at Walden Pond argued for the benefits of dropping out of the mainstream, a nod to Rousseau's belief that civilization itself was the source of its problems. In Putney, Vermont, the failed clergyman John Humphrey Noyes preached the doctrine of "perfectionism." After conversion to his doctrine, Noyes argued, one was free from sin and no longer subject to conventional morality, another take on "holy sinning." As with the Moravians, sex was an important part of Noyes' congregation, but as a socialist, he equated monogamy with private property and advocated instead a system of extended shared marriages. In essence, every woman was the wife of every man in his congregation, and vice versa. This doctrine, along with his belief that the Second Coming had already taken place soon after Christ's death, led to friction between Noyes' community and the other residents of Putney, and Noyes moved his congregation to Oneida, New York, from which his alternative society took its name. Noyes' unconventional marital beliefs elicited the kind of protests that Victoria Woodhull endured, yet the sex lives of his followers were strictly supervised. Only certain couples were allowed to have children, and from an early age offspring were cared for in a communal nursery. In effect, the Oneida Community practiced a form of eugenics.

THE PURPLE MOTHER

Tingley's "white city," located in the magnificent landscape of Point Loma, overlooking the Pacific Ocean near San Diego in Southern California, was to be a center for a new spiritual and social covenant. Tingley had a background in theater—she and Annie Besant shared a love of ritual and procession—and here the Purple Mother, as she was called, allowed her sense of drama a free hand. Expressing her belief in the unity of religions, Katherine erected Greek theaters, Egyptian gates, Muslim domes, and Hindu temples with the same disregard for taste or continuity that would ironically become associated with Southern Californian architecture. Theater and the arts were paramount here. Tingley's aim was to create a kind of Theosophical Bayreuth, modeled on Richard Wagner's aesthetic center, home of monumental productions of his operas.

Tingley also focused on education, as did other Theosophists. C. W. Leadbeater, who became Besant's lieutenant and who was the first Christian missionary in Ceylon to convert to Buddhism, was very interested in children's education, and like Besant, agreed that sex should be part of it. Leadbeater's zeal led to some trouble when he was accused of corrupting some adolescent Theosophists by instructing them in masturbation, a kind of hands-on approach to Besant's cause of birth control; suspected of less than progressive intentions, he was forced to temporarily leave the society. Rudolf Steiner, who left Theosophy because of Krishnamurti (and who had little use for Leadbeater), is best known today for the Waldorf Schools, a less questionable manifestation of pedagogy emerging from esotericism. Tingley's schools were for a time successful, if run on authoritarian lines. The children, who were made to eat and work in silence, lived apart from their parents under Tingley's personal supervision, and as in Besant's Hindu College, the curriculum included mainstream studies and Theosophical material. Tingley briefly established schools in

Cuba—where she had helped with relief after the Spanish-American War of 1898—and also founded homes for poor children.

Point Loma also supported gardens, orchards, and agricultural laboratories—a presage of the "bio-dynamic" farming that grew out of Steiner's later lectures on agriculture. Yet Tingley's authoritarian personality led to the community's ultimate failure. The Purple Mother's grandiose designs exceeded her ability to finance them, while she spent dwindling resources on holidays, which she thought of as spiritual retreats, or on lavish rituals and processions. As with other alternative communities, locals began to resent her influence on their lives. Not long after her death, this particular alternative society collapsed.

MOUNTAINS OF TRUTH

Theosophists in other parts of the world thought to establish their own communities, too, and most of these shared in the general rejection of mainstream society that has since become the signature of the counter-culture. This had its most widespread popularity in the 1960s and '70s, but the idea of an alternative society didn't start then. We can trace some sense of alternative societies back to the Rosicrucian experiment, but the idea of a counter-culture as we know it emerged in the last decades of the nineteenth century. This was something more than the "bohemia" of artists and poets that we associate with Paris and *La Bohème*. Rather than living unconventionally but still within society, alternative societies were just that—alternatives.

One such experiment was carried out in Ascona, Switzerland, on the shore of the beautiful Lake Maggiore. Today an up-market summer resort, ironically Ascona has a history of radicalism. In 1873, one of its residents was the Russian anarchist Mikhail Bakunin. In the late 1880s, Alfredo Pioda, a member of the Swiss Parliament and a devoted Theosophist, planned a "Theosophical cloister" in Ascona, which he called "Fraternitas." It was to built on Monescia, a hill overlooking the lake. Pioda's collaborators were Countess Constance Wachtmeister, a friend of Madame Blavatsky's, and the occultist Franz Hartmann, whose "magnetism," Blavatsky once remarked, "was sickening." Also in the group was the Dutch novelist, psychiatrist, and spiritualist Frederik Willem van Eeden, a pioneer dream investigator who in 1913 coined the term "lucid dream." Although Ascona itself "was always full of people experimenting with everything between palm reading and tea-leaf reading to spells and séances and Ouija boards," Pioda's Fraternitas didn't last.[1] But a few years later the hill he chose to build it on became the site of a remarkable experiment in alternative living.

Well in advance of the "love generation," anarchists, vegetarians, nature enthusiasts, free-love advocates, Theosophists, psychoanalysts, artists, poets, occultists, and philosophers who rejected an increasingly materialist mainstream society were drawn to the beautiful and curiously spiritual atmosphere of Pioda's Monescia. Two of the early pioneers arrived in 1900, a Montenegran piano teacher named Ida Hoffman, and Henri Oedenkoven, the son of a wealthy Belgian industrialist. They rechristened the hill Monte Verità, the "Mountain of Truth," and from their modest beginnings as a "co-operative vegetarian colony" grew an impressive attempt at ringing in the New Age. The site attracted a clutch of esoteric and cultural notables. The novelist Hermann Hesse, the dancer Isadora Duncan, the choreographer Rudolf von Laban, the anarchistic psychoanalyst Otto Gross, the philosopher Ludwig Klages, the occultist Theodor Reuss, the spiritual scientist Rudolf Steiner, and the anarchist Erich Mühsam (later murdered by the Nazis) were some who came to participate in what was called the "new life." This initial experiment ended in 1920, when Oedenkoven and Hoffman moved to South America, but in the 1930s the site became famous once again when the Polish socialite Olga Fröbe-Kapteyn opened her nearby Casa Gabriella. Here she invited C. G. Jung to preside over the annual Eranos Conferences, which continued for decades. Over the years, people like the historian of religion Mircea Eliade, the cabala scholar Gershom Scholem, the mythologist Joseph Campbell, the philosopher Jean Gebser, the esotericist Henry Corbin, and others met in an atmosphere of esoteric thought and natural beauty. Fröbe-Kapteyn had originally planned for the auditorium she had built to be used by the Theosophist Alice Bailey, but for some reason, Bailey declined, suggesting darkly that the area was associated with black magic and witchcraft.

One of the most radical figures associated with Monte Verità was Gustav Gräser, known simply as "Gusto." A poet and painter determined to throw off the shackles of civilization, he lived as a *Naturmensch*, a "nature man," making his own clothes and plucking food from the trees, or begging for it. For a time he lived in a cave with his wife and their several children. He even made his own furniture out of tree limbs and branches. On a trip to Monte Verità to take the cure for his nerves, Hermann Hesse was so impressed by Gusto that he submitted to his regimen, which meant exposing his naked body to the elements. Hesse later wrote of being burned by the sun, drenched by rain, and having his skin torn by thorns as he walked through the woods. Less beneficial, perhaps, were the career and ideas of the radical psychoanalyst Otto Gross, another Monte Verità inhabitant, who combined Freudian psychology and Nietzschean individualism with free love and an unfortunate morphine addiction. Gross, at the time considered Freud's most brilliant disciple, led an anarchic life, fathered illegitimate children, and expressed his contempt for bourgeois convention by refusing to bathe, a tactic adopted by many hippies of the 1960s, who would have felt right at home on the Mountain of Truth.

Cosmic Consciousness

Gusto's primitive regime shared an idea expressed by his contemporary Edward Carpenter in his book *Civilization: Its Cause and Cure*, which advocated the kind of retreat from society that in the 1960s would less graciously be called "dropping out." Carpenter's book communicated a rejection of the modern world that would, as the new century went on, be associated with both progressive and reactionary forms of occultism and would reach perhaps its greatest intensity in the years following World War I. Little read today but extremely influential in his time, Carpenter is a good example of the odd blend of progressive ideas, evolutionary vision, mystical doctrine, and radical lifestyle that characterized the original New Age movement of the *fin de siècle*. Combining ideas about higher consciousness with an assortment of reformist views, Carpenter features in Richard M. Bucke's once widely read *Cosmic Consciousness* as an example of the new form of consciousness many thought was emerging in the West in the twentieth century. In the 1960s, Bucke would find a new readership when the LSD guru Timothy Leary included him in his canon of psychedelic classics.

Bucke himself envisioned a radically socialist new century based on the triumph of technology—"The immediate future of our race," he writes, "is indescribably hopeful"[2]—pointing to Carpenter's long Walt Whitmanesque poem *Toward Democracy* as a work in which "the Cosmic Sense speaks." Yet while espousing socialist ideas and celebrating cosmic democracy, Bucke could also regard the Aryans as a undoubted "higher type" and make questionable remarks about "backward races." In *From Adam's Peak to Elephanta*, an account of his travels in India, Carpenter speaks of experiencing "consciousness without thought," and his ideas would later influence P. D. Ouspensky's exploration of higher states of consciousness in the latter's early work *Tertium Organum*. Before being exiled to Constantinople and then London after the Bolshevik Revolution, Ouspensky translated Carpenter's books and for Russian readers was the main source of new ideas emerging from England.

Along with his criticisms of Western materialism and investigations into "cosmic consciousness," Carpenter, a homosexual, was an advocate of what would be known today as "gay rights"; his own term was "homogenic love." An exponent of "nature cure," he followed a sparse vegetarian diet (as did Victoria Woodhull). Like the Christian mystic and spiritualist Anna Kingsford, Carpenter was also an anti-vivisectionist and a follower of Dress Reform. Like Besant, Kingsford, who was elected President of the London Lodge of the Theosophical Society in 1883, had an earlier career in which she campaigned for women's property rights, an issue significant to Besant. One of the reasons Besant's marriage failed was that, as a married woman, she had no rights to the income she received for her writings; it all went to her husband. Kingsford's antipathy to vivisection was so great that she claimed to have killed several vivisectors by sheer willpower.[3] How she squared her Christian beliefs with her deadly advocacy of what we would today call "animal rights" is unclear. A less fatal cause was Dress Reform, a movement to free men and women from the encumbrances of Victorian attire, to which Carpenter made a lasting contribution, helping to popularize sandals.

SUPERMEN

Dress Reform was also embraced by Carpenter's friend, the playwright and "Life Force worshipper" Bernard Shaw, who, as mentioned, along with Besant, was a Fabian; photographs of Shaw at the time show him wearing his famous Jaeger suit. Shaw was also a vegetarian, a feminist, and an advocate of spelling reform, and although he had no interest in the occult, his belief in "creative evolution" bears comparison to some Theosophical views. Unlike that of strict Darwinians, Shaw's evolution isn't mechanical but rather is driven by life's urge to understand and transcend itself. Another to emerge from the Fabian fold and to combine radical socialist views with Theosophical ones was A. R. Orage, the brilliant editor of *The New Age*, best known today as one of G. I. Gurdjieff's most intelligent disciples.[4] Following Carpenter and Bucke, and anticipating his soon-to-be esoteric teacher P. D. Ouspensky, in 1907 Orage delivered a series of lectures to the Manchester and Leeds branch of the Theosophical Society on the topic of "Consciousness: Animal, Human and Superman." Years later Orage would print a series of letters Ouspensky wrote while a refugee from Bolshevism, depicting the horrors of the Revolution.

In another example of *fin de siècle* New Age eclecticism, Orage combined Fabian socialism, Nietzschean individualism, Bergsonian evolutionism, and Theosophy with his own rhetorical brilliance and mastery of world literature. Orage argued that just as human self-consciousness is a kind of doubling of an animal's simple consciousness, which lacks an "I," with the result that that consciousness becomes aware not only of the world outside but also of *itself*, the new "super-consciousness" he saw emerging in the West was a kind of doubling of our self-consciousness. It was a kind of awareness *above* that of our ego, which could regard the ego with the same detachment with which we regard the world and which, presumably, animals lack.[5]

Orage, whom Shaw once called a "desperado of ideas," embodied the new century's appetite for experiment, risk, and adventure—what Nietzsche called "living dangerously"—that characterized the progressive ethos of the time. It's no coincidence that Orage moved through socialism, Nietzsche, and Theosophy eventually to find a spiritual home in Gurdjieff's "work" and to become its representative in America in the 1920s. It's also not surprising that in the early 1930s, after his break with Gurdjieff and shortly before his own death, Orage returned to the idea of monetary reform, a cause he had campaigned for in his socialist days.

THE OCCULT UNDERGROUND

But not everyone was keen on creating supermen. Ralph Shirley, editor of the influential *Occult Review*, remarked that a Nietzschean superman who was spiritually unadvanced "would not be the sort of person one would care to encounter alone on a dark night"—which, if nothing else, showed Shirley's misunderstanding of Nietzsche's idea.[6] Nevertheless, readers of Bulwer-Lytton's *The Coming Race* less taken with the notion of a society of subterranean super-adepts, would recall that these superior beings regarded the human race with the same cold indifference as we do cattle. Given that Orage depicts super-consciousness as an advance on ordinary consciousness in the same way as our consciousness is an advance on that of animals, this isn't surprising. Even Shaw, a very vocal advocate of supermen, recognized this danger. In his play *Man and Superman*, Shaw included a warning, admittedly voiced by the Devil (an opponent of super-humanity), counseling us to "beware the pursuit of the Superhuman: it leads to an indiscriminate contempt for the Human." Far from celebrating the discovery of these supermen, at the end of *The Coming Race*, the hero of Bulwer-Lytton's evolutionary fable warns of the danger awaiting mankind if, by the time the Vril-Ya, as they are called, leave their underground kingdom, we aren't strong enough to repel them. As the Vril-Ya are masters of a mystic force known as *vril*, which is a combination of Mesmer's magnetism and Éliphas Lévi's astral light, our chances are doubtful.

As Joscelyn Godwin shows in his fascinating book *Arktos: The Polar Myth in Science, Symbolism, and Nazi Survival*, the idea of a subterranean world is more common than we might think and may even qualify as a Jungian archetype. The idea is perhaps best known through Jules Verne's classic *Journey to the Center of the Earth*, which, in recent readings by Godwin and Richard Rudgely, is seen as not only a riveting adventure story but a psychospiritual and alchemical fable.[7] Yet perhaps the most sensational account of an underground empire was given in a work purporting to be not fiction but fact.

In *Beasts, Men and Gods*, the Polish traveler, writer, scientist, and possible spy Ferdinand Ossendowski relates his adventures in Mongolia as he fled the collapse of the Russian Civil War and the rise of the Bolshevik regime. As with many an occult adventure, it's unclear how much of Ossendowski's story is true. By the time of his escape, Ossendowski had already traveled across much of Asia; he was also deeply interested in spiritualism and is said to have met Rasputin. Originally of leftist sympathies—he was exiled from Russia at the turn of the century because of his involvement in an anti-tsarist student riot and briefly was "president of a rebel government of the Far East in the Revolution of 1905"[8]—Ossendowski later rejected communism and in the civil war was an anti-Bolshevik White Russian. Years later, during World War II, he worked for the Polish underground against the Nazis.

Ossendowski's Mongol guide told him of legends of an underground kingdom, Agharti, ruled by a mysterious "King of the World" who "in his subterranean palace prays and searches out the destiny of all peoples on the earth."[9] This "Mystery of Mysteries" began, one legend claimed, sixty thousand years ago, when "a holy man disappeared with a whole tribe of people under the ground and never appeared again on the surface of the earth."[10] Centuries ago, a Mongolian tribe trying to escape from Genghis Khan accidentally found the entrance to Agharti and was never heard from again. Others met a similar fate. Yet although local legend cast Agharti as a place of danger, a lama corrected this impression. Lamenting that in a world of constant change—an increasing concern in the new, modern century—the only thing that remains stable is evil, the lama told Ossendowski that in Agharti, "all the people there are protected against evil and crimes do not exist within its bournes." "Science," he continued, "has there developed calmly and nothing is threatened with destruction."[11] Agharti, he told Ossendowski, is a kingdom of millions, ruled by the King of the World, who "knows all the forces of the world and reads all the souls of humankind and the great book of their destiny." His kingdom "extends throughout all the subterranean passages of the whole world," which are also inhabited. It even includes the ancient peoples of lost Atlantis and Lemuria. He also "rules eight hundred million men on the surface of the earth and they will accomplish his every order."[12]

Ossendowski didn't immediately reject these remarkable claims, possibly because he had already allegedly encountered an equally remarkable "real life" ruler who, while not King of the World, was for a brief time dictator of Mongolia. Ossendowski's journey was delayed for a time by his involvement with Roman Ungern von Sternberg, a Baltic German–Russian ex-lieutenant general in the White Army, who had set himself up as an independent warlord, and whose raiding parties on both Red and White supply trains, and extreme cruelty, had earned him the sobriquet of the Bloody Baron. His eccentric behavior, extreme asceticism, and belief that he was a reincarnation of Genghis Khan earned him the additional title of the Mad Baron. Ungern von Sternberg is perhaps unique in being a passionate devotee of a Buddhism whose practice included acts of brutality and gratuitous violence both to his own men and to native Mongolians. He combined it with a virulent anti-Semitism and hatred of communism, a linkage that would appear frequently as the century progressed. Ungern von Sternberg regarded the Soviets as an "evil empire" and saw their destruction as his holy duty; as Hitler would, he lumped the Jews in with them as agents of a godless materialism. Early service in Siberia instilled in him a fascination with the nomadic tribes, and in 1917, at the start of the civil war, he was sent by the White Army to secure loyalty in the Russian Far East. Eventually he rejected both the Bolsheviks and the Whites, and after a brief involvement with the Japanese, who were interested in setting up a puppet state in Mongolia with him as their agent, he broke out on his own. A fierce and brilliant if reckless fighter, von Sternberg, like Joseph de Maistre, believed that monarchy was the only feasible form of government; and for a time he dreamed of restoring the Qing Dynasty in China and uniting the Far East under it. These grand aims would be accomplished through an "Order of Military Buddhists," an army under his command that followed the teachings of Mongolian Buddhism and lived a life of utter purity.[13] His dreams collapsed when, after successfully capturing Ulan Bator (then Urga) and proclaiming himself dictator, he was eventually defeated and executed by the Soviets. It's claimed that before being shot he *chewed* the Cross of St. George medal given to him for bravery, so that it wouldn't fall into the hands of the communists. It isn't surprising that Ossendowski—having briefly worked for Ungern von Sternberg as a political advisor and, perhaps, intelligence agent—might have an open mind about the King of the World.

AGHARTI, SHAMBHALA, AND NICHOLAS ROERICH

Agharti, like Shambhala, is an underground city, and in the literature that has grown around the two, they're often confused, with one or the other being regarded as a center of evil or of goodness, a city of light or darkness.[14] They've also enjoyed different spellings. Agharti is also "Asgartha," at least according to the French writer Louis Jacolliot. Variations on Shambhala include "Schamballah," as it appears in *The Morning of the Magicians* by Pauwels and Bergier; in their version, "Schamballah" is a "city of violence and power." A rather different account comes from the Dalai Lama; for him Shambhala isn't a place—"if you lay out a map and search for Shambhala, it is not findable"—but a state, "a pure land which, except for those whose karma and merit have ripened, cannot be immediately seen or visited."[15] Yet not everyone was satisfied with a purely spiritual interpretation of Shambhala, least of all the Russian artist, explorer, and Theosophist Nicholas Roerich.

Roerich is best known for providing the inspiration, costumes, and set design for Igor Stravinsky's revolutionary modern work *The Rite of Spring*, whose riotous performance in Paris in 1913 inaugurated the age of modernism in music. But in the 1920s and '30s, Roerich was a world-famous figure, a globe-trotting mystic-artist who hobnobbed with presidents and lamas and whose quest for Shambhala found popular expression as the Shangri-la of James Hilton's *Lost Horizon*. Roerich's first love was ancient Russia, and in his early career he searched for the remnants of its pre-Christian past. But he soon felt the lure of the East. A painting of Kanchenjunga, the sacred Himalayan mountain, at his family estate in Isvara, outside St. Petersburg, captured the young Roerich's imagination. It was an early influence that led to a life-long passion for the snow-capped peaks.

The idea of a Russian Asia inspired Roerich, and Eastern ideas soon dominated his mind. He was an early member of the Theosophical Society and was on the committee responsible for building Agwan Dordjieff's Buddhist temple in St. Petersburg. It was from Dordjieff that Roerich may have first heard of the legend of Shambhala. Dordjieff himself had used the myth in efforts to create a pan-Mongol state under Russian protection, and in later years, the idea of a new Mongol state would attract Roerich as well. Tradition said that Shambhala lay in "the north," which could mean Russia itself, a notion that surely would have helped in the Great Game. Prince Ukhtomsky had even written to Dordjieff, claiming that the Mongols recognized the Tsar as an incarnate Buddha.[16] Roerich later rejected the idea of a "northern" Shambhala, saying it was only north in relation to India. Yet, on occasion, a northern Shambhala suited his purposes.

Roerich had little love for the Bolsheviks—"Vulgarity and bigotry, betrayal and promiscuity, the distortion of the sacred ideas of human kind: that is what Bolshevism is," he wrote in 1919—and his transference from a collapsing Russia to an inviting West was helped by his early success and his association with Serge Diaghilev's Ballet Russes, although he did have to abandon his art collection, which was confiscated by the comrades. With his wife, Helena, herself a mystic and translator of *The Secret Doctrine* into Russian, and their sons, George and Svetoslav—who went on to important careers in ethnography and painting—Roerich left Russia first for Finland, then London. Eventually they reached New York, where Roerich was an immediate success, landing a major exhibition almost as soon as he disembarked.

Roerich was adept at acquiring patrons, a skill he no doubt learned from his impresario, Diaghilev. By 1923, his patrons, who were as much captured by his art as by his mystical doctrine—which involved Theosophical Mahatmas, a coming new age heralded by the Maitreya Buddha, and the mysterious Shambhala—pooled sufficient funds for mammoth projects. These included a Master Institute of United Arts, two libraries, a Roerich Press, a museum, and Corona Mundi, an exhibition center. All were to be housed in a Manhattan skyscraper, a rare edifice to esoteric work. Roerich added to his message a campaign for world peace and universal brotherhood and, like Madame Blavatsky, spoke critically of colonial powers, especially Great Britain.

Another project Roerich's American patrons funded that year was a monumental expedition to India and the Himalayas. Ostensibly to provide inspiration for his paintings—which the patrons would receive in exchange for financing the trip—and to allow his son George to collect ethnographical material, the real aim of the adventure was to locate Shambhala. Or failing this, to create it. Like Agwan Dordjieff and Ungern von Sternberg, Roerich had visions of a modern Buddhist nation, pieced together from parts of Tibet, Mongolia, China, and Russia, to be ruled by the Panchen Lama, the spiritual leader of Tibet, who was forced to flee the country in 1923 because of disagreements with the then Dalai Lama, the country's secular leader. By some accounts this expulsion was prophesied, as was the Panchen's return, which would signal the beginning of a new age. Leading an invincible army, the mysterious Rigden-jyepo, "Lord of the New Era of Shambhala" and "Ruler of the World," would then appear, ending the Kali Yuga, or current dark age. Roerich undoubtedly saw himself as a key player in these developments.

In *The Heart of Asia*, Roerich speaks of a strange stone thought to have reached earth from some distant star, possibly Sirius, part of which is located in Shambhala, while another part circulates "throughout the Earth, retaining its magnetic link with the main stone." One aim of the Shambhala project may have been to return a fragment of the stone, which we assume was in Roerich's possession, to its source. Helena Roerich suggested that the "Chintamani stone," as it was called, was sent to Europe to help establish the League of Nations. Roerich's many canvases on the Chintamani theme suggest that it occupied him deeply, and his later campaign for world peace may have been linked to it.[17]

THE SECRET OF SHAMBHALA

By now the British had begun a new phase of the Great Game, this time with the Soviets, who were making overtures to Lhasa. While in London, Roerich had written articles in support of the White Russians; nevertheless, the British, as in the case of HPB and Gurdjieff, were unsure of his sympathies. Roerich was considered a Russian national, but his expedition flew an American flag next to a Tibetan *thangka*. The expedition itself, at least according to Helena Roerich, was under the guidance of the Master Morya, one of HPB's Mahatmas, and Roerich himself believed it was his mission to reach "the heart of Asia," a center as much spiritual as geographical. If the British knew that the secret of Shambhala involved an unrecognized "force," which in many ways seems a combination of Bulwer-Lytton's *vril* and the then still-unknown atomic energy, their suspicions would have been justified. Roerich spoke of a kind of "cosmic fire" emerging from Shambhala, the symbol of which was the ancient swastika (popularized by Theosophy but already appropriated by Aryan supremacists) that would create "new conditions of life." "Numerous are the splendid new forces and achievements which are being prepared there for humanity,"[18] Roerich claimed of Shambhala, seemingly predicting the coming nuclear age and sharing with R. M. Bucke a vision of a technologically advanced future. For all his love of the primitive, Roerich was no Luddite, and he was pleased when, viewing photographs of New York, his Mongolian friends saw it as a "Promised Land" and "the attainment of Shambhala"—not surprising, perhaps, for someone who had his own skyscraper.[19] Evidently the Mongols had no problem locating the secret city in an actual place, but Roerich, who had already made an expedition to "miraculous America," might have corrected their mistake.

British concerns about Roerich's possible Russian repatriation were in any case understandable. Roerich's attitude toward the communists had to ease up, as he hoped to return to his homeland in order to collect his art and archaeological collection. With his son George he had set up the Pan Cosmos Corporation, an import-export business that dealt with Russia's new rulers. One of the company's directors was Vladimir Shibaev, a Latvian whom Roerich had befriended in London. According to some accounts, Shibaev, who became Roerich's secretary, may have been a Soviet agent.[20]

TO RUSSIA WITH LOVE

A more substantial reason for British and also American suspicions was a surprise visit Roerich made to Moscow. After enduring a four-month delay at Khotan, in China, where he claimed American citizenship and was suspected of spying for the military, Roerich headed to Urumchi, capital of Sinkiang province. From there he was expected to head to Peking. Instead, the party veered westward toward Moscow. At Urumchi, Roerich had informed the Soviet Consul that material he had gathered on their journey would be "of great use to the USSR." Even more remarkable for someone who believed that the Bolsheviks distorted "the sacred ideas of humankind," Roerich told the Consul that he had letters from the Mahatmas for Stalin, and that the Mahatmas'—and hence Roerich's—task was to "unite Buddhism with Communism and to create a great Oriental Federation." Drawing on Dordjieff's hint that the Russian bear was Shambhala, Roerich mentioned the prophecy that Tibet will be freed from foreign invaders (the British) by protectors from the north. From this, the Consul gathered that Roerich's expedition was at the behest of the Hidden Masters, and that after visiting the USSR, he was to retrieve the Panchen Lama from exile in Mongolia and then liberate Tibet from the British.

Roerich must have been persuasive. Two months later, he arrived in Moscow, courtesy of the Trans-Siberian Railway, where he was feted by a bevy of Soviet notables, among them Anatoly Lunacharsky, the Education Commissar, a devotee, at least until the Revolution, of Madame Blavatsky. Lunacharsky received a "Maitreya" painting featuring a Mahatma with the face of Lenin. Lenin himself, who had died in 1924, received a container of sacred Himalayan soil to be cast onto his tomb. The great Soviet people received a message from the Himalayan Masters. But although Roerich was pleased with his reception in Russia, the Russians were ambivalent, not sure what to make of this half-Buddhist, half-Communist who lived in America and spoke of a secret, sacred city and a coming new age. After a meeting with other hidden masters—the Soviet secret police—Lunacharsky advised his fellow Theosophist to leave the USSR as soon as possible.

Although the Soviets later regarded Roerich as an American spy, and the British thought of him as a Russian agent, getting the Panchen Lama out of Mongolia and into Tibet was something practically everyone involved in the new Great Game wanted. Yet none of the players wanted the others to get credit for it, and the British were especially concerned that Roerich's real aim was to use Tibet's spiritual leader as a rallying point for a Soviet-backed revolution. Reports of Roerich's discovery that Christ had visited India led the British to consider him a crank, yet his belief in a new Shambhala headed by the Panchen Lama could be put to communist use. Roerich himself had little love for the current Tibetan regime; his account of his journey warns about the decadence rife in Tibet and the need for a purge, a return to Buddhist basics. Hearing that Roerich was nearing the Tibetan border, the British counseled the Dalai Lama, one of Roerich's *bêtes noires*, not to allow him to reach Lhasa. He never did. Beginning in October 1927, the expedition was kept south of the Kamrong Pass, in one of the coldest spots on the planet, awaiting permission to enter Tibet. It never came. Their supplies dwindled and the party had only summer tents for shelter. Temperatures dipped well below zero, and pack animals died, as did several men. Appeals for help went unanswered. Finally in March 1928, the expedition was allowed to proceed to Sikkim, where they were escorted over the border into India. Shambhala would have to wait.

HENRY WALLACE AND THE PLAN

Roerich's failure to find Shambhala didn't prevent him from trying again a decade later, this time under the auspices of the United States government. In 1934, Roerich set out on an expedition to Mongolia ostensibly to research drought-resistant grasses to help with America's Dust Bowl, the agricultural crisis that followed the Great Depression. His real aim, known to its initiates as "the Plan," was to establish an alternative society in northern Asia, once again under the leadership of the Panchen Lama. Roerich's confederate in this second Shambhala expedition was Henry Wallace, then U.S. Secretary of Agriculture, later the thirty-third vice-president, and, in 1948, an unsuccessful candidate for the presidency.

Wallace had already read widely in many religious and spiritual traditions when he met Roerich; he was a Freemason and would gain a reputation as the only Washington politician "who dabbled in the occult and could cast a horoscope."[21] He had corresponded with AE, the pen name of the Irish poet and mystic George Russell, but he was also a serious agriculturalist, and a seed company he had started offering hardier, higher-yielding corn had made him wealthy. When Wallace met Roerich in 1929, the mystic had recovered well from his aborted Tibetan adventure. Construction had begun on his twenty-nine-story "Master Building," and at the opening ceremony for his museum Roerich had been feted by New York's mayor and applauded by foreign diplomats. President Herbert Hoover even invited him to the White House. The year 1929 also saw the start of the Roerich Peace Pact, an ambitious treaty designed to protect artistic and cultural treasures from the ravages of war; the loss of his own treasured collection may have given him the idea.[22] Supported by figures like Albert Einstein, Bernard Shaw, H. G. Wells, Rabindranath Tagore, and Eleanor Roosevelt, as well as many prominent Theosophists, the Pact led to Roerich's nomination for the Nobel Peace Prize, one of three. Roerich had devised a striking symbol for the Pact, known as the Banner of Peace: three red circles, denoting religion, art, and science, surrounded by another, laid out on a white background. Roerich claimed he had discovered it carved on stone monuments in Asia, and it became known as a kind of cultural Red Cross.

Wallace became passionate about Roerich's Pact, and, after meeting its author, started a long correspondence with him, something he later had cause to regret. In 1933, after being appointed Secretary of Agriculture by President Franklin Delano Roosevelt—a post his father had also occupied—Wallace, who had communist sympathies and, like Roerich, somehow combined these with his spirituality, began to lobby for U.S.

endorsement of the Pact. Signing it in 1935, Roosevelt remarked, "It possesses a spiritual significance far greater than the text of the instrument itself." Roerich is also thought to be responsible for Wallace's idea of putting the verso of the Great Seal, with its Masonic all-seeing eye in the pyramid, on the back of the U.S. dollar, a change that also happened in 1935. Wallace pointed out to the Treasury Secretary Henry M. Morgenthau that the words *Novus Ordo Seclorum*, found underneath the pyramid, could be read as "New Deal," the catchword for FDR's recovery plan. Only later did Morgenthau realize that the topical phrase also related to the mystical idea of a new age.

Wallace's agricultural expertise and his belief in Roerich's mission met when he suggested to FDR that Roerich be sent to Mongolia to collect grass specimens. Roerich's reputation as a possible Soviet agent, his ostensible status as a White Russian, and his mystical ideas about a new age understandably prejudiced Wallace's colleagues against the idea, but Wallace was persuasive and FDR agreed. Roerich by this time had settled permanently in India, and the northern Asia he was heading into was even more of a political hotbed than a decade earlier. Manchuria, which he needed to enter in order to reach Mongolia, was occupied by the Japanese, who ruled through a puppet government. The Soviets had by now abandoned their tolerant policy toward Buddhists and were arresting monks, leaving the Japanese the mantle of Buddhist defenders. The Panchen Lama himself visited "Manchukuo"—Japanese-occupied Manchuria—which gave rise to rumors of a coming Manchukuo-Mongolian empire. When the Thirteenth Dalai Lama passed into the next bardo in 1934, what the Panchen Lama intended to do became an increasingly important question.

Wallace's plan was a disaster from the start. To placate critics, he sent along two government botanists; understandably, their idea of the expedition differed from Roerich's, and the party soon separated into two opposing camps. Roerich didn't help matters by demanding firearms and ammunition— saying that on the previous expedition his party had been attacked. That he gathered a personal escort of White Russians attired in Cossack dress also raised complaints, as did the politically incorrect remarks he made at lectures and in conversation with local authorities. Although he did collect some grass samples,

Roerich seemed more interested in visiting Buddhist monasteries, where he spoke with the monks about Rigden-jyepo and the coming "War of Shambhala." Faced with reports of Roerich's actions, Wallace denied them and chalked the charges up to political jealousy, assuring Roerich that he had his full backing. But the botanists weren't the only ones unhappy with Roerich. The Japanese-controlled press, as well as official channels, expressed their belief that the expedition had something more than agricultural research on its agenda.

This "something more" became alarmingly apparent when Roerich reached Inner Mongolia. An expedition headed by a White Russian mystic, accompanied by an armed White Russian escort, and funded and supplied by the Americans was enough to raise Soviet eyebrows. That the leader was speaking of a return of the Panchen Lama and the arrival of the new age of Shambhala suggested the United States was backing the start of a holy war against Communist rule. Reports reached Washington, and now even Wallace was concerned. That "the Plan" would involve an insurrection hadn't occurred to him, and when Louis Horch, one of Roerich's strongest patrons, who had recently filed suit against him to recover more than $200,000 in loans, informed Wallace that Roerich had guaranteed U.S. support for a Mongolian uprising, Wallace wavered. He immediately ordered Roerich to withdraw from the Mongolia area and relocate in Suiyan province, where his pursuit of drought-resistant grass would be more profitable. Either Roerich never received this directive or he ignored it, as Wallace was soon informed by the American ambassador in Moscow that Roerich was at large in Mongolia, recruiting unhappy Mongols and former White Russians. Wallace immediately cabled Roerich that "the Plan" was finished, the expedition terminated, and he was forbidden to make any public statements whatsoever.

THE GURU LETTERS

This wasn't the only setback Roerich was to face. Louis Horch had gained legal control of Roerich's skyscraper and museum and, in lieu of unpaid loans, took possession of their contents. He also testified against Roerich in an IRS suit against the mystic for tax evasion. Roerich's appeal was denied and the $50,000 bill stood. Perhaps something more than spiritual matters compelled him to remain in India. The Master Building, now a cooperative apartment house, still retains the three balls on its cornerstone, the symbol of Roerich's Peace Pact. The Roerich Museum is nearby, on 107th Street and Riverside Drive, and is well worth a visit.

Henry Wallace, too, had to endure more than embarrassment following the collapse of "the Plan." When running for vice-president on FDR's bid for a third term, copies of his letters to Roerich, in which he discussed weighty political matters in a spiritual code, reached the Republicans. That they were headed "Dear Guru" didn't help, nor did the suggestion that FDR's running mate took political counsel from an individual many considered a charlatan. It was too late for the Democrats to bump Wallace off the ticket, but they were saved by information they had gathered about an adulterous affair their opponent, Wendell Willkie, had with a prominent New York editor. Neither party wanted a mutually destructive mudslinging match, so both kept their secrets secret.

The "Guru Letters" reemerged in 1948, when Wallace, perhaps fortified by Roerich's prediction that he would one day have the office, ran for president as the Progressive Party's candidate. A journalist got hold of the letters and made them public. Although Wallace now referred to Roerich as a "disgruntled ex-employee" and "tax evader" rather than a guru, Wallace's reputation as a mystic and these new revelations dampened his already slim chances. Yet it is possible that if the "Guru Letters" hadn't appeared, Wallace may have gathered more votes, most of which would have surely come from supporters of the democrat Harry Truman, who ran against the Republican Thomas Dewey. If so, then the *Chicago Tribune's* famously incorrect headline, "Dewey Beats Truman," might have been right after all.

SYNARCHISTS UNITE!

If Roerich's attempts to reinstate Shambhala met with failure, others looked to other secret cities for inspiration. In *Le Fils de Dieu* (The Son of God) Louis Jacolliot described Asgartha as a prehistoric "City of the Sun" (shades of Campanella), and the seat of the "Brahmatma," the chief priest of the Brahmins and "the visible manifestation of God on earth." Jacolliot heard the story from Indian Brahmins while serving as a magistrate in Chandernagoré. Yet far from advocating the kind of theocracy evidenced by the myth, Jacolliot was himself a freethinker and advocate of social liberty. His interest in Hinduism stemmed from a strong anti-clericalism, and the story of Asgartha appears in a trilogy of books he wrote, arguing that Christianity is really a degenerate form of ancient Eastern religions, a theme Madame Blavatsky also espoused.

Another who added to the Agharti myth was the eccentric nine-teenth-century French occultist Saint-Yves d'Alveydre. At thirty-five, Saint-Yves, a civil servant, had the good fortune to marry a wealthy Polish divorcée, Marie-Victoire de Riznich, fifteen years his senior, who enabled him to pursue his politico-occult interests unencumbered by the need to make a living. His devotion to his wife was so great that af-ter her death in 1895, Saint-Yves turned their house in Versailles into a shrine, where he lived in seclusion and took to dressing in purple velvet.[23] He set her place at table every day and "conversed" with her regularly. This was perhaps not as difficult as it sounds, as one of the ways Saint-Yves was to learn the secrets of Agartha—as he called it, in yet another spelling—was through astral travel.

Born in 1842 to a Breton doctor, Joseph Alexandre Saint-Yves, a lifelong devout Catholic, was given the title "Marquis d'Alveydre" by the Pope in 1880. Like Éliphas Lévi, whom he may have met, Saint-Yves is another French occultist who combined his esoteric ideas with Catholic dogma. In 1864, he left the School of Naval Medicine at Brest because of his health and moved to the island of Jersey in the English Channel, where he lived as a professor of letters and sciences. Here he seems to have met several French political exiles, one of whom may have been the poet and novelist Victor Hugo, who was also a spiritualist, mesmerist, and critic of the government. Saint-Yves also discovered the work of Antoine Fabre d'Olivet, whose speculations on prehistoric civilizations influenced his political ideas.

In 1870, Saint-Yves returned to France to serve in the army dur-ing the Franco-Prussian War. His encounters with political radicals mustn't have endeared him to their views, as they didn't prevent him from taking part in the brutal suppression of the Paris Commune that followed and that so troubled the ailing Éliphas Lévi.

Around this time Saint-Yves developed a politico-esoteric idea that would greatly influence important occult figures in the coming century. We'll return to his concept of *synarchy* further on; here I'll point out that *synarchy* is the polar opposite of *anarchy*. Whereas *anarchy* means "no" or "without" government, *synarchy* means "total" or "complete" government, a kind of super-totalitarianism. For Saint-Yves it meant a government based on universal principles, in which everyone has their proper place and purpose.

After a century of revolution, it's not surprising that a social system based on strong order would be appealing. The word *anarchy* was coined in 1840 by the socialist and Freemason Pierre Joseph Proudhon, who was also responsible for the seductive but muddle-headed equation "property is theft." One of Proudhon's followers was Mikhail Bakunin, as we've seen, an early resident at Ascona. Bakunin's own followers were responsible for the assassination in 1881 of Tsar Alexander II. Returning to his palace following an inspection of his troops, the Tsar was killed by the second of two powerful explosions—the second such attempt on his life in an era of such explosions, aimed at toppling the "establishment" in Europe and the U.S. Ironically, the anarchists killed out of a belief that man is naturally good, something the more gentle Asconians who came after Baukinin also believed. As Colin Wilson writes, the anarchists "were firmly convinced of the basic goodness of human nature, of man's ability to live in peace with his fellows in an ideal world. But in the meantime, power was in the hands of kings and police chiefs."[24] Clearly these had to go, and for the anarchists, the sooner the better. "Kill the law, exterminate the capitalists, and do it tonight"[25] was one of their murderous slogans. Small wonder that in a climate of uncertainty and violence like this one, some kind of universal order would seem attractive.

Agartha came to Saint-Yves' attention when his Sanskrit tutor, the mysterious Haji Sharif, followed the signature on his very first lesson with the intriguing phrase, "Guru Pandit of the Great Agarthian School." Like Fabre d'Olivet, Saint-Yves sought universal knowledge through a study of ancient languages, and after meeting Sharif, he became his pupil. Exactly who Sharif was is unclear, although some reports claim he left India after the Sepoy Rebellion of 1857 and worked as a bird seller in Le Havre. Sharif also referred to the "Holy Land of Agarttha"—yet another spelling—and spoke of its ruler as the "Master of the Universe." Saint-Yves learned that the "Great Agarthian School" preserves the primordial language of man, Vattan, and much of the teaching Sharif passed on to him concerned this ancient tongue.

Besides through his lessons, Saint-Yves learned of Agartha through more direct means. Through some form of astral travel, or "waking dream," he claimed to have visited the hidden city himself. He reports his findings in his book *Mission de l'Inde* (The Mission of India), one of a series of hermetic-political "missions" that he wrote and self-published between 1882 and 1887. Yet having committed his Agarthian visions to print, Saint-Yves almost immediately changed his mind. When the book appeared, he recalled all copies and destroyed them. Only two survived: one Saint-Yves kept for himself, but another was secretly saved by the printer. It was this copy that led to the book's posthumous publication in 1910. Some have suggested that an Oriental brotherhood compelled Saint-Yves to withdraw his work on pain of death for "leaking" esoteric secrets for which the world was not yet ready. Saint-Yves himself never explained his actions, and we can only speculate on why he obliterated his account of the subterranean kingdom.

Saint-Yves' Agartha, like other versions, is a vast subterranean kingdom with millions of inhabitants ruled by the Brahmatma, who in this case is an Ethiopian. This "Sovereign Pontiff" is aided by the "Mahatma" and the "Mahanga," who make their first appearance here. The Brahmatma brought his people underground in 3200 BC, at the start of the Kali Yuga. Like lost Atlantis, Agartha is a supremely technologically advanced society. It's governed under the principle of synarchy, which was the system of world government until a disastrous schism in 4000 BC disintegrated what Saint-Yves calls the "Universal Empire," a theme he adopted from Fabre d'Olivet. Before then, the whole of Asia, Europe, and Africa shared a common government and religion. After the schism, like a political Tower of Babel, the world collapsed into a plurality of governments. Some countries, like Egypt, Greece, and, not surprisingly, France, retained fragments of this Golden Age, and world teachers like Moses, Jesus, and Saint-Yves himself have periodically tried to bring the world back under synarchic rule.

The Brahmatma sends his agents to the surface world to report back on developments—much as the Rosicrucians did in their utopian fables—and the latest scientific advances, as well as the wisdom of the ages, are preserved in the Agarthian libraries, carved in stone in Vattanian, the primordial language of man. Agarthian adepts enjoy a wealth of esoteric knowledge, including the true relation between the body and the soul and the means of communicating with the departed—on which we can assume Saint-Yves drew when conversing with his dead wife—and when the upper world accepts the rule of synarchy, Agartha will reveal itself and share its wisdom with the rest of mankind. Saint-Yves was so eager to promote this desirable end that he wrote open letters to the Pope, Queen Victoria, and Tsar Alexander III, urging them to help reinstate synarchic rule. As the inhabitants of Agartha are in every way our superiors and are guided by the infallible Sovereign Pontiff, as far as Saint-Yves is concerned, the sooner we accede to this design, the better.

The similarities to *The Coming Race* and its civilization of super-beings is clear, and Saint-Yves knew Bulwer-Lytton's son, the Earl of Lytton, who was at one time Viceroy of India; the younger Lytton even translated Saint-Yves' *Poème de la Reine* (Poem of the Queen) and presented it to Queen Victoria. Saint-Yves would also have been aware of Jacolliot's work. The idea of a society of hidden masters has been with us since Baron von Hund's "hidden superiors," and as we've seen, even the Rosicrucians suggested that members of that august brotherhood left Europe for their own journeys to the East. As in the case of Madame Blavatsky, it's tempting to chalk Saint-Yves' revelations up to a fascinating if idiosyncratic variation on a familiar theme. (Ossendowski himself faced charges of plagiarism when his *Beasts, Men and Gods* appeared, his account of Agarthi including enough echoes of Saint-Yves's work for the allegation to be taken seriously.

Yet Ossendowski denied this emphatically, and, curiously, one of his defenders was René Guénon.) Yet as Joscelyn Godwin points out in *Arktos*, Saint-Yves communicates his "astral" visions in such detail that it seems something more than literary borrowing is at work here. Godwin accepts that Saint-Yves really did "see" Agartha; but even more odd, in Saint-Yves' account he speaks of himself as a kind of spy—not an "official" herald of a new Agarthian age yet an advocate of its synarchic government. Obliged by no oaths of secrecy, and calling himself a "spontaneous initiate," Saint-Yves ruminates on the shock with which the Sovereign Pontiff will no doubt greet his work and on how, once he recovers from his initial surprise, he will agree that his revelations are timely and necessary. Perhaps. Yet the Brahmatma, catching psychic wind of the book, may not have been as happy with it as this "spy" hoped and advised Saint-Yves to recall it or suffer the consequences.

We won't ever know the reason for Saint-Yves' decision, but, as we will see, he believed in synarchy and worked to promote it. The notion of a total government, in opposition to the growing chaos of modern times, became increasingly appealing as the new century moved on. Although the inspiration for it may, on occasion, have come from a higher source, the results weren't always desirable.

9

REACTIONS

Saint-Yves d'Alveydre may have withdrawn his writings on Agartha from public view, but his commitment to synarchy remained, at least for a time. He lectured on the theme as a counter-measure against anarchy frequently, drawing large crowds in France and Holland. He formed a lobbying group, the Syndicate of the Professional and Economic Press, that put pressure on government ministers, promoted discussion of his ideas, and distributed synarchic literature. This group, which included economists and businessmen, met with some success and, according to one account, embraced some important figures in French politics.[1] Saint-Yves' promotion of his synarchic ideal was convincing enough for him to be made a Chevalier of the Légion d'honneur in 1893.[2] But by this time he had apparently stopped campaigning for a pan-Europe synarchy. He spent his last years in relative seclusion, developing an equally obscure esoteric system that he called the "Archeometer," an "instrument of universal measure" that he believed would "lay the foundations for the great renewal of the arts and sciences," a project reminiscent of the Messianisme of Éliphas Lévi's mentor, Hoene Wronski.

THE JEWISH QUESTION

The Archeometer would also, Saint-Yves believed, reconstitute the ancient Vattan alphabet. Like Fabre d'Olivet, whose papers at one point came into his possession, Saint-Yves believed that the key to a spiritual renewal lay in language, and he spoke of two types: one of "the celestial city or of civilization"; the other of "wild and anarchic" barbarity.[3] Like many esotericists at the time, Saint-Yves saw the "civilized" language rooted in some Aryan alphabet, one that pre-dated Sanskrit, and his remarks about the Aryan race and its implied superiority have a uncomfortable ring. In his book *Mission des Juifs (Mission of the Jews)*, Saint-Yves exonerated the Jewish race for any "evil in the general government" and celebrated their contribution to Christianity, speaking of them as the "salt and ferment of Life amongst Christian peoples."[4] Yet the idea that Saint-Yves had to explain the Jewish "mission" grew out of the general "Jewish question" that occupied Europe in the late nineteenth and early twentieth centuries. In his last years Saint-Yves even argued that the Jewish cabala had Aryan roots. "The prototypical alphabet of all the Kaba-lim," he wrote, "belongs to the Aryan race."[5] This supposed "Aryan alphabet" was "most secret" and "most hidden," and although he wasn't anti-Semitic himself, Saint-Yves' attempts to show that an Aryan alphabet was the source of cabala run parallel to the many claims made then that Jesus wasn't a Jew but an Aryan. Thus Christianity and the esotericism associated with it could separate themselves from the non-Aryan race. Although there's also no suggestion that Nicholas Roerich was anti-Semitic, his "discovery" that Jesus—who he called "Issa"—had lived in India was made in the context of an occult revisionist history often fueled by a crude anti-Semitism. It's an unhappy truth that a strong anti-Semitism lay in much of French, and not only French, esotericism.

His remarks about Aryan alphabets may strike us as troubling, yet Saint-Yves' belief in the need for synarchy was partly prompted by what seems a surprisingly familiar concern. In his first major book, *Clefs de l'Orient (Keys to the East)*, in which the idea of synarchy made its debut, Saint-Yves he also announced the need for a united Europe, a goal that in recent years has seen some success in the form of the European Union. The need for Europe to unite into a single, synarchic state, Saint-Yves tells us, is prompted by the rise of Islam as a world power, which threatens a weak, fragmented, and materialist West. Only a strong, centralized, and renewed Christian government would be able to withstand the force growing in Muslim countries. More than a century ago, Saint-Yves seems to have predicted the very situation that, rightly or wrongly, many see facing the world today.

But what exactly is synarchy? If it means "total" government, what differentiates it from simple totalitarianism? Synarchy's basic idea is to look at the state in terms of the human body, a metaphor that goes back to ancient times and can be found in Plato. Saint-Yves' variation is to see society as formed of three different systems: thinking, willing, and feeling, or, in a different interpretation: thinking, eating, and living. We will return to this shortly. Saint-Yves claimed that the Knights Templar—whom he saw as a kind of theocratic secret society, exercising almost complete control over the economic, legal, and religious life in the lands under their protection—were synarchists, and he threw into his synarchic blend elements from Baron Hund's Strict Observance Masonry. That the idea of "hidden superiors" reached back from Baron Hund to the Templars puts Saint-Yves' synarchy in very familiar territory.

PAPUS

The person responsible for carrying on the synarchic legacy in France was Gérard Encausse, better known under his esoteric *nom de plume*, Papus, a name taken from a physician mentioned in the works of Apollonius of Tyana. A doctor and surgeon until his death from tuberculosis while serving in the medical corps in World War I, Papus was the most influential and prolific esoteric writer in France, producing dozens of volumes on practically every aspect of occultism and directing the main French occult journal, *L' Initiation*; he was also responsible for a later journal, *Voile d'Isis*, which became *Les Études Traditionnelles*. A major player in occult societies like the Ordo Templi Orientis (who later claimed Aleister Crowley as a member), the Masonic Order of Memphis-Misraïm (whose roots lay in Cagliostro's Egyptian Freemasonry), and Jules Doinel's Gnostic Church (to which René Guénon would later belong), Papus also belonged to the Hermetic Brotherhood of Luxor and the Paris branch of the Hermetic Order of the Golden

Dawn. Like Samuel Hartlib, he was a kind of esoteric "intelligencer," networking between various secret societies. He was at the heart of an occult revival that reached out to many important figures in the arts and centered around places like Edmond Bailly's esoteric bookshop in Paris, whose clientele included the composers Claude Debussy and Erik Satie, the writers J. K. Huysmans and Stéphane Mallarmé, and the artists Odilon Redon and Félicien Rops.

Papus joined the Theosophical Society in 1884, but left soon after; like Rudolf Steiner, he was unhappy with its Eastern emphasis. He established the Groupe Indépendent des Études Esoterique (Independent Group for Esoteric Studies), later known as the École Hermetique (Hermetic School). If this wasn't enough to keep him busy, Papus, who called Saint-Yves his "intellectual master," also established a new Martinist Order based on the work of Louis Claude de Saint-Martin, having been initiated, he claimed, by Henri Delage. Delage was an occultist, mesmerist, and prolific author who professed to having received a Martinist initiation from his maternal grandfather, who had been initiated by the Unknown Philosopher himself.[6] Although Papus claimed to have a notebook written in Saint-Martin's hand supposedly containing messages channeled through one of Jean Baptiste Willermoz's *crisiacs*, the authenticity of both the notebook and Papus' order has been disputed. Nevertheless, Papus' Martinist Order was remarkably successful; by the turn of the century, it had branches in the United States, Great Britain, South America, the Far East, and possibly Russia. As in Ascona and Monte Verità, Papus' Martinists had their fingers in an assortment of alternative pies—homeopathy, anarchism, anti-vivisection—and for a time Papus was involved with the feminist and Theosophical fellow-traveler Anna de Wolska.[7] Two other important *fin-de-siècle* French occultists, Joséphin Péladan and Stanislas de Guaïta, who later formed their own Rosicrucian societies, were on the order's Supreme Council.

MAÎTRE PHILIPPE

Along with their occult interests, Papus' Martinists had political aims. Before World War I changed the face of Europe, they sought to liberate Poland from Tsarist Russia. They also wanted to bring about the end of the Austro-Hungarian Empire and establish a United States of Europe.[8] Papus also had considerable political influence on the Russian court of Nicholas and Alexandra. Although the "holy devil" Rasputin is the best-known of the Tsar's spiritual advisers, Papus and his "spiritual master," Anthelme Nizier Philippe, a healer and mesmerist known as "Maître Philippe de Lyon," exercised considerable clout in a court familiar with esoteric ideas. Maître Philippe was believed to possess remarkable powers; along with healing, he was said to control lightning and, like the Rosicrucians, could travel invisibly. Papus' first contact with the ill-fated royal family occurred during their visit to Paris in 1896, when he sent them a greeting on behalf of "the French Spiritualists" in which he hoped the Tsar would "immortalize his Empire by its total union with Divine Providence."[9] In 1901, he visited Russia and was introduced to Nicholas. In 1902, Maître Philippe arrived, and during his stay he had a powerful effect on the Romanovs, which led to the Lyons mesmerist being given a state office. Along with predicting a much-wanted son for the couple, which prompted in the susceptible Tsarina an hysterical pseudo-pregnancy, Maître Philippe advised them against conceding to demands to create a constitution, an issue that would later lead to their downfall.

Maître Philippe's royal influence made him enemies, and he was forced to leave St. Petersburg, but the healer and the Tsar carried on a correspondence until Philippe's death in 1905. That year, Papus made his second journey to Russia, when he is said to have conjured the spirit of Alexander III, Nicholas' father. The resurrected Tsar predicted that Nicholas would lose the throne to a revolution, and Papus allegedly claimed that he could forestall the prophecy's fulfillment as long as he was alive. Whatever we make of this, Nicholas lost the throne a few months after Papus' death. Oddly, Rasputin made a similar prediction, telling the Tsar that if he, Rasputin, was killed by the peasants, the Tsar would continue to rule and the monarchy would prosper, but if he was assassinated by the aristocracy, the monarchy would fall. Rasputin was murdered by Prince Yusupov (according to some accounts, a follower of Rudolf Steiner) and his accomplices in December 1916, and the revolution came the next year. By this time

Papus enjoyed an influence on the Russian court equal to Philippe's, counseling them on occult matters and also acting as their physician in a Rosicrucian manner, linking spiritual and physical health. He's also alleged to have initiated the Tsar into his Martinist Order. Oddly, he warned them against seeking political advice through occult means— and especially against Rasputin—but then perhaps he was only protecting his own place as spiritual advisor.

NIET!

Papus' Russian adventures led to his association with the anti-Semitic, anti-Masonic forgery *The Protocols of the Elders of Zion*, mentioned in chapter 3. His actual part in the journey of the *Protocols* from France, where they're thought to originate, to Russia, where they were published in book form in 1905 (after appearing in serialized form in 1903) is unclear, if he had any part in it at all. But in 1901, Papus collaborated with the journalist and anti-Semite Jean Carrère in a series of articles published in the *Echo de Paris* about a secret financial syndicate hostile to French and Russian relations. Writing under the pseudonym *Niet* ("No" in Russian), Papus and Carrère attacked important figures in the Russian government, specifically Sergei Witte, the finance minister and cousin of Madame Blavatsky, and Pyotr Rachkovsky, chief of the Okhrana, the Tsarist secret police. They warned of a Jewish plot to undermine the Franco-Russian alliance and implicated Witte and Rachkovsky. (Witte was in fact alarmed at the growing anti-Semitic literature, while Rachkovksy was himself an anti-Semite.) Rachkovsky retaliated by "exposing" Maître Philippe as a charlatan employed by some Jewish secret society intent on gaining power over the Tsar; this led to Philippe's banishment from Russia. In *The Occult Establishment*, James Webb untangles the complicated web of connections that links Matvei Golovinski, said to be the *Protocols'* author and one of Rachkovsky's agents, to Yuliana Glinka, who most likely introduced the *Protocols* to Russia.[10] Glinka, an anti-Semite and Theosophist, seems to have turned on her occultist beliefs, convinced that the esoteric fascinations of the time were part of a colossal diabolical conspiracy. Although the *Protocols* themselves aren't an occult document, they pandered to Russian anti-Semitism, which, as in France, informed much Russian esoteric thought. Papus himself manifested a kind of anti-Semitic double-think; as a member of the Athanor Lodge of the Hermetic Order of the Golden Dawn, he performed magic rituals with the Jewish Moina Mathers, sister of the philosopher Henri Bergson and wife of S. L. Mac-Gregor Mathers, the head of the order. He also wrote books drawing on the cabala. In mundane matters, though, he shared in the kind of anti-Semitism made famous through the Dreyfus Affair.

ORDERS FROM THE TOP

Both Papus and Saint-Yves claimed to have contact with a "higher source" that directed their political and spiritual work. By this time, others were making similar claims as well. By the first years of the new century, MacGregor Mathers, the unstable head of the Hermetic Order of the Golden Dawn, spoke of contact with sources he called the Secret Chiefs. In 1904, Mathers' former student, Aleister Crowley, made contact with another source in a hotel room in Cairo. "Aiwass," as Crowley called his contact, dictated what would become the sacred text of the new religion Crowley would spend his dubious career promoting.

Saint-Yves' source communicated the virtues of synarchy and spiritual totalitarianism, but Crowley's had something more anarchic in mind. Crowley's *Book of the Law* envisions a new aeon of "the crowned and conquering child," presaged by wars and violent eruptions and characterized by the kind of anti-humanism that would become appallingly familiar during the days of National Socialism. The coming Law of Thelema, captured in his notorious command, "Do what thou wilt shall be the whole of the law," manifested in Crowley's own life in drug addiction, obsessive sex, and an utter disregard for the will, or feelings, of other people. Either the "unknown superiors" were as unsure as we are about what kind of government is best for us and changed their minds radically, or there was more than one source, several in fact, each with its own ideas about how society should be run and each with some divine sanction for them.

165

Crowley's own political orientation varied with the events of his colorful career, usually dictated more by expediency than conviction. As mentioned, he wrote pro-German propaganda during WWI, while in the U.S. before America got in the war. He made an impassioned anti-British speech at the feet of the Statue of Liberty, unfurled an Irish Republic flag, and tore up an envelope that he claimed contained his British passport but was more than likely empty. Had he done this in England, he would probably have been arrested for treason. In later years, Crowley claimed that he was working for both British and American Naval Intelligence at the time, but like so many of his claims, this is unsubstantiated. Crowley did later offer his services to both the British and U.S. Intelligence but was rejected, although he seems to have been paid by either Scotland Yard or MI5 (the British Intelligence service) to spy on Gerald Hamilton, the model for Christopher Isherwood's "Mr. Norris," while he and Hamilton, a supporter of the Irish Republic, shared an apartment in Berlin. That Crowley lurked in the shadows of espionage seems appropriate. He appears to have had some influence on Tom Driberg, a Labour Member of Parliament and also an MI5 spy. Driberg's superior, Maxwell Knight, was also a devotee of Crowley's "magick," as Crowley insisted on spelling it. Ian Fleming, creator of James Bond and himself an intelligence agent, devised a plan for Crowley to be smuggled into Nazi Germany to make contact with Rudolf Hess, Hitler's deputy and a known occultist, and feed him misinformation. Hess' dramatic and inexplicable flight to England in 1941 canceled this extraordinary scheme.[11]

THE SYNARCHIC STATE

For Saint-Yves' sources, synarchy meant that, much as in the Laws of Manu, everyone and everything had its proper place. It was, in fact, a version of the Cosmic State, with a rigid hierarchy reaching from the Sovereign Pontiff down to the common people. Social harmony is maintained only by strict recognition of these indisputable distinctions; any change would result in a kind of dissonance. As one's allotted place is determined by natural, universal laws—not arbitrary human decision—an act against the status quo is an act against nature; it is, in fact, a kind of disease, an idea Soviet authorities put to effective use when they argued that anti-government criticism was evidence of mental imbalance. The synarchic state took this a step further and claimed that dissension from it is an act against God, a sentiment shared by many a king and queen. As with the divine right of kings, for Saint-Yves, certain members of society were destined to rule. These were the priest-kings, individuals who, because of their inherent spirituality, were in contact with the divine and could interpret its messages. Although Saint-Yves' own symbol of infallibility lived in subterranean Agartha and not in Rome, it isn't difficult to see in the Sovereign Pontiff an image of the Pope writ large, a magnification that Joseph de Maistre would have applauded. As the human being is "only an instrument ruled by laws that are beyond him,"[12] the common people need these priests and adepts to translate inscrutable cosmic destiny into accessible forms of thought.

THE BODY POLITIC

For Saint-Yves' three distinct spheres required strict control for synarchy to be effective: the law, the economy, and religion, a variant of the political-social law of three mentioned earlier. Here "living" was equated with law, "eating" with the economy, and "thinking" with religion. Papus developed his own version of these, and he looked at the individual as a kind of "cell" in the body of a race, nation, or state. Just as the cells in our body are destined to perform certain functions, so too is the individual destined to fulfill certain functions in the state. Equally, if the cells in our body "rebel" and disregard their function, or try to perform another, they threaten both themselves and the body as a whole. Cancer, in fact, is an example of such a "rebellion," and it's tempting to look at social unrest and political disagreement as kinds of "social cancers"—tempting, but dangerous, especially for those individuals who are seen as the "sick" cells. It's a very "holistic" way of looking at society, although many advocates of holistic thinking might find the totalitarian aspects of this "body politic" metaphor unappealing. Indeed, the idea of society as a "body" and of the individual as merely one part of it would find many advocates in Germany in the years leading up to National Socialism. For many sympathetic to this view, "individuals" were, by definition, the equivalent of our own "lone nutters," and being outside the *volk* was a sign of disease, while being within it was a source of power. Rudolf Bode, a dance theorist, resident of Monte Verità, and follower of the *völkisch* philosopher Ludwig Klages, argued that "the larger the mass in movement, the stronger the effect of irrational impulses, the more powerfully the soul's innermost currents begin to roar . . . the instinctive forces are reinforced under the influence of comrades striving for the same good."[13] As mentioned, the philosopher Jean Gebser saw in the Nazi *volk* a prime example of what he called the magical structure of consciousness, which works through the *body* to circumvent the rational, critical mind.

Yet it wasn't solely the *volk* that threatened to either absorb or neutralize the individual, and not all esotericists shared Papus' and Saint-Yves' views. In his sobering *Letters from Russia*, P. D. Ouspensky, writing from Ekaterinodar, near the Black Sea, where he was stranded after the Bolshevik Revolution, spoke of those "big, two-dimensional creatures called Nations and States," which he saw as living on the "level of the zoophytes, slowly moving in one direction or the other and consuming one another." For Ouspensky "the whole life of individual men and women is a struggle against these big creatures," who are at "a far lower stage of development than individual men and women."[14] Again, this shows that there is no such thing as "occult politics" in the sense of a single socio-political doctrine or set of beliefs. Some occult or esoteric thinkers see the race or the state taking precedence over the individual, while others hold the opposite view.

THE THREEFOLD COMMONWEALTH

One esoteric thinker who saw the future in terms of the individual yet who was influenced by Saint-Yves' synarchy was the Austrian spiritual scientist Rudolf Steiner. In 1919, in the aftermath of WWI, Steiner published an *Appeal to the German People and the Civilized World*, a document aimed at guiding German and European reconstruction. Germany was in chaos. Defeat followed by financial collapse had combined with political assassinations and civil war to reduce it to anarchy, a situation amenable to the rise of National Socialism. During the war, Steiner's followers, who came from all the battling nations, worked in neutral Switzerland on building the Goetheanum, a fantastic example of anthroposophical architecture that sadly burned to the ground on New Year's Eve 1922; proto-Nazi arsonists may have been responsible, although an electrical fault may also have caused the blaze. Steiner himself had been the target of attacks for some time from a variety of opponents: Marxists, German nationalists, Catholics, Protestants, even rival occultists. He had in recent years moved beyond the esoteric fields into the public arena, and his attempts at a spiritual reformation of Europe met with much resistance.

Like Saint-Yves, Steiner spoke of the "missions" of certain races and nations, and he also thought in terms of a united Europe. The "mission" of Central Europe (which included Germany, Austria, and what is now the Czech Republic) was to act as a balance between the mega-powers of Russia and the United States. Even during the war, Steiner had been called upon by Otto von Lerchenfeld, a German diplomat and anthroposophist, to devise a plan for an acceptable peace. Like many, Lerchenfeld believed that Germany had been misled by the hysterical saber-rattling and militarism of Kaiser Wilhelm, and like Steiner he wanted to preserve the humanist Germany of Goethe and Beethoven. Lerchenfeld and Steiner collaborated on a memorandum, spelling out the wrong decisions that led to the war. But more importantly, it discussed the necessary restructuring of society. Steiner, who certainly knew of Saint-Yves's ideas, saw human beings as composed of three powers, thinking, feeling, and willing, which he associated with three functions of the body. Thinking was linked to the head and nervous system; feeling to what he called the rhythmic system, which included breathing, circulation, and the heartbeat; and willing to the limbs and metabolic system. Like Saint-Yves and Papus, Steiner took this "threefold" system and applied it to society, adapting the triune call of the French Revolution—liberty, equality, and fraternity—to his brand of spiritual politics. The thinking/head system in society is the world of culture and must be free to explore new ideas; the feeling/rhythmic system is the political sphere in which everyone must be treated equally; and the willing/metabolic system is the economy, which must work fraternally, for the good of all. One of Steiner's central concerns was education, which he linked to the cultural branch of society, and the aim of Steiner education—the most successful application of his "threefold" idea—is to produce a "free" individual in a society supportive of spiritual growth.

Steiner's memorandum was read by a few officials and not surprisingly sank out of sight, its utopian vision having little impact in the world of *realpolitik*. But following his *Appeal to the German People* Steiner published *The Threefold Commonwealth*, a book spelling out his political ideas. It became a best-seller, and for a time Steiner was a major player on the European stage, lecturing on a "threefold" European reconstruction throughout Germany and Switzerland, where unions dedicated to his ideas were formed; at one lecture, the crowds were so large they stopped traffic and hundreds had to be turned away. Steiner's ideas about "threefoldness" even made it to a ballot, during a referendum in Silesia, in northeastern Germany, where they were deciding whether to remain German or to become part of Poland. Steiner's followers canvassed voters, but by then the anti-Steiner campaign had reached its height, and one campaigner remarked that they only just missed being arrested or shot.[15] Steiner himself was physically attacked more than once and was almost assassinated in Munich.

WALTER STEIN

One follower of "threefoldness" who achieved some political influence was Walter Stein, a philosopher, historian, and student of Steiner who wrote a remarkable book, *The Ninth Century and the Holy Grail*, on the esoteric and historical context of the Grail legend. Stein is most known to students of occult politics for his inclusion in Trevor Ravenscroft's thrilling but questionable account of Hitler's occult obsessions, *The Spear of Destiny*. Ravenscroft claims to have been a student of Stein's and in the book he says, among other things, that Stein met Hitler before and after World War I and that he was invited to England to advise Winston Churchill on Hitler's occult beliefs. Like much else in the book, both claims are unsubstantiated. Yet Stein did try to introduce "threefoldness" into European politics.

Stein, who grew up in an anthroposophical household, met Steiner and became his personal student in 1913; Steiner even served as a kind of unofficial adviser for Stein's philosophy doctorate. After the war Stein campaigned for "threefoldness" in Germany, and at one point he even tried to get the philosopher Ludwig Wittgenstein, who had already given considerable amounts of his large inheritance to the poets Rilke and Georg Trakl, to donate to the campaign, but was unsuccessful. (Like Saint-Yves, Stein also believed that the Templars exhibited a form of "threefoldness.") When it was clear that "threefoldness" was a lost cause, Stein became a teacher in the first Steiner school, in Stuttgart. A few years after Steiner's death in 1925, Stein left the school, and in the early thirties, because of his Jewish background, he left Germany for England.

Stein became involved with the anthroposophist Daniel Nicol Dunlop, director of the British Electrical and Allied Manufacturing Association and chairman of the executive council of the World Power Conference. Dunlop wanted Stein to help in establishing a World Economic Conference that would promote Steiner's ideas, but Dunlop died before this could come about. Yet Stein did produce a journal, *The Present Age*, contributing articles on anthroposophical themes and campaigning for an economy based on Steiner's "threefoldness."

Through Dunlop, Stein made contact with some figures in British politics, including Churchill, whom he met through Admiral Roger Keyes, who knew Dunlop. More than likely, though, they didn't discuss Hitler's interest in the occult. Keyes was also friendly with the Belgian royal family, and through him Stein became close to Leopold III, King of the Belgians, whom he met through the pianist and anthroposophist Walter Rummel, another student of Steiner's. Stein talked with Leopold about the cosmic forces behind human evolution and the growing threat of war and how a strictly neutral Belgium could act as a balance between the Allies and the Axis powers, echoing Steiner's ideas about the role of Central Europe. Their discussions advanced as far as a declaration that Leopold presented to the seven "Oslo" states in 1939, which was influenced by Steiner's "threefold" ideas. In an attempt to avert another war, the "Oslo" states—Belgium, Denmark, Finland, Luxembourg, the Netherlands, Norway, and Sweden—tried to act as mediators between the Axis powers and Britain and France, and their efforts included an element of Steiner's "threefoldness." According to Stein's biographer Johannes Tautz, in Belgium and Holland, "peace keeping efforts were made in which pupils of Steiner's were involved."[16] In Holland, anthroposophists appealed directly to Queen Wilhelmina to suggest a World Conference "for the general settlement of spiritual, economic and political questions throughout the world."[17] Sadly, they weren't successful. But like his contemporary Henry Wallace, Stein did make esoteric inroads into politics, and he even came close to reaching President Roosevelt when an American banking magnate and adviser to FDR took an interest in his ideas.[18] Another political leader with whom Stein discussed "threefoldness" was Kemal Atatürk, founder in 1923 of modern Turkey.[19] Exactly how open to Steiner's ideas the secularist, rationalist, and modernist Atatürk was is unclear. Another esotericist, P. D. Ouspensky—after his second visit to Constantinople (Istanbul today), swept there by the Bolshevik Revolution—complained that the "enlightened rulers of the new Turkey forbade all activity to 'astrologers, fortune-tellers, and dervishes.'"[20]

RENÉ GUÉNON

The modernizing trend Ouspensky despaired of in Turkey troubled another esoteric thinker influenced by Saint-Yves' ideas, and the "crisis of the modern world," as he saw it, became the central theme of his work. René Guénon is generally regarded as the founder of the Traditionalist school, whose fundamental idea is that a primordial spiritual tradition, revealed by a divine source, existed in the ancient past but was subsequently lost.[21] Traces of this tradition can be found in the world's major religions; not in their exoteric forms, which are corrupt and decadent, but in their esoteric teachings. The modern, secular world has lost contact with this original source; the result is the burden of ills—political, social, cultural, and spiritual—with which modernity is plagued. This theme, which informs a variety of occult politics, is rooted in the *prisca theologia* that grew from Marsilio Ficino's translations of the *Corpus Hermeticum* in 1460. Traditionalism's slant is that everything was a great deal better *back then* but became corrupted through human *hubris*, an example of the non-progressive element in esotericism, or, perhaps less generously, of historical romanticism and what the literary critic George Steiner dubbed "nostalgia for the absolute."[22] Closely associated with the Traditionalists is the idea of a *philosophia perennis*, a "perennial philosophy"—the title of a once-popular anthology of spiritual writings edited by Aldous Huxley—which points to the belief that "all religions shared a common origin in a single perennial (or primeval or primordial) religion that had subsequently taken a variety of forms."[23]

The term *philosophia perennis* was coined in 1540 by the Catholic scholar Agostino Steuco to celebrate Ficino's insight that Christianity and Platonism emerged from the same primordial source—an important argument for thinkers wanting to study Plato without incurring the censure of the Church. Yet, in another example of the irony at work in the world of occult politics, for Guénon and other Traditionalists, the Renaissance which produced Ficino and the idea of a "perennial philosophy" was itself a product and cause of mankind's loss of contact with the original source. For Guénon, the Renaissance saw the rise of humanism and its poisonous growth, modernity. It wasn't, as is usually thought, a rebirth "but the death of many things."[24] As I argue in the introduction to this book, the occult as we know it (and that we can see as including esotericism) is very much a product of the modern world, and as Mark Sedgwick in his major study of Traditionalism puts it, "Traditionalism set itself against the modern world, but it was born with modernity, in the Renaissance."[25]

René Guénon was born in 1886 to parents no longer young; his father was fifty-six and his mother thirty-six. His family was Catholic, and like Éliphas Lévi and Saint-Yves d'Alveydre, Guénon combined

Catholicism with more eccentric spiritual pursuits. One of these, spiritualism, was in evidence in the Guénon household; René's parents had lost a baby girl just months before René's birth, and they attempted to contact her through a medium. Although Guénon would later warn against the dangers of occultism—specifically Theosophy and spiritualism, speaking of them as "counter-initiatic"—he, too, as we have seen, made contact with spirits, one of whom, claiming to be Jacques de Molay, directed him to establish a new order of Knights Templar.

Guénon spent much of his youth in ill health, pampered by his spinster aunt who acted as his tutor. A solitary child, he showed an early interest in mathematics, something he may have inherited from his father. Like the young Rudolf Steiner, he was drawn to "an inner unchanging reality of which mathematics and particularly geometry were in some way the symbol."[26] History and the phenomenal world didn't interest him—according to his biographer, Guénon considered "the last 2,000 years . . . relatively unimportant"—and, tellingly, he showed little aptitude for anything requiring imagination and an artistic sense. Guénon's whole bent was toward "getting it right." He defended his conclusions fiercely and early on showed signs of hypersensitivity and an inability to admit mistakes as well as a persecution mania.[27] In later years, the paranoia the young Guénon directed at one his teachers would find more formidable targets when he spoke of occult brotherhoods who sought to impede his work.

TEMPLARS RECIDIVUS

Although he seemed destined for an academic career, Guénon abandoned the academy soon after arriving in Paris, where his studies unexpectedly fared badly; competitiveness and his inability to accept "second place" seem to have been behind his decision, as well as a resurgence of his persecution mania. (He did later complete a philosophy degree, but his doctoral dissertation was rejected by the Sorbonne, and he left academia for good in 1923; the dissertation, *In-*

troduction to the Study of Hindu Doctrine, would emerge as his first book in 1921.) His academic and authoritarian character found fertile soil in the Parisian occult milieu. In 1906 Guénon joined Papus' Martinist Order, which some have argued was a major influence on the Traditionalist worldview.[28] He also became a member of the Independent Group for Esoteric Studies and, soon after, a Freemason. Freemasonry would remain one of Guénon's interests, yet his relationship to it was ambiguous. He wrote anti-Masonic articles for the journal *La France Chrétienne* (Christian France) while still a Mason; the journal later changed its name to *Anti-Masonic France*. His active involvement with Masonry apparently ended in 1917.[29] Later Guénon would also contribute to the Catholic journal *Regnabit*, associated with the cult of the Sacred Heart, a Catholic mystical society that had "political and nationalist overtones" and was linked to the ongoing Naundorffist movement.[30] Guénon was also linked for a time with Charles Maurras and the Catholic, nationalist, royalist, and right-wing movement Action Française.

His stay with Papus was cut short when, as mentioned, he was called upon by the spirit of Jacques de Molay to reestablish the Knights Templar. According to one source, other spirits were also in attendance at the Hôtel des Canettes where the group of Martinists involved in the séance met: Cagliostro, Fredrick the Great, and Adam Weishaupt were there, too, all jostling for air time through the medium Jean Desjobert.[31] When Papus caught wind of the séance, he wasn't happy, especially with the idea that one of the group had decided to help himself to his mailing list. Papus himself had caused a similar stir among the Theosophists when he branched out with his own Martinist Order, but this didn't prevent him from expelling Guénon. That Guénon had made contact with Jacques de Molay—or at least some entity claiming to be him—is suggestive, as he later argued that the suppression of the Knights Templar marked a crucial turning point in what Hinduism calls a *manvantara*, a vast cosmic cycle. *Manvantara*s, which last some 306,720,000 years, are divided into smaller units known as *mahayuga*s, and these in turn are divided into four periods, known as *yuga*s, called *satya*, *treta*, *dvāpara*, and *kali*—or golden, silver, bronze, and iron in the Western equivalent. Each *yuga* denotes an increasing separation from the divine source until a dark age is reached and a final cataclysm leads to the reinstatement of the Golden Age. For Guénon and many others, we are currently in the tail end of the Kali Yuga, or Iron Age, a period of almost irredeemable spiritual decline, and have been for some six thousand years—hence Guénon's lack of interest in the last two thousand years. For Guénon, the suppression of the Knights Templar started the modern secularist age—Philip the Fair's dominance over Pope Clement V signaling the triumph of temporal power over spiritual authority—and one imagines he believed his Order of the Temple Renewed might set things straight. The "unknown superiors" who suggested he establish the order apparently thought otherwise, and in 1911 they directed Guénon to disband it.

By this time, Guénon had become a bishop in Jules Doinel's Gnostic Church and started the journal *La Gnose*, to which he contributed articles on esotericism and spiritualism;[32] he would later take over Papus' *Voile d'Isis*. He had also met the Swedish-French painter Ivan Aguéli, a Sufi inclined toward anarchism who is believed to have initiated Guénon into a Sufi order at this time, although other sources suggest Guénon's initiation occurred after his move to Cairo in 1930. (Guénon left France for Egypt after the death of his first wife in 1927, and he remained there, living in practical seclusion, until his death in 1951; he remarried to an Egyptian woman with whom he had three children.) Aguéli was known for his eccentric behavior; he was prone to make speeches supporting anarchism while wearing a turban and Arab dress. Little is known about him, and it's possible he committed suicide in Barcelona in 1917, where he was apparently run over by a train. Aguéli seems to have taken his political beliefs fairly seriously; in a radical example of animal rights activism, in 1900 he and his lover, Marie Huet, an anarchist poet, Theosophist, socialist, and staunch anti-vivisectionist, shot a matador in protest against the introduction of Spanish-style bullfighting—where the bull is killed—into France. The matador survived, and Aguéli received a suspended sentence.[33] Earlier Marie Huet did not fare so well, when she did time for harboring a wanted anarchist.[34]

CRISIS

The Islamism of his Sufi initiator rubbed off on Guénon, and from his earlier embrace of Hinduism he turned to the faith of Allah as his source of a "living tradition." Although for a time he carried on his Sufi practice while still a Catholic, Guénon made a full conversion to Islam after settling in Cairo. Ivan Aguéli's anarchism, however, didn't find a place in Guénon's world. Far from it: the spiritual authoritarianism Guénon would advocate seems the polar opposite of what we can make of Aguéli's character. Guénon began his major work in the 1920s, after his fling with various occult orders, and his concerns about the debilitating effects of the Kali Yuga received political expression in what is probably his most influential book, *The Crisis of the Modern World*, published in 1927. Guénon wasn't alone in thinking that modernity, and the West in particular, had reached a kind of spiritual nadir. Nietzsche had said so years before, and in 1918, the historian Oswald Spengler had massive popular success with his *Decline of the West*, a huge tome of cultural pessimism that became a best-seller. In *Being and Time*, published in the same year as Guénon's work, one of Nietzsche's disciples, the philosopher Martin Heidegger, argued that since Plato, the West had experienced a kind of spiritual amnesia, succumbing to what he called "forgetfulness of being," a diagnosis G. I. Gurdjieff would confirm. Heidegger himself had more than a flirtation with authoritarian politics. While a member of the Nazi party, he infamously linked his philosophy of *Dasein* and its spiritual destiny to Nazism in speeches made as rector of Freiburg University in the early days of Hitler's regime. Spengler, on the other hand, rejected the Nazis, comparing Hitler to an operatic "heroic tenor."

In the aftermath of World War I, weariness and decline were "in the air," but Guénon's approach to the sense of aimlessness captured in T. S. Eliot's *The Waste Land* had a unique aggressiveness. As the "primordial spirituality becomes gradually more and more obscure," he tells us, the "purely material character" of the present civilization turns the modern world into "a veritable monstrosity,"[35] a true waste land that exhibits the "profound degeneracy which the Gospel terms 'the abomination of desolation.'"[36] Guénon's paranoia emerges in his remark that it "seems difficult to admit" that this situation has occurred "spontaneously, without the intervention of some directing will whose exact nature must remain rather enigmatic."[37] Even so, the urge in humans to "reduce everything to human proportions" and to "eliminate every principle of higher order"[38] served as a viable target for his critique, which shares much with the anti-Gnosticism of Eric Voeglin. Democracy and its attendant egalitarianism and individualism are particular bêtes noires. Echoing T. E. Hulme's concern about the excesses of Romanticism, Guénon sees in individualism "the determining cause of the present decline of the west, precisely because it is . . . the mainspring for the development of the lowest possibilities of mankind."[39]

Democracy fares but little better. After castigating the "pseudo-principle of equality" and "the evils of compulsory education," Guénon announces that "the most decisive argument against democracy can be summed up in a few words: the higher cannot proceed from the lower, because the greater cannot proceed from the lesser," and this, he tells us, "is an absolute mathematical certainty that nothing can gainsay."[40] In another work, *Spiritual Authority and Temporal Power*, Guénon argues that contemporary society is a complete "inversion"— one of his key terms—of the caste system, with the Sudras, the common people, now dominant, the Brahmins having been eclipsed since the French Revolution. While the majority laud this as the triumph of democracy, for Guénon it means that "while all that really matters is in fact in decline, people foolishly suppose they see progress."[41]

Guénon's familiarity with synarchy is apparent when he declares that "under the present state of affairs in the western world, nobody any longer occupies the place that he should normally occupy by virtue of his own nature; this is what is meant by saying that the castes no longer exist, for caste, in its traditional meaning, is nothing other than individual nature . . . that predisposes each man to the fulfillment of one or another particular function."[42] As in Papus' cellular state, in which each member of society must perform his allotted task or suffer the consequences, for Guénon "opposition or contrast means disharmony or disequilibrium, that is to say something which . . . can only exist from a relative, particular and limited point of view."[43] Reading this, it's no surprise that Guénon was fascinated with Saint-Yves' account of Agartha, even going so far, as we've seen, to defend Ossendowski from charges of plagiarism. In his book on the subterranean synarchic kingdom, *The Lord of the World*, Guénon argues that Agartha represents "a spiritual center existing in the terrestrial world," housing "an organization responsible for preserving integrally the repository of sacred tradition which is of 'non-human' origin . . . and through which primordial wisdom communicates across the ages to those capable of receiving it."[44] The idea of a Lord of the World itself, for Guénon, pointed to "Manu, the primordial and universal legislator."[45] In other words, the Sovereign Pontiff, the benevolent spiritual dictator, who rules over his kingdom with a loving but firm hand.

SPIRITUAL ELITES

Guénon believed that the West could be saved from its utter collapse only through the formation of a spiritual elite, a kind of modern-day Rosy Cross Brotherhood, who understood the need for the return of the primordial Tradition and were willing to take steps to ensure it. But these new Rosicrucians wouldn't espouse the progressive ideals advocated by Johann Valentin Andreae. Instead, they would act as a kind of governing secret society, a council of adepts who would lead the masses back into the light in spite of themselves. The "primordial wisdom" was only available to "those capable of receiving it," and this meant for Guénon that the burden of saving the West lay on the shoulders of the few. "Living traditions" could still be found in the East; yet these traditions weren't available to everyone. They could only be "assimilated by an elite," not by "the mass of western people, for whom they were not made."[46] "If," Guénon speculates, "a western elite comes to be formed, real knowledge of the Eastern doctrines will be . . . essential to it," but, he continues, "the remainder, the majority of people, whose lot it will be to *reap the benefits of its work* [my italics], can quite well remain unaware of this, receiving the influence from it unwittingly and in any case by means that will be beyond their perception."[47] "The true elite," he tells us, "would not have to intervene directly in these spheres [social and political], or take part in outward action; it would direct everything by an influence of which people were unaware, and which, the less visible it was, the more powerful it would be."[48] "It would be enough," he argues, "if there were a numerically small but powerfully established elite to guide the masses, who would obey its suggestions without suspecting its existence, or having any idea of its mode of action."[49]

It wouldn't be unusual if, in a kind of Jungian enantiodromia, Guénon's occasional paranoia turned around, and he himself became the source of the "hidden others," operating behind the scenes. And while his conclusions seem unacceptable, it's difficult to disagree with many of his criticisms of the modern West. Yet the kind of benevolent masterminds Guénon envisions aren't solely the concern of paranoid esotericists. The kind of governing elite proposed by Guénon was advocated, at least according to some of his critics, by the political philosopher Leo Strauss, whom we met in chapter 2. In *Leo Strauss and the American Right*, the Canadian political theorist Shadia Drury argues that Strauss is responsible for an elitist sensibility in American politics, which she links to a Christain fundamentalist imperialist agenda. For Drury, Strauss was Machiavellian. He taught that "perpetual deception of the citizens by those in power is critical because they need to be led, and they need strong rulers to tell them what's good for them." As mentioned, Strauss, like Eric Voeglin, is seen as a significant influence on neoconservative politics, and his idea of the "noble lie" goes back to figures like Joseph de Maistre and the fictional (though by no means impossible) Grand Inquisitor.

The idea of some Sovereign Pontiff and his agents masterminding society for our own good is chilling, yet it is arguable that many of us do avoid the responsibility of governing ourselves. As the Marxist Freudian Erich Fromm noted long ago, we seek some "escape from freedom," a theme Dostoyevsky, creator of the Grand Inquisitor, grappled with at length. A threat may trigger a defense of our freedom; but once it subsides, we sink back into the kind of complacent spiritual lukewarmness Guénon disdained. This isn't to argue in favor of his elite; it is only to point out that his advocacy of it isn't necessarily prompted by some nefarious appetite for political power. It may be rooted in an unflattering yet accurate assessment of human psychology.

With the rise of mass society and the politics of the "lowest common denominator," the notion of a spiritual elite and of a kind of "esoteric chivalry" appealed to those who shared Guénon's concerns. One such was the French alchemist and Egyptologist René Schwaller de Lubicz, who, like Guénon, emerged from the occult underground of *fin-de-siècle* Paris. In the years following World War I, Schwaller de Lubicz gathered a group of like-minded individuals to form his own spiritual elite. Among them was possibly a character who would be at the center of the most devestating political movement of the twentieth century. His name was Rudolf Hess.

10

Dark Sides

Contemporary readers know René Schwaller de Lubicz for his work on the metaphysics and cosmology of ancient Egypt, presented in a series of difficult but arresting books like *Symbol and the Symbolic*, *Esotericism and Symbol*, and *The Temple in Man*. His views about the antiquity of Egyptian civilization reached a wide readership in the 1990s when his notion that the Sphinx is thousands of years older than the official estimate was taken up by Graham Hancock and Robert Bauval in their bestselling books *Fingerprints of the Gods* and *The Orion Mystery*. Earlier, in the 1970s, Schwaller de Lubicz's ideas were popularized through John Anthony West's *The Serpent in the Sky*. Still other readers know of Schwaller through accounts of the mysterious early twentieth-century alchemist Fulcanelli, who some believe discovered the philosopher's stone, and who, according to some reports, worked with Schwaller in uncovering the secret of making alchemical stained glass.[1] Schwaller de Lubicz's ideas have influenced one of the leading contemporary "alternative" thinkers, William Irwin Thompson, and through Thompson's work, Schwaller's thought has become part of New Age thinking, contributing to it a rigor not usually associated with that term.

But as readers of André VandenBroeck's memoir of his time as a student of Schwaller in the early 1960s discover, this elder of spiritual thought had a dark side.[2] In the years around World War I, Schwaller formed a secret society, a Guénonian elite, antithetical to democratic and egalitarian views. Like Guénon, de Lubicz was disgusted by the modern world, and in his celebration of chivalry and rank wanted to counter-balance what was for him a growing spiritual and cultural mediocrity.

As readers of this book will recognize, a form of chivalry runs throughout esoteric politics, starting with the Knights Templar and their impact on Freemasonry. Yet in the early twentieth century, notions of chivalry moved into territories less frequented by gallant knights performing heroic deeds. As the political journalist William Pfaff writes, in the dark days surrounding the World War "the tradition of European chivalry was turned into a nihilistic counterfeit of chivalry," and ideas of nobility and heroism were "appropriated by Hitler, the SS, and subsequently by Fascist or quasi-Fascist parties from Romania to Ireland and Australia."[3] Although Schwaller's attraction to chivalry wasn't unique, his approach to it produced results that link his name forever to this dark appropriation. Like Joseph Campbell, Schwaller is one of the "good guys" who unfortunately said "bad things."

HERALDRY

Like Guénon, Schwaller was an habitué of the Parisian occult world surrounding Papus. He was close to the Chacornac brothers, who ran a bookstore near the Seine, and who took over publication of *Le Voile d'Isis* in the 1920s and later published Guénon's work. He frequented Edmond Bailly's bookshop as well as the wonderfully named Librairie du Merveilleux (Bookshop of the Marvelous) run by Pierre Dujols and Alexandre Thomas. Born in Alsace-Lorraine to a wealthy family (his father was a chemist), René started out as a student of the painter Matisse and a follower of the philosopher Henri Bergson. From Bergson and Matisse, he passed through a study of Einstein, Max Planck, and Werner Heisenberg to a deep interest in occultism. He joined the Theosophical Society around 1913, while his interests were dominated by alchemy, sacred geometry, Gothic architecture, and heraldry, the history and interpretation of coats of arms. Here Schwaller met the Lithuanian hermetic poet and later diplomat Oscar Vladislas de Lubicz Milosz. In 1919, de Lubicz Milosz bestowed on Schwaller the right to bear the title "de Lubicz"; before this he was simply René Schwaller. René and Oscar shared a deep interest in heraldry and in the possible link between coats of arms and reincarnation. This led to a strong bond between them, and when together they called each other "brothers in arms."[4] In his enigmatic book *Nature Word* Schwaller writes: "The proper path leads you first in search of your 'Totem,' that is to a spiritual Heraldry." This is because "you cannot step into the shoes of another person, for you are yourself a whole, a particular aspect of universal Consciousness," a sentiment strongly opposed to the collectivist tendencies of the time.[5] But "de Lubicz" wasn't the only name René Schwaller would receive. Although some accounts suggest he adopted it during his early days in the Theosophical Society, in an episode reminiscent of Jean Baptiste Willermoz and the "Unknown Agent," René is thought to have been given the mystical name *Aor*, which means "light" in Hebrew, from a channeled source. Indeed, it's been suggested that Milosz's association with Schwaller's elite ended because of the spiritualist practices that began to dominate the group, much as Louis-Claude Saint-Martin rejected the theurgic practices of Willermoz.[6] In later years, Schwaller's students were required to refer to him by this secret, esoteric title.

The Watchers

The exact date when Schwaller's elite first met is unclear; by Schwaller's account, the group started in 1917. He called them *Les Veilleurs*, "The Watchers," and they produced a journal, at first called *L'Affranchi*, "The Liberated" but later retitled *Le Veilleur*, "The Watcher." *Veilleur* in French is linked to the English "vigil" and "vigilance," which have an ominous association with "vigilante." Although Schwaller's Watchers weren't activists, their pronouncements on issues like race link them with groups who took a less intellectual interest in these matters. In later years, Isha Schwaller de Lubicz, René's wife, spoke of the Watchers' aims as "the common defense of the principles of human rights" and "the supreme safeguards of independence."[7] Yet her interpretation of the group's values may be open to debate.

In her account of the esoteric underground of early twentieth-century Paris, Geneviève Dubois remarks that the Watchers, who were part of the salon hosted by the American lesbian socialite Natalie Clifford Barney, were associated with a group called Le Centre Apostolique (the Apostolic Center), which had as its motto "Hierarchy-Fraternity-Liberty," a synarchic twist on the battle cry of the French Revolution. This Apostolic Center, Dubois relates, was "really a kind of occultist synarchy . . . supporting a political-social messianism that was inspired in part by the ideas of Saint-Yves d'Aleveydre."[8] The Center was itself directed by an even more mysterious group, the Frères de l'Ordre Mystique de la Résurrection (Brothers of the Mystical Order of the Resurrection).[9] According to some accounts, the Apostolic Center acted as the "exoteric" form of the Watchers, whose "esoteric" form was known by the name *Tala*, Hebrew for "place," although René Guénon translates it as "link."[10]

Along with Schwaller, the original members of The Watchers included Jeanne Germain, better known by her mystical name, "Isha," under which she wrote books on ancient Egypt, the best known of which is *Her-Bak*. Although they were together for many years before this, Isha would marry Schwaller in 1927, and it was she in fact who turned his attention toward pharaonic Egypt. Another member was Carlos Larronde, the journalist, poet, and founder of the Théatre Idéaliste, a close friend of O. V. de Lubicz Milosz. Other members included Gaston Revel, the founder and editor of the journal *Le Théosophe* (which later became *Le Veilleur*), and the chemist and astrologer Henri Coton-Alvart. The Watchers attracted some illustrious figures who weren't involved in the group's inner circle, but were sympathetic to its aims: the scientist Camille Flammarion, the novelist Pierre Benoit, the poets Paul Fort and Henri de Regnier, and the painter Fernand Leger.[11] Two other early members of particular interest to us are O. V. de Lubicz Milosz and Vivian Postel du Mas.[12]

The Hermetic Diplomat

Of Lithuanian descent, Oscar Vladislas de Lubicz Milosz wrote in French and lived much of his life in France, where he is embraced as a national poet. Starting out as a typical "decadent" of the *fin-de-siècle*, he survived a suicide attempt and disciplined himself into becoming a modern hermetic philosopher in the tradition of Louis-Claude de Saint-Martin and Swedenborg.[13] The author of evocative hermetic works like *Ars Magna* and *The Arcana*, Milosz was also an important statesman. From the end of World War I to the late 1930s, he served as a diplomat, working to secure the interests of his ancestral nationality, Lithuania; after World War I, when the European chessboard was being restructured, Milosz had to choose between being Polish or Lithuanian. But Milosz's true home was Europe in its widest sense. His father was a Polish-Lithuanian nobleman, his mother Jewish, and his paternal grandmother Italian, an ethnic blend that led to his being called "a fully realized Occidental, a true son and heir of the West."[14] Milosz's command of several languages served his poetic work as a translator and also his diplomatic duties. He was a member of the Lithuanian delegation to the Peace Conference of 1919 and was the Lithuanian representative to the French government. Between 1920 and 1925, as the chargé d'affaires, he organized the legations of Lithuania in Paris and Brussels. In Geneva he was the Lithuanian delegate to the League of Nations. For his service on behalf of Lithuanian and French relations, in 1931 Milosz was, like Saint-Yves d'Alveydre, made a chevalier of the Légion d'honneur. He was also, incidentally, the uncle of the Polish writer and anti-communist Czeslaw Milosz, winner of the Nobel Prize in Literature in 1980, himself a great reader of Swedenborg.

Milosz de Lubicz's diplomatic duties required him to write on a number of political, economic, and social issues, but he also made contributions to occult politics. In 1918, in *Le Revue Baltique* (The Baltic Review), a journal associated with the Watchers, Milosz spoke of Lithuania and Latvia as providing "the final vestiges of a high spiritual culture in the midst of a world ruled by the absurd cult of domination and of matter."[15] For Milosz, the Baltic states were "the mothers of this

Indo-European race, the spiritual center of the modern Aryan world."[16] His advocacy of the Baltic states was linked to his belief in the appearance of new values, which must arise to counteract the loss of "spirit." These values will cluster around the idea of hierarchy, which will now "be applied for the first time to the interior order of a nation, of a continent—of a world."[17] Milosz, who in his later years took on something of a messianic character (in a letter to a friend, he announced that "*I have not been sent for everybody*, but for the salvation of a few only")[18] and who in 1938 prophesied a coming "universal conflagration,"[19] believed that "after an absence of more than twenty centuries," spirit was "redescending into matter."[20] While awaiting this return, "the very foundations of Aryan civilization are shaken." "The white race," he felt, had "lost all direction," and the Baltic states would be called upon to "play a very great role . . . in the general evolution of the Indo-European race." He even believed that "independent Lithuania," a land of "ancient culture, ardent labor and wise organization,"[21] could serve as a model for the young Soviet Republic. This last suggestion may have cost Milosz some effort; he was made penniless by the Bolshevik Revolution when his savings, in Tsarist government bonds, lost their value overnight.

If Milosz's remarks about Aryan civilization and the white race prompt a grimace, we should remember that, prior to the Nazis, "Aryan" was a term used in different contexts by people who would have nothing but contempt for Nazi ideals; although it could be used in a racist, chauvinist way, it wasn't always. Not everyone who used the term "Aryan" was a Nazi, although everyone who was a Nazi used it, just as the swastika appeared as a universal symbol well before its Nazi appropriation and dates as far back as the Neolithic period. (Both, to be sure, are now unrecoverable, permanently tainted by the Nazi horror.) We should also remember that Milosz was half Jewish; and, given a Jewish mother, by the Nazi racial laws that made him Jewish, period. (His death in March 1939 saved him from the fate of other Jews in Vichy France.) Milosz had nothing but respect for the Jews, whose thought, he believed, formed "the apex of a spiritual pyramid of which Hindu, Egyptian, Aramean, Greek and Neo-Platonic philosophies form the base and the four sides," and whose "biblical poetry" he spoke of as proclaiming an "heroic affirmation." These remarks were made in a

Jewish review, in an article in which Milosz refers to himself as Jewish, speaking of "*our* contemporary spirit" and "*our* body, deprived forever . . . of the support of an absolute place" [my italics]. He also believed that it was "easier" for Jews to "rediscover the path of the immutable," although once a Jew "steps aside from the way of Knowledge—which is also that of sacrifice—he is trapped by matter."[22]

Among his many languages, Milosz taught himself Hebrew, and for years a Hebrew Bible was his bedside reading. One of his last books argued that the Jews originated from the Iberian Peninsula, the site, he claimed, of the original Garden of Eden, a thesis many considered evidence of his gentle eccentricity. There's no evidence that Milosz was ever anti-Semitic, although, like many other Jews, he wasn't shy of criticizing Jews if they behaved in a way he found reprehensible. He was also, like others at the time, concerned about "the Jewish question." Although he later returned to Catholicism and, like Éliphas Lévi and the author of *Meditations on the Tarot*, maintained that Catholic dogma contained the greatest esoteric truths, he also spoke well of the "good Jew, the good Muslim, the good Buddhist." Yet he did have some reservations about what he saw as the "pride" of René Guénon and others of the Traditionalist school.[23]

A MAN OF THE RIGHT

I've focused on the Jewish element in Milosz because it contrasts sharply with the views of his "brother in arms," Schwaller. One of the disturbing things André VandenBroeck discovered about Schwaller was that he was "a typical bourgeois French gentleman," which meant he was a "man of the right."[24] It also meant he was anti-Semitic. This was difficult for VandenBroeck to assimilate, given that he came from a Jewish background and was himself a "man of the left." Throughout his book, as the novelist Saul Bellow remarks, a tension runs between "the high spiritual level of de Lubicz's teachings" and "the residue of de Lubicz's reactionary convictions."[25] Although Bellow, who had close contact with another "man of the right," Mircea Eliade, recognizes that Schwaller is "a source of revolutionary insights," he also recognizes his connection to "the political horrors of the Twentieth Century."[26] VandenBroeck recognized this, too, and it led to his separation from his teacher.

VandenBroeck came of age during those political horrors, and, as many felt in the 1930s and '40s, he saw that "only the left resisted fascism . . . and such resistance was a priority in my time." Yet VandenBroeck's leftism didn't prevent him from appreciating the connection between some forms of esotericism and right-wing politics. With Guénon and Schwaller, VandenBroeck saw that "the true right is monarchistic and theocratic; it desires authority, preferably divine, it believes in elites." Seeing the value in this idea, VandenBroeck yet adds the caveat: "This standpoint could have much in its favor, were it not for a propensity for demagogism, with fascism as its latest flowering."[27] One form in which this "spiritual fascism" emerged was de Lubicz's ideas on evolution—or rather its opposite, devolution, his version of the Traditionalist view that it's all been downhill since Adam. Drawing on his Theosophical roots, Schwaller told his student of "the devolution of mankind in general . . . from giants who once walked the earth to a near-animal state being rapidly approached in the modern world and vowed to cataclysmic annihilation, while an evolving elite gathers all of human experience for a resurrection in spirituality," a cycle he believed had happened many times in the past.[28] Schwaller's ideas on elites had a sexual dimension, too. According to him, women have an "an inescapably congenital deficiency,"[29] making abstract thought and philosophy a "constitutional impossibility" for them.[30] VandenBroeck's account of Lucy Lamy, de Lubicz's stepdaughter, who worked as his "scribe" and whom he had "formed" for this "function" since she was a child, depicts a constrained, stunted life.[31]

VandenBroeck's interest in his teacher was in "abstract realms, intellectual, philosophical and logical," so he could ignore these unappetizing character traits while assimilating Schwaller's insights into alchemy, cognition, and what he called Egyptian "symbolique." He could even agree with de Lubicz's own version of Guénon's elite spiritual knowledge, of which the masses would be unaware.[32] This included music, and de Lubicz, who was notoriously tin-eared (tellingly, the only music he appreciated was Wagner's *Ring*), shared with

Julius Evola and Theodor Adorno a contempt for contemporary music, its "secularization" and the "disintegration of tonality" being merely another example of "the need for 'temple knowledge' accessible only to an elite."[33] Like Guénon, Schwaller had a touch of paranoia, speaking darkly of "people who would like to know what I do," of governments interested in his work, and of pages mysteriously disappearing from his books.[34] But VandenBroeck's doubts about his teacher began when he learned of the Watchers and of Schwaller's contributions to *Le Veilleur*. One contribution in particular struck an uneasy note, an article written by "Aor" for inclusion in the first issue, which served as a kind of proclamation of the group's "general statement of policy." The article was entitled *Lettre aux Juifs*, "Letter to the Jews."

LETTERS AND RIDING BOOTS

VandenBroeck had witnessed Schwaller's anti-Semitism more recently and had chalked it up to his "xenophobia coupled with religious intolerance," a sadly common trait among the French middle class.[35] What disconcerted VandenBroeck was that of all the esoteric, intellectual, or philosophical issues "Aor" could devote himself to in this announcement of his elite's aims, he chose to address an issue of race. Other "letters" addressed artists, socialists, philosophers, occultists—Isha even contributed one on femininity. But the *chef des Veilleurs* chose to write about the Jews. This "highly visible gesture in the Paris of 1919" troubled VandenBroeck. "In a new publication representing his ideas, he lets others address philosophers and artists, and he chooses to address . . . the Jews?" And what did "Aor" have to say to them? "Go build your country and construct a square tower in Zion."[36]

The idea that European Jews should repatriate to a "homeland" in the land of Israel had been around since the Jewish Austrian journalist Theodor Herzl started the Zionist movement in the late nineteenth century. But VandenBroeck couldn't ignore Aor's message. His letter was "an invitation" for French Jews to "leave France which was not really their country,"[37] a sentiment applied to African-Americans in the U.S. in the 1960s, with racist calls to "go back where they came from." "Once again," VandenBroeck wrote, "I had encountered the pernicious weed that grows wild at the extreme political right, and once again I had encountered it in the name of spirituality."

What equally troubled VandenBroeck was that throughout his subsequent career Schwaller had not only kept quiet about the Watchers and his own undeniable anti-Semitism—he led a remarkably secretive life and VandenBroeck only learned about the Watchers after his time with Schwaller—but he had never repudiated his early views. He had, it's true, refined his idea of the elite. In *Nature Word*, first published in 1963, Schwaller writes that "to be of the Elite is to want to give and to be able to give . . . to draw on the inexhaustible source and give this food to those who are hungry and thirsty in the form which is suited to them."[38] This has a philanthropic ring, but it still sees the elite in some position of privilege, distributing esoteric handouts. Schwaller never recanted his political beliefs, unlike C. G. Jung, who acknowledged that he had made mistakes in the early days of National Socialism, when he felt something good might come of it, an opinion shared by many who, like Jung, were soon appalled at the Nazis' barbarity. In a conversation with Rabbi Leo Baeck, a friend who had broken with Jung because of his remarks and who had spent time in the Theresienstadt concentration camp, Jung admitted that he had "slipped up." The two men were reconciled, and on that basis the cabala scholar and Zionist Gershom Scholem accepted an invitation to participate in the Eranos conferences, of which Jung was the unofficial focus.[39] Schwaller, by contrast, never made a public apology, and in this he is like the philosopher Martin Heidegger, who likewise never admitted to "slipping up."

But perhaps even more than Schwaller's ideas about the "Jewish question," what troubled VandenBroeck was Schwaller's admission that the Watchers' concern about cultural decline included items of dress. After discussing the inanities of the fashion industry, offhandedly Schwaller offered the information that "In Paris after the First World War, I had a group of people I worked with, and in protest against this fashion nonsense, all the men wore the same attire: boots, riding pants, and a dark shirt. *Ce qui plus tard est devenu l'uniforme des SA*" ("This later became the uniform of the SA").[40]

The SA, or *Sturmabteilung* (Storm Troopers), were the paramilitary thugs who brought Hitler to power, and who were later wiped out by Hitler and the SS, or *Schutzstaffel* (Shield Squadron) in 1934 in the "Night of the Long Knives." Needless to say, both the Sturmabteilung and the Schutzstaffel are prime examples of the "nihilistic counterfeit of chivalry" spoken of by William Pfaff.

VandenBroeck was struck by how casually Schwaller made the link between the clothes he designed and "those that would costume barbarity."[41] The abstract language neutralized the causal relation between his animus toward fashion and the uniform that would symbolize Nazi inhumanity, and VandenBroeck would have left the story as a macabre synchronicity were it not for an ominous possibility that later occurred to him.

VIVIAN POSTEL DU MAS AND RUDOLF HESS

A publisher of pornographic literature seems an odd conduit for esoteric transmission, but as head of the Olympia Press, Maurice Girodias was just that, although it must be said that he also published works by Henry Miller, Samuel Beckett, and Vladimir Nabokov. Oddly, Girodias knew both VandenBroeck and Schwaller, and while visiting Vanden-Broeck years after he had ended his apprenticeship with Schwaller, Girodias left behind a book he was reading. Entitled *La Synarchie*, it talked about Vivian Postel du Mas, mentioned earlier as one of the founding members of Les Veilleurs, although by some accounts he was associated with the group for only a short time.[42] In the 1930s, Vivian du Mas was an advocate of Saint-Yves' synarchy, writing a *Schéma de l'archetype social* (Outline of Archetypal Society), a "systematic analysis of all the levels of the visible and invisible universe," and *Le Pacte Synarchique* (The Synarchic Pact), a political tract based on the "four orders that correspond to the Hindu caste system," which argues that its "division of the people into orders is natural and conforms with tradition " and is a necessary "spiritual classification of individuals."[43] VandenBroeck remarks that he had heard about "the secret society that is said to have been a gray eminence behind the

French governments of the 1930s and early 1940s, and that is believed in some quarters to wield power in France even to this day," and he adds that du Mas' synarchic pact "made its way in the corridors of the Third Republic and during the Occupation."[44] Paging through *La Synarchie*, he came across a reference to the Watchers. Among other things, it mentioned du Mas in association with another name linked to Schwaller's elite, Rudolf Hess, the occult-oriented future Deputy Führer of Germany. One of the few high-ranking Nazis with a genuine interest in the occult, Hess was a follower of Rudolf Steiner (ironically, an early target of the Nazis), ate "biodynamic" foods, practiced alternative health, and was a passionate astrologer.

Later, reading Girodias' autobiography,[45] VandenBroeck discovered his encounter with du Mas' synarchy group at a Krishnamurti lecture in Paris in the '30s. Remarking on their riding boots, Girodias asked, "Who are they, God's own Storm Troopers?" Girodias was also at the founding of the Synarchist Order, where du Mas lectured on the ideas of his synarchic pact, in which a modern version of the caste system is based on the "psychological differences between four very distinct categories of humans" and involves "orders" that have their own "hierarchy and government."

Girodias' account, the reference to Hess, and Schwaller's casual remark about the Watchers' fashion choice led VandenBroeck to an unsettling thought. "Could it be that I had been spending those months listening to a voice that once inspired Rudolf Hess?"[46] Could, that is, Schwaller's choice of attire have become the uniform of the SA and later the SS—as well as other "chivalrous" groups—through some direct influence on one of the few Nazi figures who had a known interest in esotericism? We know the swastika was an important symbol for Schwaller, as it was for theosophy in general, well before it became associated with Hitler. (It was also important for Nicholas Roerich.) In his first book, *Les Nombres* (The Numbers), published in 1916—just a year before the Watchers started watching—Schwaller devoted much attention to it. Hess' association with the Watchers remains speculative, but as some have argued, it's possible that Hess borrowed ideas from Schwaller and took them back to Germany, where he could have introduced them to another elite group, the infamous Thule Society.

As Joscelyn Godwin points out, there's even a phonetic link between "Thule" (pronounced "too-la") and the name of the Watchers' inner circle, "Tala."[47] Among other concerns, the members of the Thule Society were, like Schwaller, deeply interested in the "Jewish question."

HYPERBOREA HO!

By now the literature on Nazi occultism constitutes a huge subgenre, populated mostly by works of dubious scholarship or esoteric fantasy. The most dependable studies are those of Nicholas Goodrick-Clarke;[48] I can also recommend a short but very impressive work that effectively undermines most of the "occult Nazis" myth, *Unknown Sources: National Socialism and the Occult* by Hans Thomas Hakl.[49] The efforts of these and other reliable historians compete with more sensational works like J. H. Brennan's *Occult Reich* and Trevor Ravenscroft's classic *Spear of Destiny*. While offering exciting reading, these and similar accounts are more often works of imagination than anything else and, unfortunately, have created an association between occultism and fascism that's difficult to shake. To be sure, in some instances the association is justified, and indeed, the link between Nazism and the occult started well before Ravenscroft and Brennan.[50] Most accounts start with the publication in France in 1960 of Louis Pauwels and Jacques Bergier's best-selling *The Morning of the Magicians*, but earlier books suggested a link between Hitler and the occult. In 1939, Dion Fortune, a member of a Golden Dawn off-shoot and founder of the Society of Inner Light, published *The Magical Battle of Britain*, a work designed magically to impede the Nazi advance across Europe, which she linked to black magic. In 1940, the British Theosophist Lewis Spence published *The Occult Causes of the Present War*, arguing that Hitler's secret aim was to plunge Europe back into paganism. And in 1941, Rom Landau, author of the best-selling *God is My Adventure*, which discussed his meetings with Gurdjieff, Ouspensky, Krishnamurti, and other spiritual figures, published *We Have Seen Evil: A Background to the War*, an account of his impressions of Hitler and Mussolini. More straightforward academic works, like Peter

Viereck's *Metapolitics: The Roots of the Nazi Mind* (1940; reprinted 1961), and, later, George L. Mosse's *The Crisis of German Ideology* (1964), saw Nazism as a particularly virulent expression of German Romanticism, of which the occult was an important part, an association that's been repeated wholesale, the reservations of other historians notwithstanding.[51] Hans Thomas Hakl traces the roots of occult Nazism to a French esoteric magazine, *Le Chariot*, which in 1934 first spoke of Hitler as an agent of "invisible spiritual forces."[52] Understandably, the French, who felt the heel of Nazi domination in the 1940s, have shown the most interest in uncovering the dark powers behind Hitler's regime. Louis Pauwels himself, one of the architects of occult Nazism, remarked that in the early days of the "phoney war" of 1939, he heard weird anti-Nazi propaganda that depicted Hitler as a demonical character.[53]

But while the reality of Hitler's and Nazism's occult roots is less sensational than many books suggest, the milieu in which they arose certainly had an occult air. Like Ascona and Monte Verità, the Munich that saw the rise of National Socialism was rife with the "alternative" thought of the time; there was even a Munich-Ascona circuit, much like the New York–San Francisco "beat trail" of the early 1960s. Proto-hippies and New Agers stressed by city life could retreat to the Mountain of Truth to chill out and get "back to nature." Characteristic of the time were the Wandervogel, bands of idealistic German youth who wore long hair, sandals, played guitar, and spent their time worshiping the sun and wandering the countryside, in a way strikingly reminiscent of the '60s flower children.

Yet as Martin Green in his history of Monte Verità writes, in the darkening political twilight "the Asconian idea proved to be . . . a precursor of Nazism."[54] Sadly, the peaceful Wandervogel would become the Hitler Youth. Especially after World War I and its ignominious defeat, Germany suffered an identity crisis that James Webb argues was a potent motivation for a "flight from reason." As the historian David Clay Large remarks, many in Munich at that time felt "a repugnance for industrial modernity, liberal rationalism, parliamentary democracy and orthodox Christianity" and looked instead toward mysticism and the occult for some means of renewal.[55] During the war, an "unprecedented orgy of destruction had been carried out in the name of 'progress and civilization.'"[56] Many at the time rejected both and sought instead for some meaning in the past.

One group who had been arguing against "civilization" well before World War I was the Cosmic Circle, whose most famous member was the *völkisch* philosopher Ludwig Klages, who held court in the bohemian suburb of Schwabing, Munich's version of Haight-Ashbury and Greenwich Village.[57] Deeply influenced by the nineteenth-century cultural theorist Johann Jacob Bachofen, whose *Das Mutterrecht* (The Matriarchy) argued that prehistoric civilization had been matriarchal, Klages rejected "masculine" logic and rationality and affirmed instead that "the oldest wisdom of humanity was the possession and privilege of women."[58] For Klages, "only men in touch with their inner woman were capable of true creativity."[59] In the ancient past he saw "a sunken world in which many of the conditions governing modern life were not yet present." Not man, "but woman, governed here; not calculating mind, but the expanding soul, filled with myth and symbolic powers."[60]

Much of Klages' thought would be welcome among New Agers, who share both his mystical feminism and belief in a primordial matriarchy—popularized by writers like Riane Eisler—and his rejection of modern civilization. Yet Klages' celebration of myth, symbol, and the past contributed to a milieu that supported the prehistoric fantasies of many Aryan-minded anti-Semites, who rejected the intellect in favor of the "expanding soul," especially as their visions of a "pure" Aryan homeland rarely stood up to rational scrutiny. Klages himself had Aryan visions and, according to the German-Jewish neo-Marxist philosopher Walter Benjamin, "made common cause with Fascism."[61]

The Thule Society, although not an occult organization, was founded by an individual who was certainly an occultist. "Thule" is the name of a mythical city of the north, a kind of polar Shambhala or Agartha. Linked to a prehistoric civilization called "Hyperborea" (Beyond the North Wind), which the historian Richard Rudgley calls the "lost continent of the European imagination,"[62] it was a land of mild climate believed by the ancient Greeks to lie in the northernmost part of the globe. In his *Pythian Odes*, the Greek poet Pindar wrote:

"Neither by ship nor on foot could you find the marvellous road to the meeting-place of the Hyperboreans." In 1897, while in prison for anti-British activities, the militant Hindu nationalist leader Bal Gangadhar Tilak wrote *The Arctic Home in the Vedas*, which argues that the birth-place of the Aryan race was not central Asia but the far north.[63] This was an idea that many German Aryanists would happily adopt.

ULTIMA THULE

Pindar may have had doubts about discovering Hyperborea, but some occultists in early twentieth-century Germany were less modest. One was Rudolf Sebottendorf, who founded the Thule Society in Munich in 1918. Sebottendorf, who's been associated with the Traditionalists, had an eccentric background.[64] A Freemason, Sufi, alchemist, Theosophist, and astrologer, Sebottendorf, whose real name was Adam Glauer (he was also known as Erwin Torre), was born in Germany but left to live in Egypt and then Turkey. He returned to Germany in the early 1900s, where he married but was soon divorced; he was also arrested for forgery. In 1911 he returned to Turkey, where he acquired Turk-ish citizenship, converted to Islam, and was adopted by the German expatriate Baron Heinrich von Sebottendorf, hence the name.

After fighting on the Turkish side in the First Balkan War, Sebottendorf returned to Germany again. In Munich in 1916, he unsuccessfully sought disciples for his system of meditation based on numerology. That year he came into contact with the Germanenor-den, a secret quasi-Masonic lodge of Aryan anti-Semites (something like the Ku Klux Klan), and was made a local group leader. He soon after formed the Thulegesellschaft (Thule Society), a "study group for German antiquity" that became an "organization of conspiring right-wing radicals with rigorous anti-Marxist, anti-liberal, anti-democratic and anti-Semitic opinions."[65] In effect, the Thule Society was a "front" for the Germanenorden. Like many at the time, Sebottendorf believed in the Jewish-Masonic conspiracy, and he advocated a mysticism based on the "purity" of German blood and a kind of *jihad* against Jews, ideas that would become central to Hitler's thinking. A clear link between the Nazis and the Thule Society was the swastika; the Thule Society's emblem was a swastika emblazoned with a dagger.

Nicholas Goodrick-Clarke argues that the Thule Society was influenced by the ideas of the rabid anti-Semitic Austrian occultist Guido von List. Devoted to the rebirth of German paganism and the mystic power of the runes, like Sebottendorf, List fantasized about racial purity. His admirer and follower, the former Cistercian monk Jörg Lanz von Liebenfels, coined the term "Ariosophy," meaning "the wisdom of the Aryans," to characterize List's teachings. In Vienna, Liebenfels published a racist journal, *Ostara*, named after the German pagan goddess of spring; one of its regular readers was a third-rate painter named Adolf Hitler. As the name implies, Ariosophy borrowed some of its themes from Theosophy, which, like it, regarded the Judeo-Christian tradition as inferior to that of Aryan India. Theosophy, too, spoke of "root" and "sub" races, ideas that in the hands of people like List and Liebenfels were put to odious use.

Under Sebottendorf the Thule Society prospered, attracting well-heeled pillars of society; industrialists, brewers, judges, doctors, police officials, and university professors were among its members. This wasn't unusual. As the historian George L. Mosse points out, "the Nazis found their greatest support among respectable, educated people," their ideas being "eminently respectable . . . after the First World War."[66] It also drew well-known figures like the biologist Ernst Haeckel, a Darwinian whose ideas would have an enormous influence on Rudolf Steiner and C. G. Jung.[67] Haeckel was an advocate of what we would call social Darwinism, a "survival of the fittest" approach to society that would become popular with the Nazis. In the late nineteenth and early twentieth centuries, Haeckel was famous across Europe; his books popularizing Darwinian evolution were bestsellers in a way that Richard Dawkins' are today. He even proposed a new religion, Monism, based on his evolutionary ideas. Another interested in the society was Alfred Rosenberg, author of *The Myth of the Twentieth Century*, which would eventually rival *Mein Kampf* as a Nazi best-seller; Rosenberg would later become the Nazi's central ideologue. Also becoming involved was Anton Drexler, who in 1919 founded the German Workers' Party, an anti-Semitic and anti-Marxist political group that accepted the myth that Germany had lost World War I because it had been "stabbed in the back" by politicians and socialists. His cofounder, Dietrich Eckart, was an anti-Semitic journalist, poet, and occultist influenced by the ideas of List and Liebenfels.

Although Hitler never joined the Thule Society, he did become a member of Drexler's German Workers' Party. The rest, unfortunately, was history. Soon after he joined, Hitler came under Eckart's wing, and if anyone is responsible for creating the monster Adolf Hitler, it was Eckart. Thought to be the dark muse behind National Socialism—the monstrous *egregore* that grew out of Drexler's German Workers' Party—Eckart introduced Hitler to Alfred Rosenberg and took part in the failed Beer Hall Putsch of 1923. He died the same year. By that time the Thule Society was no more, Sebottendorf having left for Turkey after several high-ranking Thuleans were murdered by the Bavarian Soviets in retaliation for the killings of their own members. In 1933, Sebottendorf returned to Germany and claimed credit for Hitler's rise in a book entitled *Before Hitler Came*. Understandably, Hitler didn't care for the book and had him arrested, but Sebottendorf somehow escaped and returned to Istanbul, where he is believed to have drowned himself in the Bosphorus in 1945.

THE JUNG CASE

Although Hitler apparently had little interest in the occult—as Mark Sedgwick writes, "Hitler had no sympathy for occultism of any variety,"[68]—he had close contact with people who did, and the Nazi movement, while not the product of "black brotherhoods" or diabolical "unknown superiors," was certainly amenable to some occult influences. Himmler's SS infamously incorporated runic, pagan, and Grail elements and was deeply influenced by the ideas of the occultist Karl Maria Wiligut.[69] One SS officer, Otto Rahn, wrote a best-selling book, *Crusade against the Grail*, associating the Cathars with the Grail legend. Hermann Wirth, author of the monumental *The Rise of Mankind*, used meditation to view the past and argued, like Bal Gangadhar Tilak, that the Aryan race began in the frozen north. In 1935 Wirth was a cofounder of the notorious Ahnenerbe, the Nazi "research unit" devoted to uncovering Germany's ancestral Aryan heritage, whose efforts included sending the SS explorer Ernst Schäfer to the Himalayas to measure Tibetan skulls. And while Hitler himself may have rejected occultism, he was certainly aware of "the power of myth," a phrase familiar to viewers of the journalist Bill Moyers' fantastically successful series of interviews with the mythologist Joseph Campbell.

The electrifying power of the swastika; Albert Speer's dazzling lighting effects at the Nuremberg rallies; Hitler's "demonic" oratory and his own deification as the Führer; the romantic vision of a bucolic Germany rooted in "blood and soil," as opposed to an urban, mechanical modernity—all were part of the myth of National Socialism that Hitler and his followers sold to an interested public. A myth was instrumental in Hitler's success, the dark lie voiced in *The Protocols of the Elders of Zion*. Whether the *Protocols* were "true" or not probably never occurred to Hitler; what was important was that they agreed with his own views and that, like himself, many people *believed* they were true. (The people who believed in the *Protocols* weren't necessarily unintelligent; one of their most fervent supporters was Henry Ford, father of the assembly line and mass production. Like many influential people, faced with evidence that the *Protocols* were forged, Ford refused to believe it.) Like the French syndicalist George Sorrel and the political philosopher Leo Strauss, Hitler knew that in politics, myth is often more important than the "truth," a difficult commodity to pin down at any time. Reason and rationality are boring and demand effort. Myth bypasses the inhibitions of the critical mind and reaches down to the vital forces below. This is what makes it exciting and enlivening. It is also what makes it dangerous. In saying this I am not arguing "against" myth; I am merely pointing out that it entails something more than just "following your bliss."

Yet many at the time were willing to risk the dangers of myth and embrace it over reason. One was the Swiss psychologist C. G. Jung, perhaps more than anyone else the single most important figure in the reawakening of spiritual thought in modern times. Although for much of his career Jung obscured his interest in the occult, in his later years his writings on Gnosticism, alchemy, the paranormal, spiritualism, and even flying saucers brought these otherwise marginal areas into the field of respectable research. Predictably, Jung's occult inclinations led to criticisms of irrationalism. Like Ludwig Klages, Jung has been seen by many on the left as a dangerous exponent of *völkisch* ideas. The neo-Marxist philosopher Ernst Bloch, himself no stranger to Rosicrucianesque utopias, once described Jung as a "fascistically frothing psychoanalyst."[70] Other neo-Marxist philosophers, like Theodor Adorno, likewise branded Jung a fascist. The tag was perhaps first made seriously by the German-Jewish cultural philosopher Walter Benjamin, who, unlike Adorno, had some interest in occult ideas, specifically the cabala and graphology, a discipline he shared, ironically, with the "fascist" Klages. (Benjamin was also a close friend of the cabalist scholar Gershom Scholem, who, as mentioned, was an associate of Jung at the Eranos lectures.) Adorno, Bloch, and others saw Jung's psychology as a simple celebration of the unconscious, a rejection of the rational, critical mind in the same vein as the work of the more straightforward irrationalist Klages, whose ideas about "soul" in opposition to "spirit," they argue, helped prime the German psyche for Hitler. The fact that Jung, like many others, at first believed that the creative potential of Germany might find fruitful expression through Hitler couldn't have helped. According to Jung's psychology, the "shadow" side of the psyche, though associated with "evil," can often be the source of "good," of new life and transformation, and Jung reportedly spoke of the Nazis as "a chaotic precondition for the birth of a new world,"[71] a nod to Nietzsche's remark that "one must have chaos within oneself to give birth to a dancing star." This, in a way, exemplifies the dangers of "holy sinning" and reminds us that even great men can be blinded by their ideas.

More recently, in his controversial work *The Jung Cult*, Richard Noll makes similar charges against Jung, arguing that in his early career the heir apparent to the throne of Freud immersed himself in the Aryan occult milieu of Munich and Ascona, as a devotee of *völkisch* beliefs who envisioned himself a kind of national savior. Other works suggest that in his later career Jung was, while not a full-fledged party member, at least a kind of Nazi "fellow traveler," hedging his bets before finally coming down on the winning side.[72] Jung's supporters reject this idea as well as the belief that, in the words of the novelist Thomas Mann, Jung was "always a half-Nazi."[73] Jung himself flatly denied that he was ever a Nazi sympathizer or anti-Semitic.

The debate continues.[74] What comes across in accounts of Jung's involvement with the Nazis is that, like anyone else, the great man was capable of damaging mistakes and misjudgments, a charge made against Jung by one of his closest collaborators, the Jewish psychoanalyst Jolande Jacobi.[75] Jung's misjudgments included commenting on the differences between the German and Jewish psyches at a time when such remarks, no matter how "objective" or "scientific," would be used for odious purposes by the Nazi racial hacks. Pronouncements on the "old" Jewish psyche and the "youthful" German one were bound to be misread in the dark days of the 1930s, notwithstanding that Jung made these comments in the context of others about the "Western" and "Eastern" psyches and wasn't singling the Jews out for criticism. Likewise, Jung's remark that the Jews seem "never to have created a cultural form of their own" but require a "host nation" would have been read in 1934 (when it was made) in one way only: that the Jew was a parasite, feeding off its Aryan host. No matter that Jewish philosophers like Otto Weininger and Ludwig Wittgenstein made similar remarks (and clearly, that they did doesn't make it true).[76]

Jung can also be criticized for accepting the presidency of the General Society for Psychotherapy and editorship of its journal, the *Zentralblatt für Psychotherapie*—both based in Germany—at a time when they were moving inexorably toward being *gleichgeschaltet*, "conformed," to Nazi ideologies. Jung argued that he accepted the presidency in order to prevent the society from becoming totally Nazified and that he even took steps to help its Jewish members, redrafting its statutes to make it formally international and creating a new category of membership, thus allowing Jews excluded from German membership to belong as individuals. During Jung's editorship of the *Zentralblatt*, Dr. M. H. Göring—a cousin of the Nazi Reichmarshal Hermann Göring—who had been made president of the German Section of the Society, inserted a pro-Nazi statement of principles in an issue in 1933, recommending *Mein Kampf* as a basic text for all psychotherapists and urging all members to declare their loyalty to National Socialism. Jung, who lived in Zurich and had little "hands on" control of the journal, was outraged at the statement and claimed it was included without his knowledge.

Jung eventually gave up his presidency and editorship, but that he initially stayed on has been taken as evidence that he didn't want to become an enemy of the Third Reich too early in the game. In his defense it can be said that Jung didn't want to hand over an important intellectual journal to complete Nazi rule, and along with helping Jewish colleagues and other Jews—and having important Jewish followers, like Erich Neumann and Gerhard Adler—in 1936 Jung did finally condemn Hitler as a "raving berserker," a man "possessed" who had set Germany on its "course toward perdition."[77] After this, Jung naturally became a target; his books were suppressed and destroyed and his name put on the Nazi blacklist.[78] As Deirdre Bair makes clear in her recent biography of Jung, U.S. military intelligence checked reports of Jung's Nazi sympathies, found they were unsubstantiated, and conscripted Jung to help in their plans to defeat Hitler. Along with other efforts in the Allied cause, Jung worked with the Office of Strategic Services, making psychological assessments of Nazi leaders, under the code name "Agent 488." Jung's influence reached to the upper echelons of the Allied hierarchy when, toward the close of the war, General Dwight D. Eisenhower turned to Jung's work for insight on how best to convince German civilians that defeat was inevitable.[79] Jung was even briefly involved in a German plot to overthrow Hitler, and his essay "Wotan," in which he argues that the rise of National Socialism was evidence that Germany, which he called a "land of spiritual catastrophes," had been overwhelmed by the archetype of the ancient Teutonic god, became required reading throughout the British Foreign Office.[80]

But in a sense, Jung's encounter with Nazism is a red herring. Whether he was inclined toward Nazism or not (and I don't think he was), like Schwaller de Lubicz, Jung was in many ways a "man of the right." Like René Guénon, he had little love for the modern world. He built his famous tower, Bollingen, on the shores of Lake Zurich so he could escape from modern banality and immerse himself in older, mythic forms of consciousness. He was notoriously disparaging of modern culture and saw works like James Joyce's *Ulysses* and Picasso's paintings as indications of a psychic deterioration; he was also, like Schwaller, tin eared and had little time for music.[81] There was also an authoritarian streak in Jung that made him partial to dictators like Spain's Francisco Franco, a political sentiment that put him at odds with his fellow Eranos lecturer Jean Gebser, who was on the side of the Republicans and missed being executed by the fascists by a hairsbreadth.[82] With all due respect for his undeniable contribution to the spiritual consciousness of modern times, this marks Jung as one of the "good guys" who said "bad things."

Like Joseph de Maistre and Saint-Yves d'Alveydre, Jung believed that anarchy must be avoided at all costs. Writing in 1936, Jung argued that "the loss of any firm authority is gradually leading to an intellectual, political, and social anarchy, which is repugnant to the soul of European man, accustomed as he is to patriarchal order."[83] He felt that the loss of the authority of the Church was responsible for the rise of totalitarianism and the deification of the state, which he defined as "the agglomeration of the nonentities composing it."[84] Like Ouspensky, Jung believed that the state was "intellectually and ethically far below the level of most of the individuals in it,"[85] yet he felt that modern man was increasingly moving toward some absorption in the mass. One agent of this movement was the welfare state, which Jung saw as a "doubtful blessing" that "robs people of their individual responsibility and turns them into infants and sheep" and produces a collectivist society in which "the capable will simply be exploited by the irresponsible," an argument often made by conservative politicians and right-wing thinkers like the philosopher and novelist Ayn Rand. Yet the welfare state was only one manifestation of the ills of modernity. More disturbing was "the accumulation of urban, industrialized masses—of people torn from the soil, engaged in one-sided employment, and lacking every healthy instinct, even that of self-preservation,"[86] an observation that could easily have been made by the Traditionalist and fascist sympathizer Julius Evola.

Jung argued that these conditions made something like Nazism possible, yet these are the very evils the Nazis opposed when they championed being "rooted in the soil" against what they saw as a rootless, urban, Jewish cosmopolitanism. This doesn't undermine Jung's criticism of the modern condition, which in many ways rings true, but it is another example of the complexities of occult politics. It also shows that a rejection of the modern world needn't result in a dangerous "flight from reason," or an embrace of some putative "tradition," or a plunge into fascism. It can also prompt a rational recognition that unless these troubling realities are addressed, one of these three undesirable possibilities will settle in to fill the gap.

Against these trends, Jung offered his concept of individuation, the psychological process through which, in Nietzsche's phrase, "one becomes what one is," and which Jung saw as Western man's only hope to avoid being absorbed in some homogenous social mass, the "mass man" of modern times. As Noll argues in his challenging work, it's easy to see this as Jung's own call for an elite; by Jung's admission, individuation, while theoretically possible for everyone, is really embraced only by the few, although there is nothing to stop others from doing so, except inclination. The echoes of Guénon and Schwaller are disturbing, yet Jung's individuation, like the psychologist Abraham Maslow's self-actualizing, doesn't call for some primordial tradition or temple knowledge—or even riding boots—but for us to take on the responsibility of realizing our own personality and potential, which Jung called "an act of the greatest courage in the face of life."[87] As such, it suggests a more liberal, tolerant, and creative path than the one offered by authoritarian schools of thought.

Yet those other schools of thought remained, and their reaction to the modern conditions that troubled Jung were very different.

11

ARCHANGELS OF OUR DARKER NATURE

Before I turn to this last chapter's main subjects, I should briefly mention a development in occult politics that I write about at length in my book *Turn Off Your Mind: The Mystic Sixties and the Dark Side of the Age of Aquarius*. The last major occult revival in modern times started in France in 1960, with the publication of the surprise best-seller *The Morning of the Magicians* by Louis Pauwels and Jacques Bergier, and has never really ended. In modified form it's carried on as our own New Age movement, which has been with us now for at least twenty years, taking the "Harmonic Convergence" of 1987 as a handy starting point, although New Age ideas were around before that.

As I mention earlier, in the 1960s, many of the "alternative" ideas that were popular in the early days of Monte Verità, and made the rounds in the cafés of Munich's pre-Nazi Schwabing, came to notice. By the mid-sixties, the most famous people in the world—the Beatles and the Rolling Stones—advocated a grab bag of mystical pursuits: meditation, Eastern wisdom, magic, even Satanism, as the Stones' song "Sympathy for the Devil" suggests. Among the faces included on the cover of the Beatles' ground-breaking album *Sgt. Peppers' Lonely Hearts Club Band* (1967) are C. G. Jung, Aleister Crowley, and Aldous Huxley. Huxley's gentle advocacy of the judicious, controlled use of hallucinogenic drugs to explore consciousness (as argued in *The Doors of Perception*) was soon hijacked by the psychedelic guru Timothy Leary, who notoriously championed a more widespread "democratic" approach that, ironically, led to lysergic acid diethylamide-25, popularly known as LSD, being made illegal. That Leary, a demagogue, saw himself as the leader of a new "psychedelic society" didn't help. A good portion of the calls for "revolution" that echoed through the last years of the decade and carried on briefly into the next were fueled by the mind-altering effects of LSD and, less powerfully, marijuana, although many leftist radicals saw in these drugs the same thing that Marx saw in religion, namely, a means of keeping the populace happy. What made the time exceptional is that ideas about "alternative" ways of living—which emerged in a plethora of communes and alternative societies—along with wide interest in non-Western cultures and a resurgence of mystical and occult thought, were linked by many to expectations about an imminent social reformation, in which Atlantis would rise, the saucers would land, or some other apocalyptic denouement would take place. These millennial expectations were disseminated widely through the machinery of popular culture that by the 1960s was becoming the global communication network it is today.

Another important factor was the establishment of a powerful youth culture, which acted both as a transmitter and a rich consumer market: one had to buy the albums to hear the music calling for a rejection of bourgeois society. But there was also, in James Webb's sense, a genuine preoccupation with a "transcendental scale of values." One example of the blending of political and magical consciousness that characterized the decade was the student revolution in Paris in May 1968, in which "Power to the imagination" and "Take your desires for reality" were among the rallying calls of the graffiti covering the urban battlefield.

Many current staples of modern spirituality first came to wide popular consciousness in that turbulent decade, and listing them here would be superfluous; the interested reader can turn to my book. But although much good undoubtedly emerged from that time, the '60s were not all love and peace. There was a dark side to the Age of Aquarius, the clichéd icon here being Charles Manson, the hippie mastermind responsible for the gruesome Tate-Labianca murders in Los Angeles in 1969, who had an interest in LSD, Hermann Hesse, and his own subterranean city.[1] Curiously, 1969 was also the year of Wood-stock and the first moon landing, showing that, as in previous times, in the '60s the ancient and the modern were fused: Woodstock being an attempt to cast off civilization and, in the singer Joni Mitchell's words, "get back to the garden," while Neil Armstrong's moon walk was the most powerful symbol to date of the triumph of technology.

But Manson, who also wanted to throw off civilization—in his case, in order to start a race war—was only the most visible of the darker blooms to blossom in the summer of love (Manson started to collect his "family" in San Francisco in 1967). Other forms of darkness appeared, too, and some had links to the political consciousness of the time. One example is the attempt by some leaders of the "love generation" to employ the notorious Hell's Angels motorcycle gang as a kind of hippie brown shirt to protect the "heads" from the "straights" at "tribal" gatherings like the Be-In at San Francisco's Golden Gate Park in 1967. For the most part, the violence the Angels enjoyed at this gathering went unreported—it would have been bad publicity for the cause.[2] But this wasn't the case at the scene many argue marked the end of "flower power," the Rolling Stones' disastrous concert at Al-tamont, California, on December 6, 1969 (again that important year), when the Angels, again employed as security, terrorized a small hippie city and murdered at least one individual. Anyone at that concert, or the many who saw the film of it, *Gimme Shelter*, knew that as John Lennon would say almost exactly a year later, "the dream was over."

In a broad and almost farcical sense, another example of '60s occult politics was the attempt by the filmmaker and Aleister Crowley devotee Kenneth Anger to exorcize the Pentagon, which according to the Hopi Indian shaman Rolling Thunder was a powerful symbol of evil—an idea with which, during the Vietnam War, many agreed. But in a less obvious way, leftist radicals like Abbie Hoffman and Jerry Rubin, founders of the Yippie movement, engaged in a form of "street politics" that included more than a pinch of magic. The embrace of irrationalism that characterized much of Hoffman and Rubin's tactics, which James Webb sees as a powerful element in occult politics, is clear in Rubin's mantra of "Do it!" Although now best known as a consumer ploy for Nike, at the time Rubin's battle cry was more in line with Crowley's "Do what thou wilt"—which, if you think about it, is good advertising material, too. "Action is the only reality. Don't rely on words. Rely on doing. Trust your impulses. Act. Act," Rubin tells us, a message many of today's consumers hear daily. This is another version of co-revolutionary Hoffman's declaration in *Revolution for the Hell of It* that "Reality is a subjective experience. It exists in my head. I am the Revolution"—a magical insight if there ever was one. Both pronouncements are linked to the phrase which serves as the title of my book, *Turn Off Your Mind*, which came to me by way of John Lennon, who got it from Timothy Leary, who appropriated it from the *Tibetan Book of the Dead*. For Leary, Rubin, and many others at the time, the rational mind was an obstacle in the way of the "revolution," something to be avoided or gotten rid of. How successful these and other sixties "revolutionaries" were at this campaign and how desirable some of the consequences were, I leave for the interested reader to decide.[3] Other forms of occult politics demand my attention, and it is to these I must turn now.

JULIUS EVOLA AND MIRCEA ELIADE

In this chapter I want to look at two figures who seem miles away from the "magical politics" of the 1960s. Yet, oddly, the Italian Traditionalist and Fascist sympathizer Julius Evola and the Romanian historian of religion Mircea Eliade have links to that mystical decade, too.

I've chosen to end this survey of occult politics with these two for a few reasons. One is that Evola and Eliade knew each other. Indeed, Evola was a kind of Traditionalist mentor for Eliade, although Eliade minimized and obscured his Traditionalist background in his life and work in the United States following World War II. He did so for different reasons, some having to do with politics, some with his career, and some because he had in many ways moved beyond the limits of a strictly Traditionalist outlook. While most readers probably know of Eliade, many may not be that familiar with Evola, although in recent years his cachet as a brilliant, rigorous, and highly readable esoteric theoretician has grown through the many English translations of his hitherto unavailable works, published by Inner Traditions, one of the leading esoteric publishers in the United States. It's precisely the posthumous popularity of a writer who ingratiated himself with the Nazis and argued for the veracity of the *Protocols of the Elders of Zion* that suggests a renewed association between some members of the esoteric community and Far-Right politics. Although Eliade's early participation in—to a debatable degree—his own kind of "spiritual fascism" is the subject of much controversy, it remains a part of his history unknown to most of his readers. While Evola trumpeted his anti-democratic, authoritarian, and fascist views, Eliade arguably incorporated a less blatant version of similar themes into his highly regarded academic work, enough so that it's possible to see Eliade as a kind of "stealth" Traditionalist, although one who in several instances rejected the strict Traditionalist line and took a broader, more inclusive outlook.

I've also chosen these two because their work leads up to relatively recent times. Eliade's writings on shamanism and archaic religions remain widely popular, and in the 1960s, during the years of "flower power," Evola's books were being rediscovered by individuals of a very different temperament, the neo-fascist youth of Italy. (It was precisely the rise of the radical left, associated with the '60s, that prompted Evola's rediscovery.) And while Eliade's academic stature, if not his popular appeal, has in recent years been questioned, Evola's readership has grown steadily. Books intended to be read by disaffected Italian youth, looking for guidance in an unwelcoming modern world, are now regularly stocked in New Age bookshops in the United States and United Kingdom.

But since his death in 1974, Evola's views have appealed to more than readers of esoteric literature. One example is the bombing of a Bologna railway station in 1980 by Italian Far-Right neo-fascists, most likely members of the Nuclei Armati Rivoluzionari, who fled the country for Britain when the police investigation closed in. Eighty-five people were killed, including children, and hundreds were wounded. Many "usual suspects" among the Far Right were questioned, and during the interviews, one name was mentioned by all: Julius Evola, whose work arguably provided the ideological foundation for the bombing. The only reason Evola escaped arrest was because he was dead. As one commentator remarked, "In Italy in the 1970s, it is said, you got into more trouble if the police found Evola's books during a search of your apartment than if they found plastic explosives."[4]

TRADITIONAL FUTURIST

Baron Julius Evola, or to give his full name, Giulio Cesare Andrea Evola, was born on May 19, 1898, to a noble Sicilian family.[5] A bright, self-willed child, Evola early on rebelled against his strict Catholic upbringing, and his resentment against Christianity would remain throughout his life, fueling a haughty disdain for the "weak" and "ignorant" masses. Evola never received an academic degree, nor seems to have engaged in paid employment—like that of Schwaller de Lubicz, Evola's income is a matter of mystery—but his studies in industrial engineering imbued a sense of precision, a cold clarity and logic into his aristocratic and humorless style. Yet ironically, what set Evola on the road to becoming a Traditionalist was his early embrace of the work of the Italian avant-garde Futurist poet Filippo Tommaso Marinetti, whose ideas would find favor with Italy's fascist dictator, Benito Mussolini, a position Evola himself would later try to occupy. Marinetti sang the praises of the modernity Evola would soon come to despise and seems an unlikely mentor for a philosopher whose most well-known work is titled *Revolt against the Modern World*. Yet Marinetti's own fascist sensibilities—a virulent rejection of nature, a celebration of regimen and efficiency, and an embrace of speed and violence as ends in themselves—were in line with Evola's character, and the kind of "aesthetic terrorism" the Futurists engaged in would be mirrored by Evola's followers, although on a tragically mundane level. War, for Marinetti, was an aesthetic affair, and the brutal onomatopoeia of his poetry, mimicking the sound of machine guns ("stings slaps *traak-traak* whips *pic-pac-pum-tumb*") heralded Evola's own fascination with the Kshatriya, the Hindu warrior caste. Evola never lost his warrior romanticism, and he later wrote a book about the German nationalist writer Ernst Jünger, a decorated war hero. Although he saw no action himself, Evola briefly served in the Italian army as an artilleryman in the last days of World War I.

Returning to civilian life, Evola missed the discipline and hierarchy of the military, and a sense of aimlessness oppressed him. He experimented with drugs, but this only led to a preoccupation with suicide. He was saved from this morbid fate by a work of Buddhism, and later wrote a book on Buddhist asceticism, *The Doctrine of Awakening*. Buddha, however, had competition; another avant-garde movement, Dada, had spilled over into Italy from Switzerland. Futurism's bellicose tactics by now seemed vulgar, but Dadaism, founded by the Romanian Tristan Tzara in Zurich in 1916, had an intellectual appeal. Evola threw himself into the movement, reading Dadaist poetry to the atonal music of Arnold Schönberg at the Cabaret Grotte dell'Augusteo, Rome's version of Zurich's infamous Cabaret Voltaire. He even took up painting, and one of his Dadaist works still hangs in Rome's National Gallery of Modern Art.

Evola produced an important essay on abstract art, but as with Futurism, Dada wasn't enough. Years later, Evola seems to have taken an opportunity to reprimand his younger, Dadaist self by defaming his avant-garde inspiration. In 1937 Evola published a version of *The Protocols of the Elders of Zion*, arguing that they had "the value of a spiritual tonic" that couldn't be "ignored or dismissed without seriously undermining the front of those fighting in the name of the spirit, of tradition, or true civilization" and that the Jew had a duty "to destroy every surviving trace of true order and superior civilization." Of the many examples of insidious Jewry he provided, he included Tzara and Schönberg.[6] By this time, Tzara had compounded his offense by becoming a Communist, and Schönberg was in exile from the Nazis in the United States. Evola's ideas about the evils of Jewry were influenced, ironically, by a Jewish philosopher, the brilliant but disturbed Otto Weininger, whose book *Sex and Character* argued that Jews as a race displayed a hatred of things of a "higher" nature: hence Marx's reduction of religion to an "opium of the people." Weininger, who fought feelings of homosexuality throughout his short life (he killed himself at the age of twenty-three),[7] also argued that while men were spiritual beings pursuing the celestial heights, women were dark creatures of the earth, interested only in sex and reproduction. Like Schwaller de Lubicz, Evola held very "traditional" ideas about women, and in his *magnum opus* he devotes a chapter to the virtues of the harem and the Hindu practice of *sati*, when a widow joins her husband in death by being burned alive on his funeral pyre.[8] In fact, Evola's whole esoteric history of the human race—influenced by Guénon, Madame Blavatsky, Bal Gangadhar Tilak, and Bachofen—can be seen as the conflict between what he calls a "solar," "virile," "masculine" spirituality and a "lunar," "passive," "feminine" one. In a nutshell: although the primordial civilization, which was privy to Tradition, was solar and virile and began in polar Hyperborea, it lost its way when it interbred with southern, feminine, "promiscuous" races. As you might expect, things have gone downhill ever since. Although in many ways I share Evola's assessment of the excesses of feminism, it has to be admitted that his unrelentingly "masculine" work is a good candidate for a philosophy based on the clichéd fear of the feminine.

After Dada, Evola turned to philosophy and wrote several books spelling out the metaphysics of the "absolute individual." This boiled down to the doctrine that such an individual enjoys "the ability to be unconditionally whatever he wants," and that, as with the philosopher Schopenhauer, the world is his representation. For the haughty Evola, this was an ontological rationalization of his own disregard for other people, a trait sadly not uncommon among many occultists (the "Great Beast" Aleister Crowley is a good case in point). While Evola's philosophical works have entered obscurity, his ideas about the absolute individual and the unconditional freedom of the self became the basis of the work that would give him lasting notoriety—his essays into the history and practice of esotericism.

INTRODUCTIONS TO MAGIC

Evola became interested in Theosophy, and a correspondence with Sir John Woodroffe—as Arthur Avalon, author of several books on Hindu philosophy—later led to Evola's book on Tantra, *The Yoga of Power*; another book, blending his ideas on Tantra with Weininger's, is his *Metaphysics of Sex*. But Evola's real introduction to the occult, esotericism, and, most significantly, René Guénon came through the occultist Arturo Reghini, the editor of two influential Italian occult journals, *Atanòr* and *Ignis*. According to the historian David Lloyd Thomas, Reghini was a "modern Pythagorean,"[9] and in an interesting article on Evola, the Italian literary critic Elémire Zolla suggests that much of Evola's early work was "borrowed" from Reghini without acknowledgment.[10] (In fact, Evola and Reghini did engage in a brief but vindictive legal battle, involving mutual accusations of libel and plagiarism.)[11] By the mid-1920s, Reghini had introduced Evola to an esoteric society known as the UR Group, who saw magic as "the science of the ego," a sentiment in line with Evola's own. Evola threw himself into the group's activities, studying alchemy, Taoism, Buddhism, and other esoteric and spiritual practices. Linking all of these pursuits was the idea of initiation, the sense that through them Evola was joining an initiatic chain reaching back to a lost, primordial tradition. He had found his milieu and soon became the most creative voice among the anonymous UR members. It was here that his revolt against modernity became clear. In a later version of the group's journal, *La Torre*, renamed after a battle for control between Evola and Reghini, Evola announced his aim. The new journal would be a review of "combat, criticism, affirmation and negation" on the "very plane of Western culture" and would form an "unbreachable bulwark against the general decline of every value in life."[12] What Evola had acquired on the "esoteric plane" was now to be employed on the "existential-political" one.[13] What this meant was occult politics.

TRADITIONAL FASCISM

I should point out that Evola's many writings on a variety of esoteric subjects often warrant the acclaim they've received. Reading Evola can be bracing; his articles from the UR Group collected in *Introduction to Magic*, for instance, exhibit a clarity and rigor that is rare in such material. And while Evola's esotericism and politics are really a "package deal," as with Schwaller de Lubicz, one can glean much from his insights into a variety of occult themes without having to accept his politics. This, in fact, is the argument many Evola supporters make, while nevertheless often applauding the politics for their "political incorrectness." Again, in a time when leftist attitudes are de rigueur and their excesses abound, Evola's right-wing sentiments, like those of the French novelist Michel Houellebecq, can look attractive.[14] Yet their potential to balance out Far-Left overkill shouldn't blind us to their danger.

That danger becomes clear when we recognize Evola's intentions: to use fascism to inaugurate a society based on Tradition. Like many, Evola was impressed by Nietzsche's vision of a coming world nihilism, and he was impressed enough by Oswald Spengler's *Decline of the West* to translate it into Italian. Evola shared Guénon's view about the worthlessness of modern society; with his French guru, Evola agreed that liberalism, egalitarianism, individualism, freethinking, and the rest of modernity's ills were the dry rot bringing down Western civilization. Where he differed from Guénon was in his belief that the West would be saved not by a secret elite working undercover but by bold, forthright individuals—whom he later called *uomini differenziati*, "men who were different"—who would step forth and take command, a "virile" sensibility informing some neo-conservative agendas. For a time he thought Benito Mussolini was one such *uomo differenziato*, and he tried to steer Il Duce in the direction of Tradition. At first the UR Group performed magical rituals aimed at inspiring the Fascist movement with the "virile," "warrior" spirit of ancient Rome, whose military, authoritarian rule embodied Evola's political ideals. More concretely, Evola published a series of articles in *La Torre* celebrating Mussolini's attempt to revive the Roman Empire at the expense of the Ethiopians. Yet Mussolini's fascism wasn't quite fascist enough. Evola sought a "more radical, more intrepid Fascism, a really absolute Fascism, made of pure form, inaccessible to compromise."[15] Mussolini, like Hitler, was a pragmatist, and although he shared Evola's vision of a restored Rome, he knew the present rulers of that city—the Catholic Church—would have to be part of the deal. Evola had other ideas. In *Pagan Imperialism,* he argued that paganism, not Catholicism, should be the spiritual backbone of Fascism, and that Mussolini was too involved in the Church and too ready to pander to the masses for any real "spiritual aristocracy" to arise. Understandably, Mussolini didn't care for Evola's criticism, but Evola was admirably steadfast. When told that Il Duce disagreed with some of his comments, Evola replied, *"Tanto peggio per Mussolini"* (Too bad for Mussolini). Il Duce won out, though, and after ten issues, *La Torre* was forced to stop publishing.

Although Mussolini would later adopt some of Evola's ideas to show that he was more than Hitler's puppet, and Evola himself would write for Fascist newspapers, penning a regular column "Spiritual Problems in Fascist Ethics," Evola gave up on Italy early on and transferred his attentions to the Third Reich. While others might argue that Fascism ruined Italy, for Evola it was the other way around: "Italy seems to have been incapable of providing adequate and suitable human material for the superior possibilities of Fascism."[16] Germany seemed a better prospect. The German edition of *Pagan Imperialism* was a success, and Evola was invited to the Fatherland to lecture. By this time he had written two influential books, *Aspects of the Jewish Problem* and *Outline of a Racist Education*, and he gave lectures on similar topics to university students. (Throughout the years of the Third Reich, writers and academics tried to ingratiate themselves with the Nazis by writing books either clarifying or augmenting their racist views; often sincere, the practice was also seen as a good career move.)

Evola's views on race, founded on a "spiritual" rather than a biological basis, were admittedly less crude than the Nazis'. In effect, Evola, like Weininger, argued that one might be Aryan by birth but still harbor a "Jewish soul." Likewise, one could be a Jew yet have an "Aryan soul." Evola's fastidious and cultured mind appealed to some in the Third Reich less taken with the rabid blood obsession of *Mein Kampf* (although they would never admit this in public), and Evola found himself courted by the occult-minded Heinrich Himmler, lecturing to SS groups and being treated to tours of their castles. He also addressed Berlin's elite Herrenklub, and in Vienna he spoke at the Kulturbund. Perhaps regretting Evola's departure, when Mussolini enacted Italy's own race laws in 1938, he looked to Evola as a guide. Three years later, Il Duce told Evola that his book,

The Synthesis of Racial Doctrine, was exactly what Italian Fascism needed. Evola's subtle racial ideas are often cited by his supporters as evidence that he was never really anti-Semitic. While the idea of a "spiritual aristocracy" can be applied without ideas of race (many followers of spiritual movements adopt it regularly), it's difficult to ignore Evola's less-than-encouraging remarks about the Jews. The "Judaic horde" was for him "the anti-race par excellence," and to argue that a supporter of the "tonic" virtue of *The Protocols* wasn't anti-Semitic requires a dialectical skill beyond my own. To be sure, Evola's disdain reached beyond the Jews. We've seen how he felt about jazz, to which he linked "Negro syncopation." He also worried about other "inferior, non-European races," and, in an expression set to delight feminists and male chauvinists alike, he complained about the "sexual tormentresses" who had the audacity to wiggle their hips in very tight pants.

The Nazis ultimately rejected Evola's ideas about "Aryan Jews" and their opposite; the difficulties involved in telling which from which were no doubt insurmountable. He made many important contacts, but the pragmatic Himmler eventually found no use for him, and like all others the Nazis saw as potential rivals, Evola found his activities curtailed. Being rejected by Himmler may be a point in his favor, although it's doubtful if Evola's ideas about spiritual racism ever saved any "Aryan Jews" from the gas chambers. Yet Evola didn't give up that easily. Although he had already pegged Mussolini as second rate, he was the first to greet Il Duce at Hitler's Rastenburg headquarters after his daring rescue from prison in 1943, and for a time Evola was involved in the short-lived Fascist republic of Salò. But the thousand-year Reich was coming to a close sooner than expected. In 1945, Evola was in Vienna during the Soviets' blistering attack. Rather than head for the shelters, Evola worked in his office translating stolen Masonic documents or walked the streets, wanting, he said, to "calmly question his fate."[17] He was injured in an attack and left paralyzed. One wonders if the old artilleryman—who had never seen action—saw the irony in becoming a casualty of the Russian shelling. For the last thirty years of his life he was bound to a wheelchair, the grim nucleus of a small but devoted following.

APOLITEIA

Hitler's defeat convinced Evola that esoteric politics couldn't be addressed head-on. While others, like the Austrian Hinduphile Savitri Devi, tried to revive belief in Hitler's regime by presenting him as an avatar of the New Age,[18] Evola abandoned mass movements and concentrated on the role *l'uomo differenziato* could play in the despicable modern world. Returning to Italy, affirming "neither Coca-Cola nor Marx," Evola hoped "those who were different" could drag their feet against American capitalism and Soviet communism, an aim with which many contemporary readers would agree, without, however, accepting Far-Right methods in order to achieve it. Evola wrote about the "legionary spirit" and the "warrior ethic," but his rhetoric had lost some of its triumphal tone. In 1951 a new edition of *Revolt against the Modern World* appeared, but it no longer spoke of the heroic efforts of international Fascism and instead advised a philosophy of stoic resistance. Evola's polemics aroused the authorities, and he was summoned to court, accused of trying to revive Fascism. The fact that he had never actually joined the party, as well as his eloquent defense, cleared him of the charges, and Evola was free to carry on his increasingly lonely battle against an increasingly modern world. In *Men among the Ruins*, he outlined the need for a counter-revolution, drawing much of his argument from Joseph de Maistre. Yet age and the times were against him. In *Ride the Tiger*, mentioned in the introduction, Evola delivered a meditation on how "those who were different" could survive the last days of the Kali Yuga. Advocating *apoliteia*, a kind of active nihilism, Evola argued that there was little hope of salvaging anything worthwhile from modern society; "those who were different" could display their difference through an aristocratic disdain and contempt. And although Evola himself never actually advocated violence, the vision of a world absolutely in the grip of decline argued that there was little harm in helping it in its downfall. The bitter pages of *Ride the Tiger* often read like a primer on philosophical vandalism, an ideological justification for throwing bricks through modernity's window.

Evola might have drifted into obscurity were it not for the rise of his ideological opposite, the radical Left, as often as not an agent of a nihilism and philosophical violence as bleak as *l'uomo differenziato*'s. In the midst of the '60s "revolutions," which involved their own kind of occult politics—including an attempt to levitate the Pentagon[19]— Evola was rediscovered by disaffected right-wing Italian students, who strangely linked his work to that of their other hero, J. R. R. Tolkien. Dubbed "our Marcuse," by the Italian Far-Right leader Giorgio Almirante—a nod to the then highly popular doyen of leftist ideology, Herbert Marcuse—by the early 1970s, half-paralyzed and totally pessimistic, Evola held court in his small Rome apartment to a growing band of neo-fascist followers. Along with his reminiscences of Hitler, Himmler, and Mussolini, Evola passed on his insights into Traditional politics, summed up in explosive formulas like, "Nothing in this system deserves to be saved," and,"It is not a question of contesting and polemicizing, but of blowing up everything." If your revolt is against the entire modern world, then anything in it becomes a target, including the innocent men, women, and children at a Bologna railway station. Unfortunately, being abstractions, neither modernity nor society nor the modern world can be hurt by an explosion; only people can.

ORDEALS AND LABYRINTHS

Evola's influence continued on after his death. Italian neo-fascist groups like the New Order, the National Vanguard, and the National Front were taken with his aim to topple the "corrupt and bourgeois" democratic system, and many of these "virile" radicals adopted Nazi symbols and images to promote their ideologies. Although Evola supporters try to minimize his influence on these Far-Right thugs, the neo-fascists themselves celebrated his input. When on trial for a series of assassinations and bombings carried out in 1971 and 1972, members of the New Order quoted Evola in justification of their actions.[20] Franco Freda, one-time head of the New Order, adapted Evola's *apoliteia* into a "call for action against the bourgeois state irrespective of effect," a kind of "armed spontaneity" that was really a late twentieth-century refit of old Futurist tactics, although the Futurists themselves never killed anyone.[21] In this kind of "political

Dada," the distinctions between the radical Left and the radical Right blur, as both make the status quo their target. As I point out elsewhere, the Far-Left radicals of the 1960s and '70s enjoyed a similar ideology of sudden, "motiveless" violence, which in both cases is little more than licensed mayhem aimed at a putative "system."[22] If the entire "system" is wrong, you can throw a bomb in any direction and be assured of hitting something.

One very important follower of Evola's ideas also believed in the necessity of political violence. In *Ordeal by Labyrinth*, a series of interviews with the writer Claude-Henri Rocquet, the historian of religion Mircea Eliade remarked that he became "politically aware" during his time in India, where he witnessed the same repression that angered people like Annie Besant. Eliade remarked, "One day I heard an extremist talking and I had to admit he was right. I understood perfectly well that there had to be some violent protestors too."[23] India, however, isn't the only country in which Eliade's name is associated with political violence. In his homeland of Romania, there were links between the two that, as many of his detractors believe, Eliade did his best to obscure. Although the Eliade that most readers know is the tolerant, multicultural scholar of the world's religions, in a younger guise Eliade was a fiercely nationalist writer, motivated by the same intolerant views that informed Schwaller de Lubicz and Eliade's Traditionalist mentor, Evola. In an article written in 1937, "Hungarians in Bucharest," the thirty-year-old Eliade complains that over the recent Christmas holidays, three Hungarian plays were staged in his nation's capital. But this wasn't all. In the film *Dracula's Daughter*—an admirable sequel to the Bela Lugosi classic—some of the characters call for a Hungarian Transylvania. "I would have loved to hear the audience jeer for the entire duration of the movie," Eliade wrote. "I would have loved to see a group of students tear the film to pieces and trash the equipment."[24] Like many Romanians at the time, Eliade resented what he saw as Hungarian incursions into his nation, much as the British Nationalist Party is troubled by the "economic migration" of Eastern Europeans into Britain today, made possible by the European Union. Eliade made his strident remarks in print, in a national newspaper, at a time when in Germany many "patriots"—and not only students—were doing precisely the kind of thing he yearned to do, not solely to film projectors and movie screens but to people, mostly Jews, the universally unwanted guest.

That Eliade, like Schwaller de Lubicz, might want to forget such an injudicious past—and might want others to also—is understandable. Yet the kind of esoteric politics that Evola linked to Traditionalist thought remained a part of Eliade's sensibilities. In the same series of interviews, speaking of the political power of cultural activities like literature and art—he calls them "political weapons"—Eliade echoes Schwaller de Lubicz's and Guénon's calls for an elite. "It is no longer the politicians who stand at the concrete center of history," he told his interviewer, "but the great minds, the 'intellectual elites.'" Eliade had in mind a small number of "great minds," five or six, but, exaggerated or not, "those 'five' or 'six' are inordinately important."[25] Although Eliade would speak critically of Guénon and would never publicly voice his debt to Evola, his Traditionalist roots show through the camouflage of half a century.

CLOSET TRADITIONALIST

In the late 1920s and early '30s, Eliade was a "distant follower" of Evola's and Reghini's UR Group; exactly how he made contact with them is unclear, but Eliade became acquainted with Guénon's work through Reghini, as had Evola.[26] Eliade carried on an extensive correspondence with Evola—Evola even sent him copies of his books during Eliade's time in India—and although there is little direct trace of Evola's influence in Eliade's *oeuvre*, in his early years he was clearly a follower of his thought.[27] In 1930, Eliade published an essay in which he spoke of Evola as a great thinker; in the same essay he also praised the work of other racist philosophers, like Arthur de Gobineau, Huston Stuart Chamberlain, and the Nazi ideologue Alfred Rosenberg. Eliade was so taken with Evola's ideas—and so eager to avoid a public declaration of that interest—that in 1941, at the age of thirty-four, he started writing a novel in which Evola features as a character, an occultist named Tuliu, a close approximation of Evola's own first name, who espouses an esoteric faith that he calls "traditional metaphysics." Tuliu lives in a small scholar's dwelling where the bookcases are filled with "the complete works of René Guénon and J. Evola" as well as "complete collections of *Ur, Krur* [the name of another Evolian journal] and *Études Traditionelles.*" Tuliu recommends Guénon and Evola to his friends, but a haphazard pile of books by Blavatsky, Steiner, Papus, and Annie Besant suggests the lack of importance these thinkers have for him. In the journal Eliade kept while writing the novel, he remarks that he must devote a special chapter to Tuliu's "philosophy," "lest the reader believe he is a case of a simple scatter-brained 'occultist.'" "Actually," he continues, "his theories are not completely foreign to mine," and Eliade remarks that he will use Tuliu to "say, for various reasons about which there is not room to dwell here, things I have never had the courage to confess publicly." "Only occasionally," he goes on, "have I admitted to a few friends my 'traditionalist' beliefs (to use René Guénon's term)."[28] Given remarks like these, it isn't difficult to see Eliade as a kind of "closet Traditionalist."

Why in his own journal Eliade didn't have room "to dwell" on his reasons for never publicly "confessing" to his adherence to Traditionalist beliefs is unclear, unless we recognize that he didn't want a record—even a private one—of his own admission to a kind of intellectual cowardice. What Evola himself thought of this is unknown—the novel was never finished and the journals came to light only years later—although he did once ask Eliade about his reticence to refer to him in any of his books. Eliade replied that he wrote for a general audience, not for "initiates."[29] As in the case of Jung, Eliade seems to have taken steps to see that his interest in questionable occult matters didn't hamper his having a respectable career.

Eliade met his secret mentor in 1937. Following his visit to Vienna, where he lectured at the Nazi Kulturbund, Evola carried on to Hungary and Romania. Here he met Eliade, and his Romanian disciple introduced him to Corneliu Zelea Codreanu, leader at the time of a Far-Right Christian "chivalrous" society, the Legion of the Archangel Michael, later known as the Iron Guard. It's his association with this spiritual élite, and his "fellow traveling," or worse, with Romanian fascism that, as his detractors claim, Eliade tried to keep hidden.

Much of the responsibility for Eliade's "outing" is credited to the research of his Romanian student, collaborator, and later literary executor, Ioan Culianu. Like Eliade, Culianu was a brilliant historian of religion, magic, and the occult and was himself thought to display remarkable powers of prediction and fortune-telling. Culianu was also an outspoken public critic of both the Ceauşescu regime and that of Ion Iliescu, which followed the downfall of Romanian communism. In 1991, Culianu's body was found in the bathroom of the Divinity School at the University of Chicago, where Eliade taught until his death in 1986. He had been shot once in the back of the head, execution style. Culianu's murderer or murderers were never caught. Although Chicago police initially thought Culianu's death might be the work of some occult group unhappy with his research, the most plausible explanation is that it was the work of Romanian nationalists, unhappy with his criticisms of political developments in his homeland. It's also possible that a revived Iron Guard, unhappy with Culianu's research into Eliade's past, retaliated and used his murder as a warning for other Romanian expatriates.[30]

Some of Eliade's "secret," however, was already known to many at the university and to the academic community in general, although it wasn't until his last years that the full details of his other life became widely available. In 1969, Gershom Scholem made it known that Israel could not welcome Eliade, who, like Scholem, was one of the "star" lecturers at the Eranos conferences; the reason was Eliade's past. In 2000, the novelist Saul Bellow published a book, *Ravelstein*, a thinly disguised account of the last days of his friend the philosopher Allan Bloom, who died in 1992 from complications arising from AIDS. Bloom, a student of Leo Strauss, came to nationwide prominence in the late 1980s when his book *The Closing of the American Mind*, criticizing the decline of university education under the rule of leftist professors, became a surprise best-seller. Like Eliade and Bellow, Bloom taught at the University of Chicago, and in the novel Eliade appears as the "Romanian nationalist" Radu Grielescu, who wants to mitigate his anti-Semitic past by making friends and being seen with Bloom/Ravelstein, a Jew. Bellow, no stranger to esotericism—his novel *Humboldt's Gift* is heavily influenced by Rudolf Steiner, and he once carried on a kind of "correspondence course" in anthroposophy with the philosopher Owen Barfield—makes no bones about Grielescu's "secret." "The man was a Hitlerite," Bellow writes, who likened the presence of Jews in Romania to a case of social syphilis, a reference to an article written by Eliade in 1937 in which he spoke of Romania being "conquered by Jews and torn to pieces by foreigners."[31] Even Eliade's countrymen, like the playwright Eugène Ionesco, criticized Eliade for creating a "stupid, dreadful, reactionary Romania."[32]

THE ARCHANGEL MICHAEL

The Legion of the Archangel Michael was established in Romania in 1927 by Corneliu Zelea Codreanu. Codreanu had studied law at the University of Iasi, on the Russian/Romanian border, where he became involved in anti-Semitic and anti-communist activities. In 1923 a plan to murder several Jewish bankers and politicians was aborted when Codreanu was arrested, although he did later murder the police prefect of Iasi, a crime for which he was acquitted. This murder became the prototype for later political assassinations associated with the Legion, whose philosophy embraced a kind of death fanaticism that included martyrdom, communication with the dead, and a contempt for the body—all aspects, incidentally, of the shamanism Eliade would later become associated with. Before forming the Legion, Codreanu had been a follower of Alexandru C. Cuza, a political economist at the University of Bucharest who had founded a League of National Christian Defense. Cuza's violent anti-Semitism was seen as insufficient by Codreanu, who looked to the movement to bring about the "moral rejuvenation" of Romania, which would nonetheless include its "purification" of Jews, Hungarians, and other undesirables—an early twentieth-century version of ethnic cleansing. This would come about through the creation of a "new man," a version of the "regeneration" we have encountered throughout this book. In this sense the Legion was as much a spiritual and religious movement as it was a political one. Its ideology was based on a fundamentalist form of Orthodox Christianity, and it took its name from the icon of the archangel

Michael. If Mussolini's Fascism had the state as its center and Hitler's Nazism had race, for Codreanu and his followers, Christ, paradoxically, was the heart of their vicious and intolerant creed.

Like much else in Eliade's "hidden" past, the exact nature of his relationship with the Legion is still unclear. Detractors argue that he was a "card-carrying" member and enthusiast, while supporters claim that his dallying with the Legion was a regrettable youthful faux pas and that he left before the violence associated with the later Iron Guard appeared.[33] Yet Eliade's newspaper articles praising Codreanu's elite clearly and publicly linked him to it. As with Evola's association with Fascism, the fact that he may never have literally joined the Legion seems overshadowed by his clear sympathies with it.

Most English-speaking readers are unaware that in his early career, Eliade was a kind of all-around public intellectual and that his first essay into Romanian nationalist politics was a series of articles he wrote under the heading "Spiritual Itinerary." In these he focused on political ideals favored by the Far Right. Like Evola, Eliade rejected liberalism, democracy, and modernization; he also praised Mussolini, an early sign of the admiration for "strong" leaders that he would also have for Spain's Franco and Portugal's Salazar, something he shared with Jung. Eliade approved of an ethnic nationalist state founded on the Orthodox Church; for all his interest in Oriental and "primitive" (read "primordial") religions, Eliade remained a lifelong devotee of Orthodox Christianity. The Legion of the Archangel Michael was a kind of vanguard for an Orthodox revolution that Eliade hoped for in Romania. Eliade's celebration of the Legion suggests that his Traditionalism followed Evola's emphasis on the Kshatriya, or warrior, caste rather than Guénon's more Brahmin version.

According to some accounts, Eliade was introduced into the Legion in 1935 by his friend and fellow writer Emil Cioran.[34] By 1937, the year he introduced the Legion's leader to his mentor, Evola, Eliade was recognized as one of its leading propagandists, a position acquired through his enthusiastic newspaper articles. Its aims were impressive. The Legion, he believed, would spark a Christian revolution aimed at creating a new Romania, and its leader, Codreanu, would reconcile Romania with God. The Legion's victory was part of Romania's destiny, Eliade declared, and, as mentioned, it would "bring forth a new type of man" and the "triumph of the Christian spirit in Europe."[35] Like Evola and Guénon, Eliade believed in a geographical "supreme spiritual center," a "repository of primordial tradition," a kind of Romanian Agartha or Shambhala, which in his case was located in Dacia, the Roman province from which Romanians claim they have descended. Part of the Legion's mission was to cleanse this "primordial" "sacred space" of unwanted intruders. Linked to this was the cult of Zalmoxis, a Dacian deity at the center of a monotheistic "death and resurrection" religion like Christianity, with which it could easily be assimilated. Disturbingly, notwithstanding its esoteric and occult overtones, much of Eliade's rhetoric about the Legion of the Archangel Michael has surprising echoes with similar ideals advocated by the current American Christian Right.

Along with Cioran, who professed an admiration for Hitler (and who, unlike Eliade and Heidegger, later publicly repented of it), other figures close to Eliade were involved with the Legion, most significantly his philosophy professor, Nae Ionescu, with whom Eliade and Evola lunched after their meeting with Codreanu. Like Eliade and Cioran, Ionescu was part of the influential Criterion group of new Romanian intellectuals, and Ionescu's curious philosophy, which he called "Trairism"—a blend of existentialism, Romanian nationalism, and Christian mysticism—also advocated a regime aimed at "purifying" Romania of foreign elements. While many were inspired by Eliade's "legionary spirit," others were less enthused and saw his polemics as "mystical, dense and stifling," promoting "noxious practical consequences" that boiled down to "the elimination of Jews through acts of physical repression and persecution."[36]

One reader of Eliade's articles was Romania's King Carol II, who, alarmed at the Legion's growing power, took control of it in 1938, arresting Codreanu and other members, including Eliade. Codreanu and his twelve closest supporters were strangled in their cells—an event that brought Evola to tears—and Eliade spent some weeks in prison but was eventually released. King Carol II then handed control of the Legion over to Horia Sima, a Nazi sympathizer, who transformed it into the notorious Iron Guard, a "chivalrous" order whose atrocities rivaled those of the SS and who the Allies would recognize as the Romanian Nazi Party.

FASCIST DIPLOMAT

After his arrest, Eliade refused to sign a declaration of dissociation with the Legion; he later argued that doing so would only put him on its "hit list" were they to return to power. But his association with fascism didn't end there. Through the help of his student Michel Vâslan, who had joined a separate Traditionalist group led by Vasile Lovinescu and would later become a follower of Guénon, Eliade was given a post as a cultural attaché to the United Kingdom; he was later transferred to Paris, and then to Portugal, which was then under the dictatorship of Antonio de Oliveira Salazar, for whom Eliade had high regard. For the next several years Eliade functioned as a cultural envoy for Romania, which in 1940 formed a pro-Nazi government under the new king, Michael I. Until the end of World War II and its coming under Soviet rule, Romania had a succession of fascist governments, including the short-lived National Legionary State, which had the vicious Iron Guard in near complete control. In 1941, after a failed and bloody Legionary Rebellion, when the Iron Guard made a bid for absolute control, Romania came under the fascist dictatorship of Ion Antonescu. That same year, Romania officially joined the Axis powers. At that point Eliade became the cultural attaché of one fascist dictatorship, in league with Nazi Germany and Fascist Italy, while residing in the capital of another, Salazar's. Part of his job was to distribute propaganda supporting Antonescu's totalitarian regime.

If this wasn't enough to give Eliade's apologists headaches and his detractors an excuse for righteous indignation, in Paris after World War II Eliade started an anti-communist journal called *The Morning Star*. (Its Romanian title, *Luceafârul*, suggests the connection with Lucifer more clearly.) This was funded by Nicolae Malaxa, a Romanian industrialist and financier of the Iron Guard who had been a corporate partner of the high-ranking Nazi Hermann Goering; at one point Malaxa and Goering collaborated on a scheme to seize the assets of a Jewish businessman, and during the war Malaxa had put his considerable industrial empire behind the Nazi effort. (Curiously, although a known Nazi, Malaxa was later allowed into the United States, with the support of the government and the help of a young Richard Nixon.)[37] Eliade was also known to have high regard for Alain de Benoist, founder of the French New Right, who is a professed pagan, highly influenced by Julius Evola, and also for the Nazi jurist and political theorist Carl Schmitt, whose ideas, along with those of Leo Strauss and Eric Vogelin, inform some aspects of American conservatism today.

THE POLITICS OF MYTH

In *The Politics of Myth*, Robert Ellwood argues that Eliade later repented of his youthful fascist sympathies and embraced a more tolerant, "modern" vision of religion and society. Yet as he was in his thirties by the time he was a diplomat, how "youthful" Eliade's sympathies were is debatable, and Eliade never made a public recantation of his controversial activities. Scholars have combed Eliade's later, more well-known work for its Traditionalist sources and for traces of his political philosophy, finding in his widely regarded academic works elements of his early "legionary spirit." That Evolian ideas might inform some of Eliade's later works doesn't necessarily detract from their value. Some critics, however, have taken the "hard" view that in the work that made him famous, Eliade peddled a Traditionalist ethos under the guise of "objective" scholarship.

Yet it isn't difficult to see that although much more open to modern ideas, Eliade's later vision is still one of the primacy of the past, of what we can call "ontological roots," as a look at the book that made his reputation in the English-speaking world, *The Myth of the Eternal Return*, makes clear. Eliade's "eternal return" isn't Nietzsche's notion of an eternal repetition of events but a vision of myth and ritual as a means of reenacting the original, "primordial" acts that give life its sacred character. For Eliade, "archaic" or "traditional" man had no interest in history, in the ceaseless flow of becoming; he was only interested in being, which he entered into by returning to the mythical "first time." History existed in what Eliade calls "profane time," a time devoid of meaning, escape from which was granted only by entering "mythic time," the once-and-once-only of the original, primary rites. Indeed, Eliade speaks of the "terror of history," "primordial man's" fear of being swallowed by the relentless flow of meaningless events, and we recall Guénon's lack of interest in the last two thousand years (Evola, too, showed a haughty disdain for "becoming"). Eliade is interested not in a past associated with history but in a past embraced by myth, and an ungenerous view might suggest that Eliade's later philosophy provides a justification for his own lack of interest in his own historical past. As his critic Adriana Berger writes, for Eliade "the past is not valid because it represents history but because it represents origins."[38] This fascination with origins, with beginnings, is linked to the search for Aryan—or in Eliade's case, Dacian—roots. It's at the bottom of most racist ideologies, including that of Eliade's mentor, Evola. In essence, it's a kind of snobbery. It argues that where you come from is more important than what kind of person you are or what you make of yourself. Among aristocrats, nobility, and "old money," the self-made man (or woman) is always a kind of upstart and not really "one of us." Sadly, for much of Western history, the Jew has been cast as the perennial upstart, but others have played this role as well.

Although as Ellwood argues, the vision of the past embraced by Eliade (and by Jung and many others) is really a romanticized modern vision of what this mythic time was like—if it ever existed—it still functions as a powerful attractant for those unhappy with modernity. The vision of a "homogenous, largely rural, and 'rooted' society'" with a "hierarchical superstructure," possessing a "religious or mystical tendency able to express its unity ritually and experientially,"[39] is in many ways attractive, given our own "atomistic" world of "rootless cosmopolitanism," and the idea that such a "sacred" society existed sometime in the immemorial past is seductive. But the idea of the past as preferable to the present isn't new. Indeed, the urge to return to some great good time seems as old as humanity itself: ever since Adam and Eve we've been trying to get back to the garden. And the notion that the future will be better than the past—the essence of modernity—is, quite rightly, only a relatively recent idea.

As the philosopher Leszek Kolakowski points out, the essence of conservatism is the belief that there are some things worth conserving,[40] the recognition that "in some of its aspects, however secondary, the past was better than the present"[41] and that the relentless flow of the "terror of history" in an uncertain progress may not always be desirable. Many of us, myself included, dizzied by the unending stream of technological advance and social change, may agree. Yet while the attraction of origins is great, there is something to be said for what the neo-Marxist philosopher Ernst Bloch called the "not-yet," the possibilities and potentials that lie ahead, the promise of the new. To be sure, the "not-yet" view of history has problems of its own—witness the wreckage left by the many attempts, in Eric Vogelin's phrase, to "immanentize the eschaton," to violently wrench history in order to bring about the millennium. Strangely, forces in Far-Right politics in the United States of recent years seem to combine the worst elements of the two opposing views: a return to some better time in the past and an imminent apocalypse that will bring about a new age.

Last Words

NEW WORLD ORDERS?

It may seem a leap from the Romanian nationalism of Mircea Eliade to the influence of evangelical Christian fundamentalism on American politics. But while writing the last chapter, a disturbing book came to my attention, and as I read it, it became clear to me that perhaps the most significant development in "illuminated politics" in the twenty-first century is happening now in the United States. The fact that by the time this book is published Americans will have elected a new president only adds a certain urgency and immediacy to this concern. Some believe that with the end of the Bush administration, the influence of the Christian Right on American politics will wane. Yet the Nazis dropped below the radar after the failed putsch of 1923; a decade later they were in power. If I'm beating a dead horse here, I ask the reader's indulgence.

The book in question is *American Fascists*. In it, Chris Hedges, a former *New York Times* foreign correspondent, paints a troubling picture of the rise of what he argues may be a form of American-Christian fascism. This isn't the kind of neo-Nazi "white power" sensibility that has been on the fringes of American society for some time. There are no swastikas, no Hitler salutes, and no armbands or kitschy brown shirts associated with this group, although its appeal to an increasingly disenfranchised sector of American society is similar to the appeal National Socialism had to disenfranchised

Germans in the early 1930s. The "American Fascists" Hedges speaks of belong to a huge, well-organized, well-funded, and disturbingly politically well-placed movement dedicated to dismantling the secular state and replacing it with a kind of authoritarian theocracy, based on a numbingly literal reading (or misreading) of the Bible. Through schools, the media, pressure groups, and lobbyists, and through its growing presence in the American halls of political power, the Christian Right, Hedges argues, is gearing up to alter the American way of life fundamentally (the pun would be inexcusable if the concern wasn't so real), and so, ultimately, the way of life for the rest of the world as well.

Like many encountered in this book, Hedges' American Fascists are unhappy with the modern world, especially the American modern world, which they see as decadent, depraved, and heading for disaster. Sexual license, homosexuality, feminism, liberalism, popular culture, the welfare state, foreigners, and a host of other ills are pulling what was once, in their eyes, a Christian nation down the tube. Although I hesitate to point out the parallels too strongly, as in the years leading up to National Socialism in Germany, there is among the followers of this belief a sense of some impending doom, some unavoidable cataclysm. Historians have argued that works like Spengler's *Decline of the West* and others of a similar tone, appearing in Germany in the years following World War I, helped prime the German psyche to accept the idea of some vast, irrevocable alteration in the shape of things and the need for strong leaders to find a way through the chaos. Hedges argues that the horror of September 11th created a similar sensibility in many Americans, and that the Christian Right is playing on the understandable fears that it and other terrorist attacks have generated. That the minds behind September 11th and other terrorist attacks, in the United States and elsewhere, are as narrow, fanatical, and oblivious to human suffering as those informing the Christian Right (at least according to Hedges) only adds to the sense that the affairs of the West in the early twenty-first century have reached, or are about to reach, a crisis point. A cliché, I know, but having looked in this book at a number of similar flashpoints in the last few centuries, it's difficult not to recognize this.

I will leave readers of Hedges' book to discover—if they are not already aware of it—the worryingly sophisticated network of media, educational, social, and political control that his American Fascists already have in place and that, in the event of another September 11th or similar catastrophe, they will speedily use to offer and assume a beneficent leadership of the nation. But these "illuminated" totalitarians aren't dependent on a terrorist attack, an economic meltdown, or an increasingly likely natural disaster (probably stemming from global warming) in order to take their rightful place as rulers of the land, although the downturn in the U.S. economy at the time of this writing is the sort of thing they're banking on. The central myth motivating their actions is the imminent end of the world as we know it, a version of the last days patched together from a selective reading of the Book of Revelations. At the heart of this is what they call the Rapture, when Jesus returns to earth and all his "true believers" are whisked up to heaven, while the rest of humanity is "left behind" to face an unimaginable ordeal of bloodcurdling torture and horror, the "time of tribulation."

I say "unimaginable," but this is incorrect, as a series of Christian Right best-sellers, collected under the title *Left Behind*, goes to some lengths to imagine just that. Reading the descriptions of the righteous violence meted out to those who refuse to let Jesus "into their hearts," or to those who are not quite Christian enough, with bodies bursting, heads exploding, torsos slashed in two—all in very graphic detail— I couldn't escape the feeling that this was a form of religious or apocalyptic pornography, a kind of sick spiritual sadism. Children have a front-row seat in heaven while they watch their parents, who didn't make the grade, receive the swift retribution of the Lord. Even Dante in his worst moments didn't depict the punishments of hell with such obscene relish, but then Dante is a much better writer than the authors of these holy gore fests.

The books, which rival *Harry Potter* and *The Da Vinci Code* in sales, have been made into films, featuring downgraded ex-Hollywood stars, and are big hits on the several highly popular Christian broadcasting networks. There are even video games based on them, with the righteous warriors of the Lord laying into the evil cohorts of the Antichrist.

That such books are written isn't surprising. Similar works entertain the followers of "esoteric Hitlerism," although in them, noble Aryan supermen defeat the repellent hordes of—well, you can fill in the blank.[1] It's saddening that such books are written, but it's a free country, at least so far. What's troubling is that so many Americans read them, and for all I know there are foreign translations, too. As I point out earlier in this book, popular culture is often a better indication of a society's beliefs than its "official" sources. If this is true, then a substantial segment of the American consciousness is anticipating an imminent holy crusade against all those that it believes are not "one of us." Candidates for this bill are the usual suspects: homosexuals, feminists, Jews, "people of color," liberals, socialists, Muslims (adherents of a "Satanic" religion), and so on. For the most part, these were also the targets of the "purifying" violence with which the Legion of the Archangel Michael sought to cleanse Romania of unwanted influences. Mircea Eliade believed that the murderous Corneliu Zelea Codreanu, leader of the Legion, would make Romania "right with God." That America is currently not right with God is the Christian Right's complaint, but come the Rapture, that will change. The belief in the "cleansing" power of religious violence as a means of political action, as if some holy "white tornado" will come and blow away all the social "dirt," has appeared throughout this book. Sadly, it's an option that many, confronted with the complexities of modern life, find attractive. If the sales of the *Left Behind* fantasies are any indication, millions of Americans do. Violence as a means of ushering in some putative new age is, of course, not limited to the right. Marx fantasized about the bourgeoisie hanging from lampposts. But I don't think an imminent Marxist upheaval is on the books just now. On a less violent but equally millennial note, many New Age advocates are anticipating some kind of radical change circa 2012. I haven't done the math, but I wouldn't be surprised if the prophets behind the *Left Behind* novels and those of Quetzalcoatl's return find themselves jockeying for position come the last days.

One of the main targets of the Christian Right, Hedges argues, are what they call "secular humanists," which basically means people who don't accept Jesus in the way they do and who more or less accept

236

modern life as it is, based on science and materialism, and, sadly, motivated for the most part by consumerism. Secular humanists are in the Traditionalists' bad books, too, and as Mark Sedgwick points out, some Traditionalist thought has informed some elements of Islamic fundamentalism.[2] This isn't surprising, as the Traditionalists and Islamic fundamentalists share a virulent disdain for the modern West.

Clearly, for anyone who thinks life should be about something more than reality TV, celebrity gossip, and having the "F" word misspelled on your clothes, the secular Western world leaves much to be desired. I include myself in this group. Like many people, I find much about the modern world unappealing. It's for this reason that I find critics of it like Julius Evola and René Guénon and others of their sensibilities disturbing—not because of Evola's obvious fascist sympathies or Guénon's elitist ethos, but because many of their criticisms hit the mark. Unless a more moderate rethinking of modernity comes up with something soon, the more extreme alternatives offered by Guénon and others like him will seem attractive. Notwithstanding Evola's repellent racist views, it's not surprising that some of his readers appreciated his belief that the only thing left was to "blow up" everything. Thankfully, the majority take this as a metaphor, and I'd bet that many of us feel something similar at times, although, again thankfully, we have the presence of mind not to succumb to this "purifying" release. To want to knock everything down and start anew has been a part of the human psyche for ages, probably from the beginning. It's a form of metaphysical impatience, and most spiritual practices are aimed at learning how to curb it. But no society or nation can practice Zen or any other discipline; only people can. So it's up to us to refrain from indulging in the delightful and stimulating exercise of smashing everything up.

When I began this book I didn't think of myself as particularly political, or at least as any more political than the next person who has to deal with a certain amount of politics in everyday life. I'm still not one to join marches, hit the barricades, or call for a revolution, and I believe that the best contribution that I, and people like me, can make is to try to understand things with as much clarity and insight as possible. Whether I manage to do that or not is another story. Now, finishing this book, I think I can articulate to myself somewhat more clearly what I can call my political stance. Politics deals with the possible, not the ideal; it inhabits the messy world of becoming, not the stable world of being. Ideas from the world of being can inform the politics of becoming, but they cannot take its place, which means that as long as the world is the world, there will always be change. Attempts to force some ideal, whether it be right or left, into existence will fail, or success will come at such a cost that failure would have been preferable. While watching the collapse of his beloved Russia during the Bolshevik Revolution, P. D. Ouspensky had deep insight into what he called "the impossibility of violence," "the uselessness of violent means to attain no matter what." "I saw with undoubted clarity," Ouspensky wrote, "that violent means and methods *in anything whatever* would unfailingly produce negative results, that is to say, results opposed to those aims for which they were applied." This, Ouspensky said, wasn't an ethical insight but a practical one. Violence simply doesn't work.[3] History, I think, bears Ouspensky out. If humankind and society are going to become "better," it's not going to happen overnight. As the *I Ching* counsels, "Perseverance furthers." And that, as I say, takes patience.

Given that the political world isn't an ideal one, if I was asked which I preferred, the modern world—which allows for shopping malls, dumbed-down culture, and consumer consciousness—or a variant of the spiritual authoritarian theocracies encountered in this book, I'd have to come down on the side of modernity. With Leszek Kolakowski, I'm conservative because I believe that there is much to conserve and that the new is not always better than the old. But with Ernst Bloch I'm a radical, because I believe in the promise of the new, the potential for something that doesn't yet exist to arrive. The challenge, of course, is how to combine the two until we find the Goldilocks-like state of having things "just right." Needless to say, this isn't easy, and if ever achieved, is only temporary. When I think of the kind of spiritual society envisioned by Schwaller de Lubicz and others, I can appreciate its appeal. I need only enter a shopping mall to do that. But it does seem to me an example of what the philosopher Karl Popper called a "closed society." More than likely, I'm too much of a modern to desire a theocracy, however spiritual. I grew up on television, comic books, movies, and pop music, and my introduction to the Western esoteric tradition came through cheap paperbacks, not through meeting some mysterious emissary of an initiated elite. I also realized while writing this book that in my own life I exemplify the "rootless cosmopolitanism" that so many anti-modern thinkers find reprehensible. And not only the scary ones; Jung didn't have much good to say about cities, and it wouldn't be difficult to find in Jung's remarks an echo of the Nazi "blood and soil" rhetoric. I've lived in three vast metropolises—New York, Los Angeles, and London—in two different countries on two different continents and have little, if any, connection to the soil or land outside of what can be found in the city. (When people ask about my "roots," I explain that I don't have them and think of myself as more of a spore.) I'm not arguing in favor of this and against the more rural life many anti-modern critics celebrate. It's simply turned out this way.

The modern secular world, for all its drawbacks, has in its favor its very messiness. It allows for all the things that anti-modern critics and others, like myself, dislike. But its very messiness also allows for other things. If we're going to have freedom—a loaded word, I know—we're going to have to put up with some things we don't care for. But we'll also be free to pursue the things we do care for. Even though much popular culture is at a numbingly stupefying level, I'm still able to turn off the television and pick up Dostoyevsky or Nietzsche or even Julius Evola. I'm not sure if in a world fashioned under Evolian principles I could do that. Chris Hedges argues that it is precisely the absence of community, meaningful popular culture, and an appreciable level of intelligence and integrity in modern American society that draws many people who feel "left out" into the ethos of *Left Behind*. But he doesn't argue for some means of *forcing* these desirable goods onto society, of compelling us to be more intelligent and meaningful for our own sake. As Ouspensky saw, such compulsion wouldn't work anyway. All that is left for people who care about these things is to do what they can to make them part of their lives. There's no formula for this, no recipe, no things to put on your "to do" list. For all its emptiness and echoes of a wasteland, we're still free in the modern world to "become who we are." How we do this is up to us. If I have to put up with the messy stuff in order to do it, it seems a fair trade.

NOTES

INTRODUCTION

1. James Webb, *The Occult Establishment* (La Salle, IL: Open Court, 1976), p. 419.
2. Leszek Kolakowski, *Modernity on Endless Trial* (Chicago: University of Chicago Press, 1990), p. 12.
3. For more on my time in "the work," see Gary Lachman, *In Search of P. D. Ouspensky* (Wheaton: Quest Books, 2004).
4. For more on Webb's death, see my article "The Strange Death of James Webb" at http://www.forteantimes.com/features/articles/264/the_damned_the_strange_death_of_james_webb.html. The interested reader can do no better than to track down Webb's books themselves. Sadly, they are no longer in print, but the determined reader can no doubt find them on the Internet.
5. Webb, *The Occult Establishment*, pp. 127, 133, 134.
6. Gary Lachman, *Turn Off Your Mind: The Mystic Sixties and the Dark Side of the Age of Aquarius* (New York: The Disinformation Company, 2003).
7. See Paul Krassner's remarks in *One Hand Jerking: Reports from an Investigative Satirist* (New York: Seven Stories Press, 2005).
8. For more on Joseph Campbell in this context, see Robert E. Ellwood, *The Politics of Myth* (Albany, NY: SUNY Press, 1999).
9. Umberto Eco, "Ur-Fascism," *New York Review of Books*, June 22, 1995.
10. Julius Evola, *Ride the Tiger: A Survival Manual for the Aristocrats of the Soul* (Rochester, VT: Inner Traditions, 2003), pp. 162–163.
11. Theodor Adorno, *Minima Moralia* (London: Verso, 1984), p. 241.
12. See Gary Lachman, *A Dark Muse: A History of the Occult* (New York: Thunder's Mouth Press, 2005).
13. Webb, *Occult Establishment*, p. 309.

14. Christopher McIntosh, *The Rosicrucians* (Wellingborough, UK: Crucible, 1987), p. 30.
15. Nicolas Campion, *The Great Year: Astrology, Millenarianism, and History in the Western Tradition* (London: Penguin Arkana, 1994), pp. 44–45.
16. His name was Gabriel Green. See Ronald Story, *The Encyclopedia of UFOs* (London: New English Library, 1980), pp. 155–57.
17. Gary Lachman, "Foraging in Atlantis," in *The Dedalus Occult Reader: The Garden of Hermetic Dreams* (Sawtry, UK: Dedalus, 2004), p. 15.
18. René Guénon, *The Crisis of the Modern World* (Ghent, NY: Sophia Perennis, 1996) and Julius Evola, *Revolt against the Modern World* (Rochester, VT: Inner Traditions, 1995).

1. ROSICRUCIAN DAWN

1. Manly P. Hall, *The Secret Teachings of All Ages* (New York: Tarcher/Penguin, 2003), p. 441.
2. Frances Yates, *The Rosicrucian Enlightenment* (Boulder: Shambhala, 1978), p. 57.
3. *Fama Fraternitas*, in Yates, *Rosicrucian Enlightenment*, p. 239.
4. As we will see, Johann Andreae Valentin is known to be the author of one Rosicrucian text. He is also thought to have been involved in the *Fama* as well as its follow-up, yet whether these were the work of one or more individuals remains inconclusive. Hence my use of "author(s)."
5. Ibid., p. 245.
6. Ibid., pp. 245–46.
7. Frances Yates offers the date of the "discovery" of Christian Rosencreutz's tomb as 1604. If he died in 1484, this would mean he lay in state for 120 years.
8. *Fama Fraternitas*, p. 247.
9. The Brethren of the Free Spirit were an antinomian, millenarian lay Christian movement that flourished in the thirteenth and fourteenth centuries. They were declared heretical by Pope Clement V at the Council of Vienne (1311–12) and fell victim to the same persecutions as befell the Knights Templar and Cathars.
10. *Fama Fraternitas*, p. 250.
11. Quoted in Yates, *Rosicrucian Enlightenment*, p. 47.
12. *Fama Fraternitas*, p. 253.
13. *Fama Fraternitas*, p. 260.
14. Christopher McIntosh, *The Rosicrucians* (Wellingborough, UK: Crucible, 1987), p. 36.
15. Ibid., p. 32.
16. Ibid., p. 44.
17. Ibid., p. 17.
18. Philip Ball, *The Devil's Doctor* (London: William Heinemann, 2006), p. 385.

19. "Fruit-bringing" in this context relates to "fructify," "to make fruitful."

20. As Christopher McIntosh points out, there was a rich esoteric tradition in Germany preceding the appearance of the Rosicrucian manifestos, so rich that I cannot possibly do it justice here. Paracelsus I've mentioned; others in this line include Meister Eckhart (1266–1327); Johannes Tauler (1300–60), whose work influenced Luther; Johannes Ruysbroek (1293–1381); Nicholas of Cusa (1401–64); Johannes Reuchlin (1455–1522); and Heinrich Cornelius Agrippa (1486–1533).

21. For more on the Cathars and Gnosticism, see Richard Smoley's *Forbidden Faith: The Gnostic Legacy from the Gospels to the Da Vinci Code* (San Francisco: HarperSanFrancisco, 2006).

22. Joscelyn Godwin, *The Golden Thread* (Wheaton, IL: Quest Books, 2007), pp. 107–8.

23. McIntosh, *Rosicrucians*, p. 48.

24. Yates, *Rosicrucian Enlightenment*, p. 137; McIntosh, *Rosicrucians*, p. 44.

25. Neither Rudolph II nor his brother, Matthias, produced an heir—which was taken as a sign that things were not right in the world. With Matthias' death, next in line for the crown was Ferdinand.

26. For an interesting account of a visit to the remains of the gardens and castle, see David Ovason, *The Zelator* (London: Arrow Books, 1999), pp. 146–50.

27. Frances Yates goes into great detail about the similarities between the *Chemical Wedding* and the marriage and life of Frederick and Elizabeth, some of which I draw on here. See Yates, *Rosicrucian Enlightenment*, pp. 59–69.

2. INVISIBLE COLLEGES

1. Frances Yates, *The Rosicrucian Enlightenment* (Boulder: Shambhala, 1978), p. 161.

2. Christopher McIntosh, *The Rosicrucians* (Wellingborough, UK: Crucible, 1987), p. 51

3. Khunrath was for a time at the court of Rudolph II in Prague, where he met John Dee and more than likely became his student. He was later court physician to Count Rotmberk in Trebon.

4. P. D. Ouspensky, *Tertium Organum* (New York: Alfred A. Knopf, 1981), p. 277.

5. For more on Ouspensky's search and its consequences, see my *In Search of P. D. Ouspensky* (Wheaton, IL: Quest Books, 2004).

6. Paul Foster Case, *The True and Invisible Rosicrucian Order* (York Beach, ME: Samuel Weiser, 1985), p. 5, quoted in Richard Smoley, *Forbidden Faith: The Gnostic Legacy from the Gospels to the Da Vinci Code* (San Francisco: HarperSanFrancisco, 2006), p. 134.

7. Manly P. Hall, *The Secret Teachings of All Ages* (New York: Tarcher/Penguin, 2003), p. 539.
8. More than one book was found in the tomb, and accounts of the discovery differ, as does much in the Rosicrucian literature.
9. Hall, *Secret Teachings*, p. 462.
10. McIntosh, *Rosicrucians*, p. 56.
11. Peter Marshall, *The Theatre of the World* (London: Harvill Secker, 2006), p. 132.
12. For the place of De Bry's publishing house in the events leading up to the Bohemian Tragedy, see Yates, *Rosicrucian Enlightenment*, pp. 70–90.
13. Included in the *Utriusque Cosmi Historia* is Fludd's "Theatre Memory System," one version of the Hermetic mnemonic techniques mentioned earlier. Fludd's imaginary *Theatrum Orbi*, or Theatre Globe, is, according to Yates in *The Art of Memory*, based on the rebuilt Globe Theatre—Shakespeare's theater—that had burned down in 1613 and that James I contributed great sums toward reconstructing. Thus we have another Shakespeare-Hermetic-Rosicrucian link. The imaginary theater, which Fludd employed as a mnemonic device to house his Hermetic world system, was based on an actual "world" (Globe) theater. The plays on "theater" as "world" and "world" as "theater" are too suggestive to pursue here.
14. It's been claimed that a Mason's Hall stood near Fludd's house in Coleman Street in London.
15. Yates, *Rosicrucian Enlightenment*, p. 169.
16. Ibid., pp. 182–83.

3. MASONIC MANEUVERS

1. Jasper Ridley, *The Freemasons* (London: Robinson, 2000), p. xi.
2. Ibid., p. 116.
3. James Webb, *The Occult Establishment* (LaSalle, IL: Open Court, 1976), p. 129.
4. Searching for "Hillary Clinton" and "Freemasons" on the Internet produces some interesting results, one such I list here: http://www.cuttingedge.org/news/n1259.cfm.
5. See David Ovason, *The Secret Zodiac of Washington, D.C.* (London: Arrow Books, 2006), and Robert Hieronimus, *Founding Fathers, Secret Societies: Freemasons, Illuminati, Rosicrucians, and the Decoding of the Great Seal* (Rochester, VT: Destiny Books, 2005).
6. Manly P. Hall, *The Secret Teachings of All Ages* (New York: Tarcher/Penguin, 2003), p. 282.
7. Ibid., p. 283.
8. Ibid., p. 658.
9. See Christopher Knight and Robert Lomas' *The Hiram Key, The Second Messiah,* and *Uriel's Machine*; Graham Hancock's *The Sign and*

the Seal; Lynn Picknet and Clive Prince's *The Templar Revelation*; and Colin Wilson and Rand Flem-Ath's *The Atlantis Blueprint*.

10. "Vatican Book on Templars Demise" http://news.bbc.co.uk/2/hi/Europe/7029513.stm.

11. See note 9.

12. Michael Baigent and Richard Leigh, *The Temple and the Lodge* (London: Arrow Books, 1998), p. 159.

13. Ibid., p. 160.

14. The official Rosslyn Chapel website, however, links the dragons to Yggdrasil, the Tree of Life in Norse mythology.

15. Mark Sedgwick, *Against the Modern World* (Oxford: Oxford University Press, 2004), p. 50.

16. René Guénon, *The Lord of The World* (North Yorkshire: Coombe Springs Press, 1983), p. 48.

17. Ridley, *Freemasons*, pp. 26–27.

18. Baigent and Leigh, *Temple and the Lodge*, p. 208.

19. Frances Yates, *The Rosicrucian Enlightenment* (Boulder: Shambhala, 1978), p. 211.

20. Ibid.

21. Thomas De Quincey, "Historico-Critical Inquiry into the Origins of the Rosicrucians and the Freemasons," originally published in the *London Magazine*, January, 1824. http://www.freemasons-freemasonry.com/dequincey_rosicrucians-freemasons.html.

22. Richard Smoley, *Forbidden Faith: The Gnostic Legacy from the Gospels to the Da Vinci Code* (San Francisco: HarperSanFrancisco, 2006), p. 141.

23. Ridley, *Freemasons*, p. 1.

24. The classic work on the esotericism of the Gothic cathedrals is still *Le Mystère des Cathédrales,* attributed to the enigmatic alchemist known as Fulcanelli.

25. Jean Gimpel, *The Cathedral Builders* (London: Michael Russell, 1983), pp. 68–69.

26. Ridley, *Freemasons*, p. 17.

27. Ibid., p. 18.

28. Ibid., p. 15.

29. Baigent and Leigh, *Temple and the Lodge*, p. 247.

30. Ibid., p. 244.

31. Ibid., pp. 264–67.

4. EROTIC ESOTERIC REVOLUTIONS

1. In his mammoth *London: The Biography* (London: Chatto & Windus, 2000, p. 230), among other possible derivations, the novelist Peter Ackroyd suggests that Fetter Lane is so called because it was the site of the

workshops that made the *fetters* or lance vests for the Knights Templar, who were familiar in the area. According to Ackroyd, the neighborhood has a long history of attracting religious, political, and social outcasts, as well as other characters who lived "on the edge."

2. For the following account of Count Zinzendorf, the Moravians, and their influence on Swedenborg and William Blake, I am indebted to the fascinating research of Marsha Keith Schuchard and her absorbing work *Why Mrs Blake Cried: William Blake and the Sexual Basis of Spiritual Vision* (London: Century, 2006).

3. Lars Bergquist, *Swedenborg's Secret* (London: Swedenborg Society, 2005), p. 204.

4. The classic work on Sabbatai Zevi remains Gershom Scholem's *Sabbatai Zevi: The Mystical Messiah* (Princeton, NJ: Princeton University Press, 1973).

5. William Blake, *The Complete Poetry and Prose*, edited by David Erdman (Berkeley and Los Angeles: University of California Press, 1982), pp. 35–36.

6. For an account of the influence of the ideas of "holy sinning" and being "beyond good and evil" on a generation, see my *Turn Off Your Mind*.

7. Unfortunately, I can touch on only some of the aspects of Zinzendorf's and the Moravians' beliefs and practices here. Readers wanting to know a bit more may be interested to read my review of Marsha Keith Schuchard's *Why Mrs Blake Cried* at http://arts.independent.co.uk/books/reviews/article350877.ece.

8. In Gary Lachman, *Into the Interior: Discovering Swedenborg* (London: Swedenborg Society, 2006), I give an overview of Swedenborg's scientific and philosophical ideas, many of which seem centuries ahead of their time.

9. For more on Swedenborg's possible activities as a Jacobite secret agent, see once again the fascinating work of Marsha Keith Schuchard, specifically her articles "Yeats and the Unknown Superiors: Swedenborg, Falk and Cagliostro," in *The Hermetic Journal*, no. 37 (Autumn 1987); "The Secret Masonic History of Blake's Swedenborg Society," in *Blake: An Illustrated Quarterly*, vol. 26, no. 2 (Fall 1992); and "Swedenborg, Jacobites and Freemasonry," in Erland J. Brock, ed., *Swedenborg and His Influence* (Bryn Athyn, PA: Academy of the New Church, 1988). Material from these articles, along with a wealth of other research, is included in Schuchard's *Why Mrs Blake Cried*.

10. Swedenborg used the term *conjugial* rather than the more common *conjugal* to emphasize the spiritual aspect of the relationship.

11. Bergquist, *Swedenborg's Secret*, p. 169.

12. Schuchard, *Why Mrs Blake Cried*, p. 70. As well as his own position as a bishop in the Bohemian Brethren, Comenius had a more direct link to Zinzendorf through his grandson, David Ernst Jablonski. While official pastor of the court of King Fredrick I of Prussia, Jablonski met Zinzendorf, who may have inducted him into the Order of the Grain of Mustard Seed.

13. Ibid, pp. 169–70.

14. Lachman, *Into the Interior*, pp. 86–87.
15. Joscelyn Godwin, *The Theosophical Enlightenment* (Albany, NY: SUNY Press, 1994), p. 103.
16. Bergquist, *Swedenborg's Secret*, p. 170.
17. Blake, *Complete Poetry and Prose*, p. 605.
18. Schuchard, "Why Mrs Blake Cried," a paper that her full-length book is based on, available at http://www.esoteric.msu.edu/volumeII/BlakeFull. html.
19. Godwin, *Theosophical Enlightenment*, p. 97.
20. Ibid., p. 223. In his account of the origins of the Golden Dawn, the occult scholar R. A. Gilbert recounts that W. Wynn Westcott, one of the order's founding members, suggested that the society was in a line of succession of occult groups that were connected by a direct lineage to the one Falk started in London in the 1740s. While not impossible—he was separated from Falk by only a century—the link seems unlikely.
21. Marsha Keith Schuchard, *Restoring the Temple of Vision: Cabalistic Freemasonry and Stuart Culture* (Leiden, Neth.: E. J. Brill, 2002).
22. For more on Swedenborg's correspondences, see my *Into the Interior*, pp. 82–84.
23. Lynn R. Wilkinson, *The Dream of an Absolute Language* (Albany, NY: SUNY Press, 1996), p. 20.
24. Robert Darnton, *Mesmerism and the End of the Enlightenment* (Cambridge, MA: Harvard University Press, 1968), p. vii.
25. Raine discusses Blake's esoteric pursuits, specifically his study of the Hermetic tradition, in her seminal work *Blake and Tradition* (London: Routledge & Kegan Paul, 1969) and also in *Golgonooza City of the Imagination: Last Studies in William Blake* (Hudson, NY: Lindisfarne, 1991). Readers may be interested in an interview I did with Kathleen Raine for *Lapis* magazine a few years before her death. See: http://www.lapismagazine.org/archive/L04/raine_lachman_iint.html.
26. Peter Ackroyd, *Blake* (London: Sinclair-Stevenson, 1995), p. 158.
27. Ibid., p. 163.
28. Ibid., p. 46.
29. Jasper Ridley, *The Freemasons* (London: Robinson, 2000), p. 96.
30. Michael Baigent and Richard Leigh, *The Temple and the Lodge* (London: Arrow Books, 1998), p. 295.
31. Ridley, *Freemasons*, p. 100.

5. ILLUMINATIONS

1. Robert Darnton, *Mesmerism and the End of the Enlightenment* (Cambridge: Harvard University Press, 1969), p. 34.
2. Gary Lachman, ed., *The Dedalus Occult Reader: The Garden of Hermetic Dreams* (Sawtry, UK: Dedalus, 2004), p. 4.

3. Gary Lachman, *A Secret History of Consciousness* (Great Barrington, MA: Lindisfarne, 2003), p. 106.

4. Ibid., pp. 256–67.

5. For more on Orage and the New Age, see my *In Search of P. D. Ouspensky* (Wheaton, IL: Quest Books, 2004).

6. T. E. Hulme, *Speculations* (London: Routledge & Kegan Paul, 1959), p. 116.

7. Ibid., p. 118.

8. Richard Smoley, *Forbidden Faith: The Gnostic Legacy from the Gospels to the Da Vinci Code* (San Francisco: HarperSanFrancisco, 2006), p. 177.

9. Jacques Barzun, *The Use and Abuse of Art* (Princeton, NJ: Princeton University Press, 1974), p. 67.

10. Isaiah Berlin, *The Crooked Timber of Humanity* (London: Pimlico, 2003), p. 118.

11. Isaiah Berlin, "Two Enemies of the Enlightenment," p. 5, at http://berlin.wolf.ox.ac.uk/lists/nachlass/maistre.pdf.

12. Joscelyn Godwin, *The Theosophical Enlightenment* (Albany, NY: SUNY Press, 1994), p. 121.

13. Quoted in ibid.

14. Jasper Ridley, *The Freemasons* (London: Robinson, 2000), pp. 138–50.

15. Gary Lachman, *A Dark Muse: A History of the Occult* (New York: Thunder's Mouth Press, 2005), pp. 49–57.

16. Robison's book is available online at http://www.sacred-texts.com/sro/pc/index.htm.

17. Lachman, *A Dark Muse*, p. 50.

18. John Bruno Hare, introduction, http://www.sacred-texts.com/sro/pc/index.htm.

19. Pernety's Avignon group spawned a rival, the Illuminés d'Avignon, led by the Sabbataian and cabalist Count Thaddeus Grabianka. As Marsha Keith Schuchard relates, Count Grabianka was one of the agents of esoteric cross-fertilization between France and England, and in 1785 he brought his sexually and magically charged mesmerism to Swedenborg's London followers. See *Why Mrs. Blake Cried*, pp. 218–21.

20. Christopher McIntosh, *Eliphas Levi and the French Occult Revival* (London: Rider, 1972), p. 96.

21. Ibid., pp. 84–85.

22. Darnton, *Mesmerism and the End of the Enlightenment*, p. 88.

23. Ibid., p. 86.

24. Space doesn't allow more than a mention of a fascinating book exploring the links between mesmerism, politics, and the rise of psychiatry in the late eighteenth century: Mike Jay's *The Air Loom Gang* (London: Bantam, 2003).

25. Darnton, *Mesmerism and the End of the Enlightenment*, p. 79.

26. Ibid.

27. Ibid., pp. 91–92.

28. Lachman, *A Dark Muse,* p. 31.
29. Ibid., p. 287.
30. Ibid., p. 288.
31. Lynn Picknett and Clive Prince, *The Sion Revelation* (London: Time Warner Books, 2006) pp. 360–62.
32. Darnton, *Mesmerism and the End of the Enlightenment*, p. 69.
33. McIntosh, *Eliphas Levi and the French Occult Revival*, p. 26.
34. Iain MacCalan, *The Seven Ordeals of Count Cagliostro* (London: Century, 2003), p. 210.
35. Quoted in Frances Mossiker, *The Queen's Necklace* (New York: Simon & Schuster, 1961), p. 554.

6. Spirits Rebellious

1. Eliphas Lévi, *The History of Magic*, trans. A. E. Waite (London: Rider, 1982), p. 313.
2. Christopher McIntosh, *Eliphas Levi and the French Occult Revival* (London: Rider, 1972), p. 46.
3. Ibid., p. 42.
4. *Meditations on the Tarot: A Journey into Christian Mysticism* (New York: Tarcher/Penguin, 2002), pp. 419–20. It is generally accepted that the author of this remarkable but controversial work is the anthroposophist and Catholic convert Valentine Tomberg.
5. Joscelyn Godwin, *The Golden Thread* (Wheaton, IL: Quest Books, 2007), p. 50.
6. Morris Berman, *Coming to Our Senses* (London: Unwin, 1990), p. 299.
7. Robert Darnton, *Mesmerism and the End of the Enlightenment* (Cambridge: Harvard University Press, 1969), p. 117.
8. Again, I refer the interested reader to my book *A Dark Muse.*
9. See http://weuropeanhistory.suite101.com/article.cfm/histories_mysteries.
10. Lachman, *A Dark Muse*, pp.136–41.
11. For simplicity's sake, although during his career as a radical, Lévi was still Alphonse Louis Constant, in the following I refer to him as Lévi throughout.
12. Thomas Williams, *Eliphas Levi, Master of Occultism* (Tuscaloosa, AL: University of Alabama Press, 1975), p. 22.
13. Lévi, *History of Magic*, pp. 355–57.
14. Williams, *Eliphas Levi*, p. 17.
15. Ibid.
16. Ibid., p. 18.
17. For an account of Lévi's other arrests and an analysis of his political writings, see Lynn R. Wilkinson, *The Dream of an Absolute Language; Emanuel Swedenborg & French Literary Culture* (Albany, NY: SUNY Press, 1996).

18. Eliphas Lévi, *Transcendental Magic* (London: Rider, 1982), p. 376.
19. McIntosh, *Eliphas Levi and the French Occult Revival*, p. 142.
20. Lévi, *History of Magic*, p. 32.
21. Ibid., p. 41.
22. Colin Wilson, *Afterlife* (New York: Doubleday, 1987), pp. 73–108.
23. For an account of Steiner's experiences with the dead, see Gary Lachman, *Rudolf Steiner: An Introduction to his Life and Work* (New York: Tarcher/Penguin York, 2007).
24. Rudolf Steiner, *The Occult Movement in the Nineteenth Century and its Relation to Modern Culture* (London: Rudolf Steiner Press, 1973).
25. Ibid., p. 20.
26. Alex Owen, *The Darkened Room: Women, Power, and Spiritualism in Late Victorian England* (London: Virago Press, 1989), p. 1.
27. Barbara Goldsmith, *Other Powers: The Age of Suffrage, Spiritualism, and the Scandalous Victoria Woodhull* (New York: Harper Perennial, 1999).
28. Colin Wilson and Donald Seaman, *Scandal!* (London: Weidenfeld & Nicolson, 1986), p. 23.
29. One of the earliest and most famous women's rights supporters, Wollstonecraft was vilified by friends and foes alike for her "scandalous" libertinism and forthright attitude toward sex. See the excellent biographies *Her Own Woman: The Life of Mary Wollstonecraft* (London: Abacus, 2001) by Diane Jacobs, and *The Life and Death of Mary Wollstonecraft* (London: Penguin, 1992) by Claire Tomalin.
30. Wilson and Seaman, *Scandal!*, p. 1.

7. JOURNEYS TO THE EAST

1. Jasper Ridley, *The Freemasons* (London: Robinson, 2000), p. 208.
2. Sylvia Cranston, *The Extraordinary Life and Influence of Helena Petrovna Blavatsky* (New York: Tarcher/Putnam, 1993), p. 79.
3. Peter Washington, *Madame Blavatsky's Baboon* (London: Secker & Warburg, 1993), p. 41.
4. Rudolf Steiner, *The Occult Movement in the Nineteenth Century* (London: Rudolf Steiner Press, 1973), p. 31. Although he was one of the most intelligent and progressive of modern esotericists, Steiner seems to have shared the prejudices of his day. Remarking on the predominance of women mediums, he comments that "the female organism is adapted by nature to preserve atavistic clairvoyance longer than the male organism," which, in Steiner's evolutionary system, means that women are closer to the previous forms of human consciousness than are men. Ibid., p. 30.
5. A Leyden jar is a device for storing electrical charge. It was invented in 1745 by Pieter van Musschenbroek.

6. Steiner, *The Occult Movement*, p. 34.

7. Nicolas Goodrick-Clarke, *Western Esoteric Masters Series: Helena Blavatsky* (Berkeley, CA: North Atlantic Books, 2004), pp. 2–3.

8. Paul Johnson, *In Search of the Masters: Behind the Occult Myth* (South Boston, VA: by author 1990); and *The Masters Revealed: Madame Blavatsky and the Myth of the Great White Lodge* (Albany, NY: SUNY Press, 1994).

9. Christopher Hale, *Himmler's Crusade* (London: Bantam Press, 2003).

10. P. D. Ouspensky, *Tertium Organum* (New York: Alfred A. Knopf, 1981), p. 108.

11. P. D. Ouspensky, *A New Model of the Universe* (New York: Alfred A. Knopf, 1969), pp. 443–44.

12. P. D. Ouspensky, *Letters from Russia 1919* (London: Arkana, 1991), p. 2.

13. Indeed, Ouspensky once remarked to his student J. G. Bennett that the difference between one man and another can be greater than that between a sheep and a cabbage. See J. G. Bennett, *Witness* (Tucson, AZ: Omen Press, 1974), p. 53.

14. See Abraham Maslow, "Humanistic Biology: Elitist Implications of the Concept of 'Full-Humanness,'" in *Future Visions: The Unpublished Papers of Abraham Maslow*, ed. Edward Hoffman (Thousand Oaks, CA: Sage Publications, 1996).

15. Washington, *Madame Blavatsky's Baboon*, p. 39.

16. Jacolliot's "unknown nine" have had a varied career, turning up in the supernatural adventure fiction of the Theosophist Talbot Mundy, as part of the cast of characters in Pauwels and Bergier's 1960s best-seller, *The Morning of the Magicians*, and as the source of paranormal communications received by Uri Geller. See my *Turn Off Your Mind: The Mystic Sixties and the Dark Side of the Age of Aquarius* (New York: The Disinformation Company, 2001), pp. 158–59.

17. James Webb, *The Harmonious Circle* (New York: G. P. Putnam's & Sons, 1980), pp. 48–73.

18. Ukhtomsky and the Tsar-to-be visited the headquarters of the Theosophical Society on the Tsarevitch's journey around the world in 1891; on the same voyage they met Colonel Olcott in Colombo. Ukhtomsky was the main advocate of Russian Asia, and in Blavatsky's success in India he saw evidence of the readiness of the Indians to embrace their ties with the "irresistible North." Ibid., p. 58.

19. Karl Meyer and Shareen Brysac, *Tournament of Shadows* (London: Little, Brown & Co., 2001), p. 242.

20. Ibid., p. 512.

21. Washington, *Madame Blavatsky's Baboon*, p. 94.

22. In 1968, Sri Lanka (Ceylon in Olcott's day) issued a stamp commemorating his efforts on behalf of Buddhism and education. When Blavatsky and he arrived, there were only two Buddhist schools; the rest were run by Christian missionaries who eschewed Buddhism in their curriculum.

By 1900, through Olcott's efforts, two hundred Buddhist schools had appeared. His work promoting Buddhism in Ceylon was so impressive that he was invited by the Japanese to do the same in their country. (See Cranston, *Extraordinary Life and Influence of Helena Petrovna Blavatsky*, p. 195).

23. The plight of the untouchables continues today. http://news.nationalgeographic.com/news/2003/06/0602_030602_untouchables.html.

24. Cranston, *Extraordinary Life and Influence of Helena Petrovna Blavatsky*, pp. 194–96.

25. See my *Turn Off Your Mind*, pp. 81–86.

26. Andrei Bely, *Petersburg* (London: Penguin, 1995), p. xix. For more on Bely and Steiner, see my *A Dark Muse: A History of the Occult* (New York: Thunder's Mouth Press, 2005), pp. 212–18, and *Rudolf Steiner: An Introduction to his Life and Work* (New York: Tarcher/Penguin York, 2007), pp. 167–69.

27. Nicolai Berdyaev, *The Russian Idea* (New York: Lindisfarne, 1992), p. 19.

28. Ibid., p. 24.

8. KINGS OF THE WORLD ON THE MOUNTAINS OF TRUTH

1. Martin Green, *Mountain of Truth: The Counterculture Begins, Ascona 1900–1920* (Hanover and London: University Press of New England, 1986), p. 176.

2. R. M. Bucke, *Cosmic Consciousness* (New York: Dutton, 1966), p. 4. For more on Bucke, see my *Secret History of Consciousness* (Great Barrington: Lindisfarne, 2003), pp. 3–16.

3. Peter Washington, *Madame Blavatsky's Baboon* (London: Secker & Warburg, 1993), p. 73.

4. For more on Orage and Gurdjieff, see my *In Search of P. D. Ouspensky* (Wheaton, IL: Quest Books, 2004).

5. For more on Orage's lecture, see my *Secret History of Consciousness*, pp. 34–88.

6. Ralph Shirley, quoted in Alex Owen, *The Place of Enchantment* (Chicago: University of Chicago Press , 2007), p. 134.

7. Richard Rudgely, *Pagan Resurrection* (London: Century, 2006).

8. James Webb, *The Occult Establishment* (La Salle, IL: Open Court, 1976), pg. 199. Webb also points out that Ossendowski was saved from a death sentence for his revolutionary activities by Count Witte, cousin of Madame Blavatsky and a future Prime Minister of Russia.

9. Ferdinand Ossendowski, *Beasts, Men and Gods* (London: Edward Arnold, 1923), p. 300.

10. Ibid., p. 302.

11. Ibid.

12. Ibid.
13. Webb, *The Occult Establishment*, pp. 200–201.
14. Joscelyn Godwin, *Arktos: The Polar Myth in Science, Symbolism, and Nazi Survival* (Kempton, IL: Adventures Unlimited Press, 1996), pp. 79–80.
15. Tenzin Gyatso, *The Kalachakra Tantra* (London: Wisdom Publications, 1985), pp. 166–67.
16. James Webb, *The Harmonious Circle* (New York: G. P. Putnam's & Sons, 1980), p. 59.
17. Roerich's mission also provided a classic UFO sighting, decades before Kenneth Arnold's famous account in 1947. In *Altai-Himalaya: A Travel Diary* (Kempton, IL: Adventures Unlimited Press, 2001), pp. 361–62, Roerich speaks of seeing a "huge oval moving at great speed" across the sky from north to south. "Crossing our camp this thing changed in its direction from south to southwest. And we saw how it disappeared in the intense blue sky." One of the lamas traveling with the group told them it was a sign that Rigden-jyepo was "looking after them" (see Nicholas Roerich, *Shambhala*, Rochester, VT: Inner Traditions, 1990, p. 244). Roerich also speaks of an "exquisite breath of perfume" that accompanied the sighting, which he recognizes as a sign of Shambhala (ibid., p. 7).
18. Ibid., p. 4.
19. Roerich, *Altai-Himalaya*, p. 359.
20. Karl Meyer and Shareen Brysac, *Tournament of Shadows* (London: Little, Brown & Co., 2001), p. 455.
21. Ibid., p. 480.
22. Sadly, the pact did little to stop the plundering or destruction of art works during the coming Second World War; and in recent years, the pillaging of Baghdad museums following the U.S.-led invasion of Iraq was precisely the kind of cultural vandalism Roerich wished to prevent.
23. Geneviève Dubois, *Fulcanelli and the Alchemical Revival* (Rochester, VT: Destiny Books, 2006), p. 13.
24. Colin Wilson, *A Criminal History of Mankind* (New York: G. P. Putnam's Sons, 1984), p. 519.
25. Ibid., p. 520.

9. Reactions

1. For material on Saint-Yves d'Alveydre in this and the previous chapter, I'm indebted to Lynn Picknett and Clive Prince's *The Sion Revelation: The Truth about the Guardians of Christ's Sacred Bloodline* (London: Time Warner Books, 2006), p. 376.
2. Ibid.
3. Saint-Yves d'Aleveydre, foreword to Papus, *The Qabalah: Secret Tradition of the West* (Wellingborough, UK: Thorson's, 1977), p. 33.

4. Quoted in James Webb, *The Occult Establishment* (La Salle: Open Court, 1976), p. 236.
5. Ibid., p. 30.
6. Geneviève Dubois, *Fulcanelli and the Alchemical Revival* (Rochester, VT: Destiny Books, 2006), p. 11.
7. Mark Sedgwick, *Against the Modern World* (Oxford: Oxford University Press, 2004), p. 48.
8. Picknett and Prince, *The Sion Revelation*, p. 368.
9. Webb, *The Occult Establishment*, p. 168.
10. Ibid., pp. 241–49.
11. See Richard McNeef, "Crowley and the Spooks," *Fortean Times* 231, January 2008.
12. Picknett and Prince, *The Sion Revelation*, p. 373.
13. Quoted in Martin Green, *Mountain of Truth: The Counterculture Begins, Ascona 1900–1920* (Hanover and London: University Press of New England, 1986), p. 244.
14. P. D. Ouspensky, *Letters from Russia*, (London: Arkana, 1991) pp. 2–3.
15. For more on the opposition to Steiner, see my *Rudolf Steiner: An Introduction to his Life and Work* (New York: Penguin, 2007).
16. Johannes Tautz, *Walter Stein* (London: Temple Lodge, 1990), p. 218.
17. Ibid.
18. Ibid., p. 212.
19. Ibid., p. 183.
20. P. D. Ouspensky, *A New Model of the Universe* (New York: Alfred A. Knopf, 1969), p. 342.
21. Other Traditionalists include Ananda Coomaraswamy, Julius Evola, Fritjoff Schuon, Seyyed Hossein Nasr, Huston Smith, Martin Lings, and Titus Burckhart.
22. George Steiner, *Nostalgia for the Absolute* (Toronto: Anansi Press, 1997)
23. Sedgwick, *Against the Modern World*, p. 24.
24. René Guénon, *The Crisis of the Modern World* (Ghent, Belgium: Sophia Perennis, 1996), p. 15.
25. Sedgwick, *Against the Modern World*, p. 15.
26. Robin Waterfield, *René Guénon and the Future of the West* (London: Crucible, 1987), p. 31.
27. Ibid., pp. 25–26.
28. Ibid. See also Steven Wasserstrom, *Religion after Religion: Gerschom Scholem, Mircea Eliade, and Henry Corbin at Eranos* (Princeton, NJ: Princeton University Press, 1999).
29. Dubois, *Fulcanelli and the Alchemical Revival*, p. 15.
30. Waterfield, *René Guénon and the Future of the West*, p. 53.
31. Ibid., p. 14.
32. Doinel founded his Gnostic Church in 1888, but in 1895 he shocked the Parisian occult subculture by abandoning Gnosticism, returning to the Church, and writing a book, *Lucifer Unmasked*, in which he

argued that Gnosticism, Martinism, and Freemasonry were the work of Satan.

33. Sedgwick, *Against the Modern World*, pp. 60–61.

34. Waterfield, *René Guénon and the Future of the West*, p. 41.

35. Guénon, *The Crisis of the Modern World*, pp. 15–16.

36. Ibid., p. 18.

37. Ibid., p. 16.

38. Ibid., p. 17.

39. Ibid., p. 55.

40. Ibid., p. 73.

41. Sedgwick, *Against the Modern World*, p. 25.

42. Ibid., p. 69.

43. Ibid., p. 34.

44. René Guenon, *The Lord of the World* (North Yorkshire: Coombe Springs Press, 1983), p. 5. Guénon's fellow Traditionalist, the Buddhist scholar Marco Pallis, criticized Guénon for his credulous acceptance of the geographical reality of Agartha, arguing that in fact "nobody heard in India or Tibet about Agartha and the Lord of the World." See Mirua A. Tamas, *Agarttha: The Invisible Center* (Toronto: Rose Cross Books, 2003), p. 13.

45. Ibid.

46. Guénon, *The Crisis of the Modern World*, p. 27.

47. Ibid.

48. Ibid., p. 80.

49. Ibid., pp. 108–9.

10. DARK SIDES

1. For a brief account of Schwaller de Lubicz's life and work, see my "René Schwaller de Lubicz and the Intelligence of the Heart" at http.//www.unitedearth.com.au/lubicz.html.

2. André VandenBroeck, *Al-Kemi: Hermetic, Occult, Political and Private Aspects of R. A. Schwaller de Lubicz* (New York: Lindisfarne, 1987).

3. William Pfaff, *The Bullet's Song: Romantic Violence and Utopia* (New York: Simon & Schuster, 2004), pp. 90–91.

4. Geneviève Dubois, *Fulcanelli and the Alchemical Revival* (Rochester, VT: Destiny Books, 2006), p. 66.

5. R. A. Schwaller de Lubicz, *Nature Word* (West Stockbridge, MA: Lindisfarne Press, 1982), p. 129.

6. Dubois, *Fulcanelli and the Alchemical Revival*, p. 71.

7 Schwaller de Lubicz, *Nature Word*, p. 51.

8. Dubois, *Fulcanelli and the Alchemical Revival*, p. 68.

9. Ibid.

10. Joscelyn Godwin, *Arktos: The Polar Myth in Science, Symbolism, and Nazi Survival* (Kempton, IL: Adventures Unlimited Press, 1996), p. 54.

11. Dubois, *Fulcanelli and the Alchemical Revival*, p. 71.
12. Dubois refers to Du Mas as "Henri" (p. 71), but the other references use "Vivian."
13. For an account of de Lubicz Milosz's life and work, see my *Dark Muse: A History of the Occult* (New York: Thunder's Mouth Press, 2005), pp. 245–53. For his relation to Swedenborg, see my essay "Space: the Final Frontier. O. V. de Lubicz Milosz and Swedenborg," in *Between Method and Madness: Essays on Swedenborg and Literature. Journal of the Swedenborg Society* vol. 4, edited by Stephen McNeilly (London: Swedenborg Society, 2005), pp. 81–93.
14. Christopher Bamford in O. V. de Lubicz Milosz, *The Noble Traveller: The Life and Writings of O.V. de L. Milosz*, (West Stockbridge, MA: Lindsfarne, 1985) p. 50.
15. Ibid., p. 453.
16. Ibid.
17. Ibid.
18. Ibid., p. 463.
19. Ibid., p. 477.
20. Ibid., p. 453.
21. Ibid., p. 457.
22. Ibid., p. 464.
23. Ibid., p. 475.
24. VandenBroeck, *Al-Kemi*, p. 25.
25. Ibid., in the foreword by Saul Bellow.
26. Ibid.
27. VandenBroeck, *Al-Kemi*, p. 25, pp. 25–26.
28. Ibid., p. 35.
29. Ibid., p. 160.
30. Ibid., p. 39.
31. Ibid., p. 44.
32. Ibid., p. 13.
33. Ibid., p. 66.
34. Ibid., pp. 51, 123–24.
35. Ibid., pp. 166–67.
36. Ibid., pp. 168–69. For a translation of "Letter to the Jews" in full, see pp. 268–69.
37. Ibid., p. 170.
38. Schwaller de Lubicz, *Nature Word*, p. 102.
39. Gerhard Wehr, *Jung: A Biography* (Boston: Shambhala, 1987), pp. 325–26.
40. VandenBroeck, *Al-Kemi*, p. 166.
41. Ibid.
42. Dubois, *Fulcanelli and the Alchemical Revival*, p. 71.
43. VandenBroeck, *Al-Kemi*, pp. 274–75.
44. Ibid., p. 240. For more on this, see Lynn Picknett and Clive Prince's *The Sion Revelation: The Truth about the Guardians of Christ's Sacred Bloodline* (London: Time Warner Books, 2006).

·45. Maurice Girodias, *The Frog Prince* (New York: Crown Publishers, 1980).

46. VandenBroeck, *Al-Kemi*, p. 245.

47. Godwin, *Arktos*, p. 55.

48. Nicholas Goodrick-Clarke, *The Occult Roots of Nazism* (New York: NYU Press, 1993); *Hitler's Priestess: Savitri Devi, The Hindu-Aryan Myth and Neo-Nazism* (New York: NYU Press, 2000); *Black Sun: Aryan Cults, Esoteric Nazism and the Politics of Identity* (New York: NYU Press, 2003).

49. Hans Thomas Hakl, *Unknown Sources: National Socialism and the Occult* (Edmonds, WA: Holmes Publishing Group, 2000).

50. Later neo-Nazis like the Hinduist Savitri Devi and the Chilean diplomat Miguel Serrano fantasized Hitler as an "avatar" of a new age and wrote books that became influential in the extreme right-wing fringes of "alternative thought," with green and animal-rights activists, among others. With René Guénon, Savitri Devi was an opponent of modernity and agreed with the Traditionalists that we are embedded in the Kali Yuga: "Human history, far from being a steady ascension towards the better, is an increasingly hopeless process of bastardisation, emasculation and demoralisation of mankind, an inexorable 'fall'" (Goodrick-Clarke, *Hitler's Priestess*, p. 115). Serrano, who befriended an elderly Hermann Hesse and C. G. Jung and through his diplomatic contacts knew the writers Arthur Koestler and Aldous Huxley and the historian Arnold Toynbee, is the author of a series of books celebrating esoteric Hitlerism. With Savitri Devi, he views Hitler as a cosmic "avatar" who has come to battle the evil influences of the materialistic Jewish race. Along with denying the Holocaust, Serrano believed Hitler survived the fall of the Third Reich, escaping a burning Berlin in a flying saucer; he now resides in a subterranean hideout at the South Pole (Godwin, *Arktos*, p. 70). Serrano is worryingly popular among many extreme right-wing esotericists, and the fact that he was very familiar with the corridors of political power makes this doubly so. That Hitler and Nazism has spawned a disturbing subculture of fascist occultism is undeniable. The point is that the kind of *direct* occult influence commonly believed to have been behind Hitler's rise is simply unsubstantiated.

51. See the 2003 edition of Peter Viereck's *Metapolitics: The Roots of the Nazi Mind* (Piscataway, NJ: Transaction Publishers), which includes the historian Jacques Barzun's review of the original edition. Barzun's own defense of romanticism can be found in his work entitled *Classic, Romantic, Modern* (Chicago: University of Chicago Press, 1975).

52. Hakl, *Unknown Sources*, pp. 22–23.

53. See my *Turn Off Your Mind: The Mystic Sixties and the Dark Side of the Age of Aquarius* (New York: The Disinformation Company, 2001), p. 32.

54. Martin Green, *Mountain of Truth: The Counterculture Begins, Ascona 1900–1920* (Hanover and London: University Press of New England, 1986), p. 238.

55. David Clay Large, *Where Ghosts Walked: Munich's Road to the Third Reich* (New York: W. W. Norton, 1997), p. 25.

56. Ibid., p. 27.

57. Others included the scholar Alfred Schuler and the Jewish poet and professor of literature Karl Wolfskehl. A figure on the perimeter of the circle was the mystical poet Stefan George. Another figure associated with the Cosmic Circle was the novelist and free-love enthusiast Fanny Reventlow. See David Clay Large, above, and Richard Noll's *The Jung Cult* (London: Fontana Press, 1996).

58. Large, *Where Ghosts Walked*, p. 26.

59. Ibid.

60. Ibid., p. 30.

61. Walter Benjamin, *Illuminations* (London: Fontana Press, 1992), p. 153.

62. Richard Rudgley, *Pagan Resurrection* (London: Century, 2006), p. 53.

63. Ibid., p. 56.

64. Mark Sedgwick, *Against the Modern World* (Oxford: Oxford University Press, 2004), pp. 95–98.

65. Lynn Picknett and Clive Prince (with Stephen Prior and Robert Brydon), *Double Standards: The Rudolf Hess Cover-Up* (London: Time Warner Books, 2002), pp. 32–34.

66. George L. Mosse, *The Crisis of German Ideology* (London: Weidenfeld & Nicholson, 1966), p. 1.

67. For Haeckel's influence on Steiner, see my *Rudolf Steiner: An Introduction to His Life and Work*; for his influence on Jung, see Richard Noll above.

68. Sedgwick, *Against the Modern World*, p. 97.

69. Rudgley, *Pagan Resurrection*, pp. 136–51.

70. Quoted in Gerhard Wehr, *Jung: A Biography* (Boston: Shambhala, 1987), p. 352. For Bloch's "utopianism," see his monumental *The Principle of Hope* and *The Spirit of Utopia*.

71. Cyprian P. Blamires and Paul Jackson, eds. *World Fascism: A Historical Encyclopedia* (Santa Barbara: ABC Clio, 2006), p. 358. Unfortunately, the only reference work used for Jung in this entry is Richard Noll's controversial and (to my mind) biased book.

72. See, though, Sonu Shamdasani's critique of Noll in his *Cult Fictions: C. G. Jung and the Founding of Analytical Psychology* (London: Routledge, 1998). For Jung and National Socialism, see Ronald Hayman, *Jung: A Biography* (London: Bloomsbury, 1999).

73. Quoted in Hayman, *Jung*, p. 319.

74. The reader can join it at http://www.kingseyes.demon.co.uk/answ-postjung.htm. For a concise summary of the controversy, see "C. G. Jung and National Socialism" in Aniela Jaffé, *From the Life and Work of C. G. Jung* (Einsiedeln: Daimon Verlag, 1989).

75. See Deidre Bair, *Jung: A Biography* (London: Little Brown, 2004), p. 512.

76. Weininger's remarks can be found in his *Sex and Character* (London: William Heineman, 1906); for Wittgenstein, see his *Culture and Value*,

translated by Peter Winch (Chicago: University of Chicago Press, 1980), pp. 18–19.

77. C. G. Jung, *Essays on Contemporary Events* (Princeton, NJ: Princeton University Press, n.d.), pp. 16–17.
78. Ibid., p. 79.
79. Bair, *Jung*, pp. 492–94.
80. Ibid., pp. 471, 482.
81. Anthony Storr, *Music and the Mind* (London: HarperCollins, 1997), p. 155.
82. See my *Secret History of Consciousness* (Great Barrington: Lindisfarne, 2003), p. 226.
83. Jung, *Essays*, pp. 34–35.
84. Ibid., p. 37.
85. Ibid.
86. Ibid., p. 56
87. C. G. Jung, *Psychological Reflections* (New York: Harper & Row, 1961), p. 280.

11. ARCHANGELS OF OUR DARKER NATURE

1. See my *Turn Off Your Mind: The Mystic Sixties and the Dark Side of the Age of Aquarius* (New York: The Disinformation Company, 2001), p. 35.
2. "Have You Seen Your Critic, Baby?" Interview with Ralph J. Gleason in *Altamont*, edited by Jonathan Eisen (New York: Avon Books, 1970), pp. 252–53.
3. For Anger, Rolling Thunder, Hoffman, and Rubin, see *Turn Off Your Mind*, pp. 355–60. For Leary, Lennon, and the *Tibetan Book of the Dead*, see ibid., pp. 279–81.
4. Mark Sedgwick, *Against the Modern World* (Oxford: Oxford University Press, 2004), p. 5.
5. A version of this section appeared as my article "Mussolini's Mystic" in issue 191 of *Fortean Times*, special issue (no date) 2004, pp. 40–45. Sources for the article are: Richard Drake, "The Revolutionary Mystique and Terrorism in Contemporary Italy," in *Political Violence and Terror*, ed. Peter Merkl (Berkeley: University of California Press, 1986); Julius Evola, *Revolt against the Modern World* (Rochester, VT: Inner Traditions, 1995); Joscelyn Godwin, *Arktos: The Polar Myth in Science, Symbolism, and Nazi Survival* (Kempton, IL: Adventures Unlimited, 1996); and Nicholas Goodrick-Clarke, *Black Sun* (New York: NYU Press, 2002).
6. Umberto Eco, "The Poisonous Protocols," *Guardian*, August 17, 2002.
7. See Gary Lachman, *The Dedalus Book of Literary Suicides: Dead Letters* (Sawtry, UK: Dedalus Books, 2008) pp. 192-199.
8. Evola, *Revolt against the Modern World*, pp. 157–66.

9. David Lloyd Thomas, "Arturo Reghini: A Modern Pythagorean," http://www.geocities.com/integral_tradition/reghinihtml.

10. Elémire Zolla, "The Evolution of Julius Evola's Thought," *Gnosis* no. 14 (Winter, 1989–90), pp. 18–20.

11. Renalto de Ponte, preface to *Introduction to Magic*, by Julius Evola and the UR Group (Rochester, VT: Inner Traditions, 2001), p. xix.

12. Ibid., p. xxi.

13. Ibid.

14. See Houellebecq's novel *Atomised* (London: Vintage, 2001), among his other works.

15. Sedgwick, *Against the Modern World*, p. 101.

16. Ibid., p. 104.

17. H. T. Hansen, "A Short Introduction to Julius Evola," in *Revolt against the Modern World*, by Julius Evola, p. xxii.

18. See Nicholas Goodrick-Clarke, *Hitler's Priestess: Savitri Devi, The Hindu-Aryan Myth and Neo-Nazism* (New York: NYU Press, 2000).

19. During the October 1967 anti-war march on Washington. In *Turn Off Your Mind*, I outline some examples of "occult politics" not usually associated with '60s radicalism. See chapter 12, "The Magical Revolution," pp. 335–74.

20. Sedgwick, *Against the Modern World*, p. 181.

21. Ibid., p. 183.

22. See note 19 above.

23. Mircea Eliade and Claude-Henri Rocquet, *Ordeal by Labyrinth* (Chicago: University of Chicago Press, 1982), p. 55.

24. Marta Petreu, *An Infamous Past* (Chicago: Ivan R. Dee, 2005), p. 72.

25. Eliade and Rocquet, *Ordeal by Labyrinth*, pp. 80–82.

26. Sedgwick, *Against the Modern World*, p. 109.

27. An indication of the regard Eliade had for Evola is seen in his diary entry on hearing of Evola's death. "Today I learn of the death of Julius Evola. . . . Memories surge up in me, those of my years at university, the books we had discovered together, the letters I received from him in Calcutta. . . ." Mircea Eliade, *Journal III* (Chicago: University of Chicago Press, 1989), p. 161.

28. Liviu Bordaş, "The Secret of Dr. Eliade" in *The International Eliade*, ed. Bryan Rennie (Albany, NY: SUNY Press, 2007), pp. 101–30. See also Natale Spineto, "Mircea Eliade and 'Traditional Thought,'" pp. 131–47, in the same volume.

29. Sedgwick, *Against the Modern World*, p. 111.

30. See Ted Anton's *Eros, Magic, and the Murder of Professor Culianu* (Evanston, IL: Northwestern University Press, 1996).

31. "Final Report of the International Commission on the Holocaust in Romania," http://www.inshr-ev.ro/pdf/Final_Report.pdf.

32. Petreu, *Infamous Past*, p. 55.

33. On the side of the detractors, the most forceful is Adriana Berger, for whom Eliade is "one of the most influential intellectuals of his generation

and an active Fascist ideologue." See "Mircea Eliade: Romanian Fascism and the History of Religions in the United States" in *Tainted Greatness: Anti-Semitism and Cultural Heroes*, ed. Nancy A. Harrowitz (Philadelphia: Temple University Press, 1994), p. 51. On the supporters' side there is Bryan Rennie, editor of several books dedicated to Eliade's work. For Rennie, "Eliade's rightist leanings may be seen as lamentable, but they have not been proven culpable." See *Reconstructing Eliade* (Albany, NY: SUNY Press, 1996), p. 161.

34. Petreu, *Infamous Past*, p. 60.
35. Sedgwick, *Against the Modern World*, p. 114.
36. Petreu, *Infamous Past*, p. 61; Adriana Berger, "Mircea Eliade," p. 60.
37. Berger, "Mircea Eliade," pp. 64–65.
38. Ibid., p. 57.
39. Robert Ellwood, *The Politics of Myth: A Study of C. G. Jung, Mircea Eliade and Joseph Campbell* (Albany, NY: SUNY Press, 1999), p. 29.
40. This applies to areas other than politics. In this sense, anyone interested in "saving the planet" is a conservative.
41. Leszek Kolakowski, *Modernity on Endless Trial* (Chicago: University of Chicago Press, 1990), p. 5.

LAST WORDS: NEW WORLD ORDERS?

1. See for example the work of Wilhelm Landig and Jean Parvulesco, examined in Joscelyn Godwin's *Arktos: The Polar Myth in Science, Symbolism, and Nazi Survival* (Kempton, IL: Adventures Unlimited, 1996), pp. 63–76.
2. Although Traditionalism is ultimately incompatible with Islamic fundamentalism, see, however, Mark Sedgwick, *Against the Modern World* (Oxford: Oxford University Press, 2004), pp. 257–60; and also the Web site http://www.livingislam.org/trg.html.
3. P. D. Ouspensky, *In Search of the Miraculous* (London: Routledge and Kegan Paul, 1983), p. 266.

INDEX

Quest Books

encourages open-minded inquiry into
world religions, philosophy, science, and the arts
in order to understand the wisdom of the ages,
respect the unity of all life, and help people explore
individual spiritual self-transformation.

Its publications are generously supported by
The Kern Foundation,
a trust committed to Theosophical education.

Quest Books is the imprint of
the Theosophical Publishing House,
a division of the Theosophical Society in America.
For information about programs, literature,
on-line study, membership benefits, and international centers,
See www.theosophical.org
or call 800-669-1571 or (outside the U.S.) 630-668-1571.

Related Quest Titles

City of Secrets, Patrice Chaplin
The Golden Thread, Joscelyn Godwin
Hidden Wisdom, Richard Smoley and Jay Kinney
In Search of P. D. Ouspensky, Gary Lachman
The Light of the Russian Soul, Elena Fedorovna Pisareva
Nicholas and Helena Roerich, Ruth Drayer
The Secret Doctrine, Helena Blavatsky
Shambhala, Victoria LePage
The Templars and the Grail, Karen Ralls

To order books or a complete Quest catalog,
Call 800-669-9425 or (outside the U.S.) 630-665-0130.

In the 1970s and '80s Gary Lachman was a composer and performer with the rock group Blondie, a guitarist with Iggy Pop, and leader of his own group, The Know. His *New York Rocker*, written as Gary Valentine, recounts this time in his life. Lachman later became involved in Gurdjieff's "work," earned a degree in philosophy, managed a new age bookshop, and did post-graduate literary studies at the University of Southern California.

His books include *Turn Off Your Mind: The Mystic Sixties and the Dark Side of the Age of Aquarius*; *A Secret History of Consciousness*; *In Search of P. D. Ouspensky*; *Into the Interior: Discovering Swedenborg*; and *The Dedalus Book of Literary Suicides*. Recently his *Rudolf Steiner: An Introduction to His Life and Work* was named a finalist in the 2008 Coalition of Visionary Resources awards.

Lachman has appeared in the BBC documentaries *Magic: Art of Darkness* (2001) and *The Menace of the Masses* (2007) as well as in other television and radio programs. In 2006 he, along with other members of Blondie, was inducted into the Rock and Roll Hall of Fame. He lives in London.

Praise for Gary Lachman's
Politics and the Occult

"The invisible Rosicrucian Brothers of the seventeenth century, the 'unknown superiors' of high-grade Freemasons, French utopian occultists, and Traditionalists of the twentieth century trace a continuous tradition of esoteric idealism applied to political thinking. Gary Lachman offers a panoramic spectacle of occultists and millenarian visionaries who seek to translate an absolute gnosis into a radical programme of regeneration."

—Nicholas Goodrick-Clarke, Professor of Western Esotericism,
University of Exeter

"Gary Lachman has become an increasingly prolific engine of literate, well-written, and clear-headed books about esoteric history and 'occulture.'"

—Erik Davis, author of *Techgnosis*